The Upper Room

*D*isciplines

1996

The Upper Room
*D*isciplines
1996

Coordinating Editor
Glenda Webb

Copy Editors
Mary Ruth Coffman
Rita Collett
Janet R. Knight
Cathy Cole Wright

Proofreaders
Deborah L. Gallaway
Carl Gilliam
Cathy Cole Wright
Tom Page

Editorial Secretary
Betty Estes

UPPER
ROOM BOOKS
NASHVILLE

The Upper Room Disciplines 1996
© 1995 by The Upper Room. All rights reserved.

No part of this book may be used or reproduced in any manner
whatsoever without permission except in the case of brief quotations
embodied in critical articles or reviews. For information write:
Upper Room Books, P.O. Box 189, Nashville, TN 37202-0189

Cover photo © 1992 Frances Dorris
Cover design: Jim Bateman
Typesetting: Nancy Cole

ISBN 0-8358-0727-4
Printed in the United States of America

CONTENTS

Joy

Grant me today, Lord,
    a new heaven and a new earth.
Grant me the wonder of a child who for the first time
    opens her eyes upon the world;
the joy of a child who discovers
    Your splendor in each object,
in each encountered being,
    a reflection of Your glory.

Grant me the joy of one whose steps are new.
Grant me the happiness of one whose life is each day
fresh and innocent and hopeful, each day pardoned.

from *Prayers for My Village*
by Michel Bouttier
trans. Lamar Williamson

FAITH INCARNATED IN THE WORLD

January 1–7, 1996　　　　　　　　**Minerva G. Carcaño✤**
Monday, January 1　　　　　　　Read Isaiah 42:1-4.

Israel would not remain in exile forever. Already the Lord had called forth a liberator from the east who would be an instrument of God in their freedom (Isa. 41:2). But there is more. The Lord God has a wider vision and an even greater plan: salvation for all the nations. What a queer word to hear in the midst of exile and slavery. As the chosen people, Israel has a special claim on God's time and mercy, yet here is God talking mercifully about all those other folks, perhaps even the enemy Babylon.

Israel could not see beyond its own suffering; had not even conceived of any other solution to their pain other than their own freedom. But if all nations, even tyrannical, idol-worshiping Babylon, could be touched by God's love and be transformed into a nation of light and justice, Israel would be blessed!

We, not unlike Israel, continue to live in a world of exile and slavery, evil injustices, and great hatred. We, too, are assured of God's merciful presence in our lives and more. Spirit-filled, quiet, affirming, faithful without ever fainting or giving up, God's servant, the Christ, is at work in the world. And because of this, God's justice will be established on the earth. Can we hope for this justice, not just for ourselves but for all people?

Prayer: **Lord of mercy, forgive our self-centeredness. Help us to overcome our fears, and give us a new spirit as we pray and hope for all your people. Amen.**

✤Head pastor of the South Albuquerque Cooperative Ministry; clergy, Río Grande Annual Conference of The United Methodist Church; Albuquerque, New Mexico.

Tuesday, January 2   Read Isaiah 42:5-9.

Leave it to God to always have something for us to do. There is no way that God is going to simply let us sit back and observe divine grace in action. No, no, no, no! "Listen," says the Lord. "I am the one who created all things. . . . I imagined creation, stretched it out before me, and brought it to life with a single breath. . . . And do not forget that I made you as well and that I have always kept you. Now, I am calling you, for I am your Lord" (AP). How does one say no to that?

Well, one does not say no unless one wants to turn from God and deal with the consequences. But this is not a passage about judgment; it is an exciting invitation to be part of God's redemption.

Israel is special to God, and even though its faith vision is often shortsighted, God is going to allow Israel to share in the glory of salvation. They will lead off in the day of redemption, bearing the light that will bring the nations out of darkness. From prisons and dungeons and the deepest darkness of spirit they will come, surefooted and free because of Israel's guiding light. And all will give glory and praise to the Lord our God.

So what is the promise for Israel and for us, their descendents in the faith? Blessed assurance! The invitation is to a covenantal partnership with God, who gifts us with the firstfruits of salvation. In faithfulness, God's mercy will unfold before our very eyes.

Prayer: **Praised be your name, merciful Lord, for your blessed assurance! Strengthen us to be your covenant people working side by side with you for the redemption of your world. Amen.**

Wednesday, January 3   Read Psalm 29.

King David praised God for a tempest of wonderful rain that had fallen upon the land and then called upon the great heavenly beings to join him in giving thanks to God and worshiping the Almighty. Some suggest that the tempest came after Israel's three years of drought brought on by King Saul's slaughter of the Gibeonites to the point of near extermination (see 2 Samuel 21:1-10). If so, then this was no ordinary rain. Rather, it was a washing of Israel's sin after which, and only after which, Israel's physical thirst could be quenched.

Saul had tried to annihilate the Gibeonites out of zeal for Israel and Judah. His sin fell on all Israel. In punishment God withheld the rain for three years. David sought to atone Saul's sin, and the cost was the lives of two of Saul's sons and five of his grandsons who were impaled on the mountain at Gibeon. Then Rizpah, the mother of Saul's sons, sat with the seven corpses so that they would not be devoured by the birds or the wild beasts. She stayed until God's rain fell.

I cannot help but think of all the spiritual droughts that I am aware of and even a part of. Might it be that the people of God again need wise and loving mediators like David and Rizpah? Mediators who had the courage to inquire of God as to the cause of human pain and suffering, who were willing to risk leading God's people to repentance, and who were willing to sit among the carnage of life's struggles until God responded.

Suggestion for meditation: **There is no comfort in sin, but Nature herself will speak with God's voice in our repentance. God's forgiveness will gush forth in torrents of grace and glory.**

Thursday, January 4   Read Acts 10:34-46.

Peter had had a most unusual vision in which he was asked to eat creatures, reptiles, and birds that under the Jewish dietary laws were profane or unclean (10:12-13). His vision turned out not to be about food at all but about people. Peter learned that nothing that God has made clean should be considered profane, for all are God's creatures.

God used an aspect of Peter's life that he knew and understood well to teach Peter a new lesson, to push Peter's boundaries, and to lead him to even greater blessings of community. Through the vision God gave him, Peter's sight of who his community was multiplied a hundredfold as he realized that God's salvation was not just for Israel but for all who fear the Lord and do what is right. Jesus Christ is Lord of all, bringing peace to all.

I wonder what things we know well that God is using on this day to open our sight and push our boundaries that we might be that much more blessed in the fellowship of community. Could our knowledge of the injustice of racism and sexism be that God is helping us see how wrong it is to exclude others whose faith may be waiting to be acknowledged, affirmed, and received? Could our knowledge of God as Creator of all things be calling us to reconsider how we respond to brothers and sisters whose lifestyles are very different from our own? Could our knowledge of the mercy of God in our own lives be challenging how we live with others?

Suggestion for meditation: **Where is God challenging you? Remember that, like Peter, we will experience the affirmation of God's spirit when we respond in faithfulness.**

Friday, January 5   Read Acts 10:37-43.

God's salvation in Jesus Christ is for everyone regardless of race, culture, or national origin. It is a gift of grace offered universally to all. Yet, although all persons *can* claim it, claiming it is a prerequisite to *receiving* it; "everyone who *believes* in him receives forgiveness of sins through his name."

The faithful testimony of the earliest witnesses proclaims that in the life, ministry, death, and resurrection of Jesus of Nazareth, God's presence and power were made manifest. Healing and wholeness are the experience of those who believe in Jesus. The response of faith is twofold: we proclaim our belief in the Lord and then we share it with others that they also may believe in the "one ordained by God as judge of the living and the dead."

God meets all people with the mystery of divine love in Jesus Christ. In the encounter, persons are free to believe or not. But it is only in Jesus Christ that God's salvation for humanity is to be found.

Do we too often as Christians demonstrate syncretic tendencies? In our efforts to be loving and charitable, do we lean every which way to be accepting of others' concepts of faith, even when these do not affirm Christ's role as the sole Savior of the world? While we must be loving, leaving judgment to God, we must also be obedient to God's command to preach and testify about Jesus who alone is Lord, calling all people to respond in faith to him.

Prayer: **God, you who gave us Jesus, help our unbelief. Grant us the vision to be your faithful witnesses. Amen.**

Epiphany

Nature, which is ever mindful of the movement of life's changes, marks the amazing good news of the Messiah's birth by making a magnificent star rise up in the darkness of night. It is no surprise that men who observed the stars would notice this radiant message of birth. They became yet another sign of the coming of the Messiah. But, neither is it surprising that those who were not looking for the coming of the Messiah would miss the signs. Epiphany is an action of God's loving faithfulness. It is also a moment of God's judgment.

Through a star and the journeying of wise ones, God called humanity to welcome the Messiah. It appears that at the moment of epiphany only the wise strangers from the East were disposed to worship and pay homage to the Messiah. Evil King Herod "and all Jerusalem with him" were filled with fear at the very thought of the Messiah's arrival.

Even today the signs of the Messiah are present. Jesus comes to us without formal announcement but always giving us clear signs. The signs may come through the movement of nature or through the voice of a stranger. The signs of the presence of the Messiah in our lives may come most clearly through a frightened heart. Whatever the signs may be, we are each given the opportunity to be led to Jesus Christ and his joy—this is God reaching out to us! Responding is up to us.

Prayer: **Lord of light and truth, forgive us when we ignore the signs of your presence. Calm our fearful hearts, open our eyes, and send anew the signs of your salvation that we may be led straight to Jesus, the Messiah. Amen.**

Sunday, January 7   Read Matthew 3:13-17.

John's discomfort with baptizing Jesus is understandable. In Jesus, John saw the One whose coming he had preached about; the One who was without sin. Jesus was for John the model par excellence of faith and righteousness. For this precise reason Jesus had to be baptized. The action was necessary for him to model for others the way to God.

In his mother's womb John had been filled with the Holy Spirit, chosen to be the one to turn Israel to the Lord. In baptizing Jesus, John would be fulfilling his calling by turning people's attention and faith to the Messiah.

By his baptism Jesus confirms John's message. The people must "repent, for the kingdom of heaven has come near" (Matt. 3:2). The public expression of the believer's repentance is coming to be baptized, and baptism is the sacrament of God's grace. In Jesus, theology is incarnated.

If there is one clear message from Jesus' baptism, it is that faith *must* be incarnated. Faith must be made flesh, must be lived out if it is to fulfill all the righteousness that God expects of us. It is in the incarnation of his message that Jesus is declared the Son, the Beloved, with whom God is well pleased. When we take our faith and make it incarnate—when we turn our faith into action—God is well pleased.

Prayer: **God of grace, as we seek to follow the example of Jesus, help us to keep our faith fleshed out in our daily lives. Amen.**

TO WAIT, TO FOLLOW, TO WITNESS

January 8–14, 1996   **Randolph M. Cross**♣
Monday, January 8   Read Isaiah 49:1-4.

On cold mornings, I hear a river of sounds as I "open my ears" to the world: trucks grumble down the street outside; the house groans and cracks as the wind blows by; the wind chimes sing their five-note song; even Caesar, our tomcat, sighs before his midmorning nap. There are times, however, when the "river" seems to dry up, and I hear only my own preoccupation.

The servant of Isaiah 49 apparently has a good ear for listening to important things. He tells the world, "The LORD called me before I was born, while I was in my mother's womb he named me. . . . [God] said to me, 'You are my servant, Israel, in whom I will be glorified.'" God communicates—calling, naming, employing, and *revealing*. The twofold revelation reveals that God is One who actively works in our lives and that we are created for a life task as we assume the role of a servant of God—as we listen.

Listening to God requires spiritual energy as we open ourselves to God's call to us in time of silence and stillness. Be well aware that God will not compete in a shouting match with the noise of the world in order to try to get our attention! Instead, God invites us to listen for the call, to hear our name, and to receive the tasks of loving and glorifying God.

Suggestion for meditation and prayer: **Listen. What do you hear God saying to you?**

♣Pastor, Faith United Methodist Church, Fargo, North Dakota.

Tuesday, January 9   Read Isaiah 49:5-7.

How big God's plans are! If I had created the earth, for instance, I shudder to think what would have been left out of the blueprint. Would I have settled for only one shade of yellow, only a dozen kinds of trees? I surely don't think I have the depth of imagination to create dimples or hoarfrost!

God's intention for us also goes far beyond our wildest dreams. Look at Israel: they were given the original task of raising up a nation that would be that peculiar people of God and a blessing through their obedience to God's will. It was a heavy, all-consuming job that gave Israel trouble all along, but now God says, "It's too light a thing that, as my servant, all you would do would be to raise up the tribes of Jacob! No, let's go one better; and I will give you as a light to the nations, that salvation may reach everywhere!" (AP) There is a bit of wit here—to tell Israel that its present role is too light, so they will become a light itself. The fact remains that God stretched their calling, their work, and even their core identity so that the divine purpose of salvation for this world would be worked out.

Are you aware of any "stretching" in your spiritual life? Is your present important work still "too light a thing" for God's intention for you? Beyond our greatest expectations and desires, God makes a gift of you and me to bring world-changing, light-sharing love in the name of Jesus Christ. Most importantly, we live up to this divine intention when God's own strength and grace are present and growing in our lives.

Suggestion for meditation: **What are God's "big plans" for me? How may I be open to hear them?**

Wednesday, January 10   Read Psalm 40:1-5.

Anyone who has gone through a hard time in life knows what the psalmist is describing in Psalm 40. Some especially difficult times do feel like being dropped in a dirty desolate pit with steep sides and no perspective of a horizon. Or standing in a bog trapped up to your knees with no firm footing possible and slowly sinking. You know that the more you struggle the more bound you become. We give those places all sorts of exotic names like cancer, depression, the teen years, unemployment, death, or a thousand other scary words that are scary precisely because they seem to overpower our even-keeled, predictable lives. The "pit" and the "bog" are horrible places in which to find oneself. Even worse is knowing that most of the time a person is there not because of something he or she has done to deserve it but simply because one is human and human beings often suffer.

The psalmist begins by telling his experience of God's grace while crying in the pit, but then he recounts a marvelous happening. "I waited patiently . . . and [the Lord] heard my cry. He drew me up from the desolate pit, and out of the miry bog, and set my feet up on a rock, making my steps secure!" What a great feeling—yanked from the muck, pulled free by the very hand of God! Two of the great truths this psalm tells us of our relationship with God are that 1) God hears our cries; and that 2) we need to wait patiently.

The third truth is that God will "put a new song in [our mouths]," and it will be a song of praise to God. As we sing, others "will see and fear* also and put their trust in" God's saving grace and trustworthiness.

Prayer: **O God, grant me the patience of heart to wait this day upon your healing and salvation. Amen.**

---

*respect

22

Thursday, January 11   Read Psalm 40:6-11.

"Have you been to the new restaurant yet?" "I've just seen the best movie ever." "I've just read a great book." "Let me tell you about my shampoo." Recount in your mind how often someone shares some less-than-earthshaking good news that has excited them. We eagerly tell others what we have just found out or discovered or experienced, no matter how trivial it may sound.

Eager, yes—unless it involves our faith. At that point we would not dream of pushing our religion on someone else or of being seen as "one of those fanatical types." The blessings of God, the experiences of grace, the outpouring of holy love is held as news for a select few, while we boast instead about our children's achievements or praise a new breakfast cereal.

The psalmist offers us a different image: "I have not restrained my lips, . . . O LORD. I have not hidden your saving help within my heart, I have spoken of your faithfulness and your salvation." Pulled up from the pit with his feet set firmly on a rock, the psalmist makes a point of proclaiming the news of deliverance to everyone, even the "great congregation." "Is there someone here today who will witness?" the preacher challenges.

There are two reasons to tell what we know of the love of Jesus Christ. First, in doing so we praise God for the blessing we have received, a sort of a holy thank you. Secondly, our word of witness also becomes a powerful word of hope to others: "See what God can do!"

Will you witness today?

Prayer: **Thank you, gracious God, for the opportunity to speak out and to share our witness of your salvation and blessings. Amen.**

Friday, January 12　　　　　　　Read 1 Corinthians 1:1-9.

"To Whom It May Concern:" "Dear Mary, How are you? I am fine." "FAX: From: _____ To: _____." Whether sent through e-mail, typed on a letterhead, or written on fine linen rag with perfect Palmer method, the greetings and hellos that we offer set the tone for the communication that follows.

Consider, then, the way in which Paul greets the Corinthians:

> Paul, called to be an apostle by the will of God, . . .
> To the church of God that is in Corinth, to those who
> are sanctified in Christ Jesus, called to be saints,
> together with all those who in every place call on the
> name of our Lord Jesus Christ: Grace to you and peace
> from God our Father and the Lord Jesus Christ.

Do you sense the value Paul places on the Corinthians? It is a heady and empowering thing to be identified in this way! The addressees are not *just* the receivers of a letter; they are saints, filled with grace and peace, who call on Jesus Christ! Words are powerful when used to describe someone beyond a compliment, when we use them instead to speak of a person's relationship with Jesus Christ. The words become transformational, and we become transformed by the truth the words carry.

It may not always be appropriate to begin each phone conversation or interoffice memo by describing yourself as an apostle of God and the receiver of the message as a sanctified saint. There may, however, be opportunities that you as a "follower of Christ" will have to open others to the revelation of their place before God and so bring grace to their lives.

At least, this sharer of the gospel by the grace of God thinks so.

***Suggestion for meditation:* As you call on Jesus Christ today, pray with the confidence of a saint!**

Saturday, January 13   Read John 1:29-34.

January 14 is my birthday, and every year I have to struggle to keep my family from telling me what gifts they have gotten for me. Please understand—I don't pry or ask for hints! I love being surprised, but sometimes (most of the time) somebody can't keep a secret. Before long the secret is out, and I know what I am getting.

John the Baptist did not keep secrets well either! As soon as he saw Jesus, John began to tell everyone who this Jesus was: the Lamb of God, who takes away sin—the Spirit descended on him like a dove—he is greater than me—he baptizes with the Holy Spirit! He is the Son of God! John was a bit—how do you say—more passionate than restrained in his comments. In fact, if we heard John on our street, we would at least take a step or two away or even shush him if we could.

John's testimony, however, will not be shushed. His life's work is to herald the coming of the Lamb and to point out to all who will turn their heads that here is the Christ, and because he has come, the sin of the world is taken away. God and God's children are together once again!

Perhaps in this world where bad news gets shouted from skyscraper roofs while good news is buried on the back page, we should see where we could "let the secret out" of this Jesus Christ and where we could help to reveal the love of Christ present and active in our world. After all, it is a secret worth sharing.

Prayer: **Loving God, give us boldness to share what we have heard and have come to know of Christ. And may we do so in words and actions acceptable to you. Amen.**

Sunday, January 14   Read John 1:35-42.

Two of John's disciples hear Jesus called "the Lamb of God" and just begin to follow him. They do not say anything—they just walk a little behind him. It is almost comical, for Jesus soon turns around and says, "What are you looking for?" They are hot on his heels, but Jesus is asking them if they know what they have found. They answer, "Rabbi (which translated means Teacher), where are you staying?" as if to say, "We really don't know for sure, but we want to find out!" Jesus says simply, "Come and see." End this hide-and-seek game, and just seek. Seek me. And they do.

At the end of the day, one of the two finds his brother and says, "Simon, we have found the Messiah." We experience at that moment the first witness, the first sharing of the faith, and, in a way, the birth of the church three years before Pentecost. In our own congregations, don't we gather to hear the gospel from each other? "Look whom I've found! Come and join me as we follow!"

What is most amazing is that twenty centuries after Andrew spoke with Simon, we seek the same Messiah; and we ask where he is staying, because we, like millions before us, want to know who this Lamb of God is.

Equally amazing is that Jesus also says to us today, "Come and see." We are invited to begin the journey, to follow and to come to know how deep and yet how amazingly close God's grace is to us. As close as Christ.

Prayer: **Most loving God, we thank you for revealing yourself in Jesus Christ. Give us the strength to follow, to speak out, to love in your name and as your people. It is in loving so that we find you. In Christ's name we pray. Amen.**

To See a Great Light

January 15–21, 1996   **Jean M. Blomquist✠**
Monday, January 15   Read Isaiah 9:1-4.

Upon reading this passage, a parishioner turned to her pastor and exclaimed, "Isaiah must have read Handel!"

From their graves, Isaiah groans, Handel grins, and I chuckle at the anachronism. I chuckle perhaps because I, too, can scarcely read this passage without hearing the "Air for Bass" in Handel's *Messiah* running through my head. We who have experienced God manifested in Christ's birth know this "light" as the Light that is Christ.

Yet, it may be helpful for us briefly to set aside our twentieth-century lens and imagine that we are hearing these words of Isaiah for the first time. Imagine that we live in the eighth century B.C.E. in the midst of the Syro-Ephraimite war. Chaos, anguish, and fear batter us daily. Our faith wavers and wanes. The darkness around us deepens. There is no way out. Then a wise one voices the yearning that lies hidden by our despair. He calls us back, even in the midst of our fear, to the heart of our faith: God's covenant. Today the voices of Handel, of the Gospel writers, and of countless others join Isaiah in calling us back that we may see the great Light that shines in our midst.

Suggestion for meditation: **Where is the darkness in your life today? Where do you yearn to see the great light of God? Speak to God of your yearning.**

✠Writer; Berkeley, California.

Tuesday, January 16   Read Psalm 27:1, 4-9.

Confident praise, deep yearning, fear, desperation. This psalm runs the gamut of emotions. How, in just a few lines, can the psalmist express so wide a range of emotions? Scholars suggest that Psalm 27 is actually two psalms combining one of thanksgiving and one of supplication. Although the juxtaposition of stark opposites may unsettle us, perhaps a deeper wisdom was at work when these two seemingly disparate psalms were joined.

This wisdom challenges us. It challenges us to acknowledge the contradictory mix of feelings we often hold but frequently seek to deny. Even more difficult, it challenges us to place all these feelings—our yearnings, our fear, our desperation—within a larger context: thanksgiving for and confidence in the God who is our light and salvation.

But how can we honestly and authentically give thanks in those difficult times when we see nothing to give thanks for? Would it not be better *not* to give thanks at such times than to give thanks and be hypocritical?

Perhaps thanksgiving is at times proleptic—that is, an experience of the "now and not yet." In the mix of our feelings now, we offer thanks in the realm of the not yet, trusting, perhaps feebly at times, that the not yet will someday come to be: resolution, healing, courage, hope—whatever we most deeply need. In thanksgiving to God we are invited both to hold and to release all that we are, all that we do, all that we think, and all that we feel. Everything is held in the holy hands of light and salvation. For that we can be thankful, even when we do not feel thankful.

***Suggestion for meditation:* Quietly read and reflect on words from today's reading in the Psalms that best express your feelings right now. Then reread the entire passage. Use verse 1 as your closing prayer.**

Wednesday, January 17   Read 1 Corinthians 1:10-16.

Paul's plea to the Corinthians sounds eerily contemporary. Factions and factionalism reign among those who claim to be followers of Christ. Spiritual arrogance is eating the heart out of this fledgling Christian community.

Yet, perhaps like the Corinthians, we may ask Paul, "What does it mean to 'be in agreement' or to 'be united in the same mind and the same purpose'?" Surely it must have been simpler in those early years of the church, roughly twenty years after the death of Christ, than it is today. What part of Paul's words to the Corinthians can we hear today? Whom do *we* follow?

Though we may identify ourselves as Christian (instead of saying "I belong to Wesley," or "I belong to Luther," or "I belong to Jerry Falwell," or whomever), we are quite adept at making distinctions among ourselves: left/right, liberal/conservative, progressive/evangelical, social justice workers/soul savers. Paul's words challenge us, as they did the Corinthians, to drop those designations and focus on the true source of our identity: Christ. As hard as it may be to believe, being "united in the same mind and the same purpose" does not necessarily mean everyone else will be brought around to *our* point of view. Instead, we are all to be brought around to see with the eyes of Christ.

Prayer: **Gracious God, there are many Christians with whom I do not see eye to eye. All too easily I slip into the arrogance of believing people like me are right and all others are wrong. Help me to see others with the eyes of Christ that all may be one in your holy Son. Amen.**

Thursday, January 18   Read 1 Corinthians 1:17-18.

   Skilled rhetoric was highly prized by the Corinthians. Just as we might channel surf to see what TV program captures our attention and time, so the Greeks haunted the public forums seeking, listening to, and admiring fine rhetoric and philosophy. Perhaps this was why some were attracted to Christianity—it captured their attention and imaginations. It was novel and, for those who liked to go against the grain, countercultural. But the good news of Christ went further than the usual rhetoric and new ideas. It was meant not only to be listened to but to be *lived*. That *living* involved not only changing patterns of thinking but also changing patterns of behavior.

   Like the Corinthians we are often more attracted to the eloquence of slick politicians, the entertainment of advertisers, or the tease of ubiquitous pollsters than to someone who speaks simply and unpretentiously the wisdom of God. As Paul challenged the Corinthians, he also challenges our attraction to the slick, the smooth, the perfectly prepared. What he offers reaches beyond new ideas or intellectual truths. He preaches and proclaims a power that permeates all of life.

   Paul clearly does not see himself as an eloquent speaker, but that is a gift, because eloquence could lure people away from the heart of the gospel message. The heart is this: that through the cross, through Christ's death and resurrection, we are brought into this power that permeates all of life, brought into the loving embrace of God. For those who do not hear, that is foolishness; for those who do, it is the power of God.

Prayer: **Loving God, the world can be so alluring. Help me turn from the wisdom of the world to the wisdom of the Holy, so that your power may fill every part of my life. Amen.**

Friday, January 19   Read Matthew 4:12-22.

Matthew echoes the passage from Isaiah we read earlier this week. Jesus, Matthew makes clear, is the fulfillment of Isaiah's prophecy. Jesus is the great light.

But what, I wonder, *was he to Peter and Andrew, James and John?* Matthew makes it sound so simple: Jesus called and they followed—*immediately*. But I have all kinds of questions about this call. What did they see in Jesus? What did he say and what did they hear? Why in the world would they follow someone who said, "I will make you fish for people"? Was this just a lark, or did Jesus touch something deep within them, which allowed them—even compelled them—to leave family and livelihood?

Peter and Andrew, James and John must have seen something in Jesus—in his demeanor, in his words, in his eyes. *Did they*, I wonder, *see a glimmer of that great light in him, a light that they perhaps did not fully understand but still chose to follow?*

How often do we see a glimmer of that great light? How often do we follow the light of Jesus, even if we do not fully understand? We tend to read back into the gospel story what we now know of Jesus. We think, *Surely, if Jesus came to me, I'd follow, but it's just not that clear today.* I strongly suspect that it was not that clear for these fishermen either. Yet they followed the glimmer, the glimpse, of the light. May we do the same.

Prayer: O Holy One, you came to Peter and Andrew, James and John. Come to me also. Open my eyes to the glimpse of your great light that I may follow you. Amen.

Saturday, January 20   Read Matthew 4:23.

After his baptism, his temptations in the wilderness, and his calling of a few people to join him, Jesus begins his ministry. He teaches, proclaims the good news, and cures every disease and sickness. His ministry is one of encounter, engagement, and encouragement. The people to whom he ministers learn, listen or receive, and are healed. This dynamic movement between teaching and learning; proclaiming and listening or receiving; curing and the experience of healing exemplifies the activity and receptivity that is key to the life of faith. We are called to teach, to proclaim, and to heal. We are invited to learn, to listen, to receive, and to be healed. What enables this movement is a continual turning of our whole being toward the Christ-light.

The writer and priest Henri J. M. Nouwen identifies the temptations of Jesus* as the compulsions to be relevant, spectacular, and powerful. Perhaps it is no accident that Jesus begins his ministry *after* he has faced and turned aside the power that is the source of these temptations. Only then can he say, "The kingdom of heaven has come near" (4:17*b*).

Whatever form ministry takes in each of our lives, we frequently face the temptations to be relevant, spectacular, and powerful. By continually turning our lives away from those temptations and turning toward the light of Christ, we enter into the dynamic activity and receptivity that is a mark of faithful living.

Suggestion for prayer: **Reflect on how the desire or pressure to be relevant, spectacular, and powerful affects you and your ministry each day. Pray for guidance and release that you may be freed to experience the light of Christ in both your activity and your receptivity.**

---

*Matthew 4:1-11 and Luke 4:1-12; compare Mark 1:12-13.

Sunday, January 21   Read Psalm 27:4.

One of my great loves is the Pacific Ocean, which lies a few miles west of my home. I am drawn by its beauty and power and mystery. Ever changing yet ever the same, the ocean inspires, consoles, nourishes, and delights me. At times, it overwhelms me. It is too immense, too majestic, too powerful, too wild for me to take in. I stand in awe of it. The ocean feels totally "other"; and yet, as I walk slowly along the sand watching wave after wave roll to shore, the ocean and I also become one. Somehow I am drawn into its life and being.

Today's verse from the Psalms holds an allure similar to that of the ocean. Somehow these words voice my desire to enter into the fullness that is God: to ask, to seek, to live, to behold, to inquire. Though totally other, I seek to become one with the Holy, drawn into its very life and being.

How can words written long ago, prayed long ago, articulate my own and others' needs and desires today? Certainly, the answer has something to do with our humanity, which, in its similarities and peculiarities, we share with people of all time. But perhaps more important in the lives of people of faith through the ages is the yearning for the Divine and for the presence of God. Ever changing, ever the same, the vastness of the Holy draws us to itself as the ocean draws us to its shore.

Suggestion for meditation: **Slowly read Psalm 27:4 (below). Ponder any word or image that speaks to you or that expresses your deepest desire. Then sit quietly, listening for and resting in the Holy.**

> **One thing I asked of the LORD,**
> **that I will seek after:**
> **to live in the house of the LORD**
> **all the days of my life,**
> **to behold the beauty of the LORD**
> **and to inquire in his temple.**

January 22–28, 1996   **Luther E. Smith, Jr.✤**
Monday, January 22   Read Psalm 15.

Dare we ask if we may enter God's house? Dare we risk hearing expectations that bar us from entering?

Clergy and laity extol the importance of attending church. This attendance benefits the spiritual formation of the individual and the fellowship of believers. Active participation in the life of a religious community is taken for granted as our duty and perhaps even as our privilege. How jolting, then, to be challenged by the psalm's discriminating questions: "O LORD, who may abide in your tent? Who may dwell on your holy hill?"

The answer which follows is also disturbing. The standards of entry require us to take inventory of our lives. Coming before the holy of holies is no casual matter. Yet, the psalm's characterization of one who may enter is not intended to reject all who fall short of keeping the standards. If this were the case, who could enter? Being with God is necessary for our transformation into becoming who God has called us to be.

As we approach God's house, may a spirit of desire for God and devotion to God assure entry. Be prepared, though, because our being with God always leads us to examine and account for how we have been with God's people.

Prayer: **Receive us into your presence, O God. And help us seek right relationship with your people. Amen.**

✤Associate Professor of Church and Community, Candler School of Theology, Emory University, Atlanta; ordained clergy, Christian Methodist Episcopal Church.

Tuesday, January 23   Read Micah 6:1-5.

God is angry. All creation comes to attention.

God remembers the people's oppression and their dependence on God's mighty act of deliverance. This remembering is more than historical perspective; it is re-presenting the reality of God's steadfast compassion. The biblical sense of "remembering" is never just the ability to recall past events. Remembering involves being faithful to the claim of history upon our present existence. For example, whenever the prophets admonished the people to remember the Law, they were not invested in the people's ability to recite it. They called upon the people to demonstrate how what they remembered held power over their present belief and behavior.

The crisis of God's anger is caused by the people's failure to remember. Life is lived as if having been with God makes no difference.

We can join the chorus of disappointment over Israel's forgetting. But first let us ask, Does God have a controversy with you and me because of *our* forgetfulness? Assess your own response to this history. Do you live the significance of "O my people, remember now . . . that you may know the saving acts of the LORD"? Surrounded by our ancestors of faith, we remember God's saving acts of deliverance and are ushered into the presence of God.

Prayer: **God, help us to discover you anew through our heritage and to know salvation and assurance from remembering your steadfast compassion throughout history. Amen.**

Wednesday, January 24   Read Micah 6:6-8.

The price exacted to be with God is great. The prophet's registry of offerings exceeds will and capacity. The enormity of sacrifice increases as the list is read: burnt offerings, valuable calves, thousands of rams, ten thousands of rivers of oil, one's first child. But God does not desire such tribute. God exacts an even greater price than our possessions or the treasures of our heart. God wants *us*.

To give ourselves to God is to give ourselves to the passions of God's heart. And we already know what that means, for God has told us what is good—doing justice, loving kindness, and walking humbly with God. This is a commitment that is both simple yet total.

The simplicity takes hold and rescues us from religious ritualism and moral inertia. Our hearts rejoice in opportunities to express their devotion and please God. However, we also come to realize that our lives are not our own—we belong to God. Giving ourselves to God is the ultimate surrender; our all is given to All. Possessions collected to appease God and possessions withheld for our personal enjoyment, loving relationships we sacrifice and those we secure at all cost—all these must be transposed for doing justice, and loving kindness, and walking humbly with God.

As you walk with God, be at peace. Whatever is required of you can be fulfilled by remembering—remembering the good about which God has spoken so clearly and often, and which you have already experienced more times than you can count.

Prayer: **Thank you, God, for talking and walking with us. Help us to listen and to remember and to keep company with you, O God, wherever you choose to lead us. Amen.**

Thursday, January 25   Read Matthew 5:1-12.

To whom is Jesus speaking? Some biblical scholars believe Jesus is addressing the "great crowds [that] followed him from Galilee, the Decapolis, Jerusalem, Judea, and from beyond the Jordan" (Matt. 4:25). Others conclude he is speaking to a small group of "his disciples [who] came to him." The social and spiritual predicament of his hearers is also debated. One perspective argues that Jesus sees a people who are desperate for consolation and hope. They are the poor in spirit. They mourn. They are meek. They hunger and thirst for righteousness. They are merciful, pure in heart, peacemakers, and persecuted for righteousness sake. Jesus *assures* them that they are the blessed of God who will experience spiritual fulfillment. A second perspective sees Jesus teaching people who need to know the principles of God's realm. Jesus' message is a *call to transform* their lives into blessed commitment. He preaches to inspire them to pursue God and do God's work.

Each interpretation shines a distinct and illuminating light on the text. Rather than making these competing interpretations, perhaps we can accept both of them as true. Jesus may have been speaking to the crowd *and* his disciples . . . those mired in sinful ways *and* desperate people of faith. The words were the same for all those who listened, but the impact was as unique as the condition of each hearer.

More importantly for us today is the question, Is Jesus speaking to us? What is the significance of his message in my life?

Prayer: **Teach me your ways, O God. Touch tenderly my spirit when I need assurance. Tutor my spirit when I need to be challenged, to know the blessed satisfaction of being your faithful disciple. Amen.**

Friday, January 26   Read Matthew 5:1-12.

I could hardly believe my ears. Never before had I heard this interpretation of the Sermon on the Mount. The preacher explained, to his national radio audience, how Jesus' sermon (see Matthew 5:1–7:27) was not intended as instruction for behavior during our earthly existence. If it applied to our daily living, we would be subjected to a miserable life; the attitudes and behaviors prescribed in the sermon could leave us vulnerable to abuse by others. Jesus' message, he argued, intended to describe what we would experience only once evil was annihilated and God's reign was established.

A careful reading of the text annuls this preacher's interpretation. Throughout the sermon, Jesus portrays living God's rule in a social climate fraught with hostility, religious legalism, anxiety, and indifference—a climate that cries out for God's radical care here and now.

This radio minister, however, may speak our actual *response to* the sermon. After hearing Jesus' message, our witness too often reveals that we do not believe our ears. The sermon is inspiring, but seems impractical for immediate needs and capacities. Consequently, even the Beatitudes section of the sermon (today's lesson) causes us consternation. Our disbelief about the sufficiency of God's blessings leaves us stranded in our anxieties and thirsting for controlling power.

We have heard the message of the Beatitudes. Even when we refuse to believe what we hear, God's radical care is still our supreme blessedness. Blessed are those who live the truth of the Beatitudes, for they shall know the joy of being with God.

Suggestion for meditation: **How have you felt blessed by living one of the Beatitudes? Were others blessed by your witness? What were the risks of your commitment? Why did you not allow the risks to cancel your commitment?**

Saturday, January 27   Read 1 Corinthians 1:18-25.

We crave the assurance of signs and wisdom. Signs are easily dressed in religious apparel as garments of faith. For example, some people consider health and wealth to be sure signs that reveal faithfulness and being in favor with God. The wisdom of this world is also a tempting locus for faith. Testimonies of history, verification from scientific method, fierce reasoning by philosophical and theological inquiry—all these can become our idolatrous evidence for debating belief or non-belief.

As Paul writes to the church at Corinth, he yearns for its members not to be deceived by the promises of false signs and earthly wisdom. They are not the means by which God's truth is ultimately revealed. When we journey with God, we may ask for signs, such as the power to "remove mountains" (1 Cor. 13:2). Being with God seems opportune for seeking wisdom—so that we "have prophetic powers, and understand all mysteries and all knowledge" (1 Cor. 13:2). Too often we pursue the world's signs and wisdom to satisfy our hunger for certainty and control. But to build shrines of devotion to such signs and wisdom is foolishness.

God leads us to a greater revelation. Keep company with God, the ultimate source of all wisdom and power. Keep company with God, for before us is a sign that reveals wisdom and power beyond human achievement. The sign is believably clear—the executed Savior. We are called to proclaim this revelation with our words and by our lives.

Prayer: **God, our hearts crave assurance. Our fears and desires urge us to seek a faith that submits to them. Help us to entrust our lives to you, and to realize that you are closer to us than we are to ourselves. May we be comforted and assured by your presence with us. And may we experience strength and wisdom in the message of the cross. Amen.**

Sunday, January 28   Read 1 Corinthians 1:26-31.

"God chose . . . God chose . . . God chose." Today's scripture passage is unequivocal: *God* is doing the choosing. This selecting is not a tribute to being the "foolish," the "weak," and "what is low and despised in the world, things that are not." Of themselves, they suffer a terrible fate of degradation and oppression. But when God chooses them, they become a creative and powerful force with which the world must contend. Just as importantly, when God chooses them, they are able to fulfill the "call" upon their lives.

Paul's message must have inspired the church members at Corinth. Acknowledging their status within the society, these members knew they were in no position to compete for the prestige and privilege accorded the ruling classes. Perhaps this inability to influence their social reality led to the internal competition that plagued their church fellowship. (See 1 Corinthians 10–17.) However, in these declarations of social reversals, Paul was not seeking to assure the members that they would now occupy coveted positions of power. God is doing something more revolutionary than merely choosing outsiders to play at being insiders. God is choosing to establish a whole new order.

We also have a choice—to say yes or no to God. To the call upon our lives, what will we answer? To the mission before us to serve God's will for a new order of love, what will we answer? To the invitation to be with God, will we answer yes or no?

Prayer: **God, help us to choose what you choose for us. To do this, we desire and need your presence. May we remember by heart the many times and ways you have loved us. May we remember the vocation you give us to love others. And may we remember the saving sign of the cross. This we pray, O God, as we seek to walk humbly with you throughout all the days of our lives. Amen.**

THE BLESSINGS OF RIGHTEOUSNESS

January 29—February 4, 1996   **Harriet E. Crosby**✤
Monday, January 29   Read Psalm 112:1-12.

The scripture readings for this week link the fortunes of rich and poor, bind the fate of the free to that of the oppressed. These passages empower the powerless with love and bestow wisdom on those who are not wise in the world. The readings from the Hebrew scriptures (the Old Testament) view doing justice not as a responsibility but as a blessing. The New Testament readings show that the gospel's blessing springs from Christ crucified.

Psalm 112 speaks of abundance for those who fear the Lord, obey God's commandments, and provide for the poor. Not only is there the promise of prosperity, but a promise of immortality is made to those who do justice. "Their descendants will be mighty in the land; the generation of the upright will be blessed. Wealth and riches are in their houses, and their righteousness endures forever."

Now, I am not preaching a gospel that declares prosperity as a divine right. But Psalm 112 does seem to indicate that a just society reaps many blessings, prosperity being one of them. Various scarcity theories that suggest there is not enough (money, food, power, love, etc.) for everybody have no place in the Bible. According to scripture *there is plenty for everyone, rich and poor together, because God provides.* God blesses us when we live out of plenty instead of scarcity. Generous hearts know a bountiful God.

Prayer: **Lord, in you I know there is enough and more than enough. Help me share my plenty with others. Let me receive your blessing. Amen.**

✤Professional writer; Presbyterian layperson; Oakland, California.

41

Tuesday, January 30   Read Isaiah 58:1-5.

Israel's sin was not lack of worship but lack of integrity. I believe that integrity is living one's life seamlessly, as though every part of life is a piece of one fabric instead of a patchwork quilt made up of many independent pieces. In Israel's case, the people lived as though their fasting had nothing to do with the rest of their lives, how they treated people at work or their use of violence.

Fasting as a spiritual practice can help us consciously experience scarcity as an act of repentance. It is a cleansing discipline. The scarcity experienced during a fast throws God's abundant mercy in bold relief.

When we practice the spiritual discipline of fasting, we practice living under God's mercy alone. It is under God's mercy that we fall on our knees and worship. It is under God's mercy that we can repent and try again. It is under God's mercy that we come to show mercy to our families, our co-workers, our neighbors. It is under God's mercy that we live in peace.

Prayer: **Lord God, your mercy alone is enough. Let my fasting be acceptable and pleasing to you. Grant me the courage to be merciful as you are merciful. In Jesus' name. Amen.**

Wednesday, January 31   Read Isaiah 58:6-12.

In 1991 a firestorm ravaged the Oakland/Berkeley hills, where I live. The entire area, including my neighborhood, was evacuated until the fire could be controlled. When I returned, I saw how badly the fire had ravaged the hillsides. The earth was completely scorched—nothing, absolutely nothing was left. Three thousand people lost their homes; twenty-six people lost their lives. The community decided to build a memorial to the victims of the firestorm. But they did not build a monument made out of stone. Instead they planted what is now known as the Hiller Highlands Memorial Garden, a living symbol of healing, hope, and promise in a scarred, sun-scorched land.

Every Christian is a memorial to hope. Christians throughout Oakland and Berkeley were crucial in feeding, clothing, and housing the victims of the firestorm. When we loose the bonds of injustice, share our bread with the hungry, house and clothe the homeless, God makes each of us like a well-watered garden whose healing springs up quickly. Like the Hiller Highlands Memorial Garden, the people of God are places of healing. In Christ, God calls us to become a refuge to people whose lives have been scorched by adversity and pain.

Prayer: **Lord God, reveal to me how I can become a refuge of hope and healing to someone who needs me. Water me with your strength, and sustain me to minister in your name. Amen.**

Thursday, February 1   Read Matthew 5:13-16.

Years ago I was on a business trip in New York. As several colleagues and I prepared to go out in search of dinner in Manhattan, my boss appeared smiling and said, "Remember who you are and what you represent." Of course, he meant that as representatives of the corporation we should comport ourselves with all due decorum and not subject ourselves to all the late-night temptations New York City has to offer.

As I study the Beatitudes, my boss's words, slightly changed, come back to me—remember who you are and *whom* you represent. When we are abroad in the world we are Christ's representatives, the salt of the earth, the light of the world. How we live in the world is a matter of life and death. How we live with our families, our neighbors, our communities and churches points to God's presence in our midst—or denies God's kingdom at work in the world. For example, if I tell a friend in pain that I am available to help any time, day or night, she might see Jesus in my eyes. On the other hand, if I treat my employees disrespectfully, it is no wonder their cynical views of Christ deepen. Living as Christ's representatives we must not lose our saltiness or hide our lamps under bushels. Too much is at stake.

Prayer: **Lord Jesus, help me to remember who I am and whom I represent. Grant that I may be a representative of your love for the world. And should I stumble, have mercy on me, and do not let me hinder your grace. In your name. Amen.**

Friday, February 2   Read Matthew 5:17-20.

I once heard author Becky Manly Pippert preach. She told a story that perfectly exemplifies righteousness which exceeds that of the Scribes and Pharisees. Becky was enjoying a Sunday worship service at a large church—the music was wonderful, the preaching magnificent. In the middle of the sermon a homeless person wandered down the center aisle. Uncomfortable, people began to murmur. The homeless man walked up to the front of the church and sat down quietly on the floor before the podium. No one knew quite what to do. But a deacon of the church got up from his seat, walked down the center aisle, and sat on the floor next to the man for the rest of the service, which continued without interruption.

I believe that that deacon did what he did because, first and foremost, he loves Jesus. The deacon knew that Jesus is the fulfillment of the law and the prophets. But such fulfillment comes from loving those who are "outside," ignored, or powerless. Because Jesus kept God's commandment to love God and to love our neighbor as ourself, we strive to do the same. Like the deacon, we do not do good for goodness' sake—we do good for Christ's sake. We do not belong to an ethical or moral system of rules and regulations—we belong to Christ. And all our acts of love and mercy flow because we have known mercy from Jesus' hand.

Prayer: **Lord, help me to obey your commands today out of the love and mercy you have shown me in Jesus Christ. Amen.**

Saturday, February 3   Read 1 Corinthians 2:1-5.

I have a friend who, in my opinion, has some very strange and decidedly unorthodox ideas about God. She does, however, pray. In fact, she prays almost all the time, and she is very direct with God about what she needs for herself, her family, and her community. Amazingly, God answers many, if not most, of her prayers. It finally occurred to me that God answers my friend's prayers not because she is or is not theologically correct or even wise but because God loves her.

"My speech and my proclamation were not with plausible words of wisdom, but with a demonstration of the Spirit and of power, so that your faith might rest not on human wisdom but on the power of God."

When I read these words of Paul to the Corinthians, I thought of my friend and her prayer life. I began to realize that, like my friend, my faith does not rest on orthodoxy or theological constructs. My faith rests on God, revealed in Spirit and power. And the power of God is love, Jesus Christ, and him crucified for all of us, regardless of how much or how little theological wisdom we may possess.

Prayer: **Lord Christ, let me know you through the power of the Holy Spirit. For you, O God, are more than orthodoxy and theology. You are mystery revealed in love crucified. Amen.**

Sunday, February 4   Read 1 Corinthians 2:6-12.

Today's passage opens to us the heart of mystical experience. "We speak of God's wisdom, secret and hidden, which God decreed before the ages for our glory." Unlike human wisdom, the wisdom of God is not learned—it is acquired through intimate experience of the Spirit of God. It is a mystical experience which transcends the life of the mind to inspire and transform our whole being—heart, spirit, and body as well as mind.

God's wisdom has nothing to do with common sense or social acceptability. The wisdom of God is made incarnate in Christ crucified. The secret of God's wisdom is revealed in love made strong through weakness, made alive through death. We are called to be ordinary mystics on a journey to seek God's wisdom rather than the "wisdom of this age." The mystic who seeks God's wisdom is contrary—contrary to culture and convention. As Christian mystics open to experiencing "the Spirit that is from God," we look for God's love in all the places that may seem wrong—among the weak and powerless. We look to find life in the midst of death.

Prayer: Lord, help me to know your wisdom in the power of the Spirit. By your Spirit sustain me to be contrary to the wisdom of this world that I may enjoy you and glorify you forever. Amen.

OBEDIENCE—A LIFE-GIVING CHOICE

February 5–11, 1996   **George W. Bashore✣**
Monday, February 5   Read Psalm 119:1-8.

In both the Hebrew and Greek languages "to obey" and "to hear" are often interchangeable. On Mount Sinai God told Moses to tell the Israelites, "If you obey (hear) my voice and keep my covenant, you shall be my treasured possession" (Exod. 19:5). God is revealed through the divine word and voice; however, hearing is more than a physical response. It is an obedience which trusts that God will supply the resources to enable participation in the divine purpose and action. Obedience is faith accompanied by action.

The psalmist knows that those who walk in the way of the Lord will know happiness. Obedience gives a dance to one's step; disobedience burdens the journey. "I shall walk at liberty, for I have sought your precepts" (Psalm 119:45).

This psalm speaks not of heaviness but only of delights in obedience to God's ways. "Your decrees are my delight, they are my counselors" (v. 24). "Your decrees are . . . the joy of my heart," (v. 111). Thanks be to God who in Christ has destroyed our disobedience and opens for us the pathway of a delightful freedom of spirit. Obedience is a life-giving choice!

Prayer: **Gracious God, give us such a mighty love for you, that our hearing may be true obedience in Christ. Amen.**

✣Bishop, Pittsburgh Area, Western Pennsylvania Conference, The United Methodist Church.

Tuesday, February 6   Read Psalm 119:1-8.

At first glance the first verse appears to be hard and impossible to fulfill. "Happy are those whose way is blameless." The Hebrew translation for *blameless* means "without blemish." Sacrifices offered to God were the best offerings—the animals without blemish. Happy are those who give the best in following the purposes of God. They are upright in life, always striving to give to God and God's children the highest quality of discipleship. Our greatest joy is in the giving of our best to God.

It is only through God's justifying grace in Jesus Christ that the burden of this unattainable standard is lifted. Jesus Christ, the totally obedient one, has released through the cross a creative power for the perfecting of human life. This gift is sanctifying grace, and we, as new creatures in Christ, can take giant steps toward walking in the way of the Lord. Keeping our eyes upon Jesus we see the obedient way, find the obedient way, and walk with him in living the obedient way.

Charles Tindley, the great hymn writer, helps us to give our best, when he calls for all disciples to have "nothing between" our souls and the Savior. We are to "keep the way clear," knowing that "happy are those . . . who seek [the Lord] with their whole heart." Purity of heart—life without blemish, keeping the way clear—is facing the right direction, seeking God with all of heart, mind, and strength. That is obedience—a life-giving choice!

Prayer: **O Christ, whose obedience unto death has given us life, we pray for purity of heart—to will only your way to our lives. Amen.**

Wednesday, February 7   Read Deuteronomy 30:15-20.

A young woman in the Austin airport was wearing a shirt with the words, *Break the rules!* It led to a reflection, *How many persons have known sadness from breaking the rules?* The Israelites in their wilderness journey, like you and me, vacillated between faithfulness to God and choosing their own ways, breaking the rules. But Moses knew the possibilities for greatness and joy for his people, so he called them to choose God's ways. In verse 16 he reminds them that the way of obedience to God leads to life and blessing.

We need constant reminders about our focus and the way to life. Moses knew this, so he reminded the people of the *Shema* (v. 6). The Israelites repeated the *Shema*. It was on their doorposts; they taught it to their children. On airplane trips to the Holy Land you can see Orthodox Jews binding the words of the *Shema* on their arms and foreheads. This great commandment, "Hear, O Israel: the LORD is our God, the LORD alone. You shall love the LORD your God with all your heart, and with all your soul, and with all your might" (Deut. 6:4-5), reminds Jews and Christians of the faithful love of God for us and the response from us which leads to life.

Scripture verses and other phrases of adoration to God can pull us toward God, who is the Giver of life in Christ. In times of anxiety I have prayed, "I will sing of your grace, O Christ," and again I have felt the magnetic tug of God. What have you memorized to give you focus?

Prayer: **Great Giver of life, we praise you that your drawing power pulls us ever closer to you. Amen.**

Thursday, February 8   Read Deuteronomy 30:15-20.

Life is filled with choices. Some of these choices are small, and others have great significance. Yet all choices determine our future. Even our daily decisions done routinely can have a major cumulative effect, such as the food we eat, TV shows we watch, and patterns of exercise. They can lead to blessings or curses.

Moses pleaded with the Israelites to make right choices: "I have set before you life and death, blessings and curses. Choose life . . . loving the LORD your God, obeying him, and holding fast to him; for that means life to you." One pattern of decisions will lead to life and blessings; the other series of choices will result in death and curses.

Holding fast to God is the only way to life! The choice of obedience to God eventuates in making life-enriching decisions for God's people and universe. Albert Schweitzer, a great missionary doctor, was an advocate for reverence for life. He honored the "will-to-live" in all of creation, and in the footsteps of his Master called all of us to choose to enhance life-enriching values. Our choices also can bring blessings or curses to others. Cling to God and the ways of God's reign, so we will give life to God's children around us.

Prayer: **O life-giving Lord, forgive our participation in life-negating behavior, and give us your heart only to love. Amen.**

Friday, February 9   Read 1 Corinthians 3:1-9.

There is a pervasive "over-againstness" in our society which sets people at odds with one another. Perhaps as children of the Enlightenment our training has given precedence to critical analysis rather than appreciation. Competition on the ball field and in the marketplace so often deteriorates into an individualistic non-ethic with little or no regard for others. It is corrosive to community and loving relationships.

The Apostle Paul decried the divisions in the church at Corinth. People were becoming polarized, choosing sides, and ridiculing others who did not think in the same way. The arrogance in this kind of individualism hindered the people from hearing God's purpose. Their own brand of "rightness" caused separation within the Christian community. In strong language Paul, writing to the Galatians, says that jealousy, quarrels, and factions will cause such advocates to miss the kingdom of God.

God's purpose is that everything and everyone in the whole universe be brought into a unity in Christ. An exclusive "rightness" can be destructive to that purpose. Labels such as conservative and liberal are not helpful, for they perpetuate stereotypes and deny persons freedom to be heard as contributors of creative insights. Diversity of understandings of God's revelation in Christ enriches our life together. Paul rejoices that he and Apollos with varying gifts are servants of the one Lord Jesus Christ. Obedience is kindness and love, giving God the glory and life to all, so that the world might believe.

Prayer: **O God of hospitality, make my spirit restless until you are glorified in all of my relationships and I love as Christ loved. Amen**

Saturday, February 10   Read 1 Corinthians 3:1-9.

Several years ago a group of political, business, religious, social welfare, and educational leaders gathered in Boston to discover solutions for problems confronting that urban setting. The complex areas of homelessness, employment opportunities, housing, and health concerns emerged; however, underlying the low morale and discontent was isolation. Hours were spent seeking ways to establish community—a sense of belonging.

Paul, attempting to bridge the divisions in Corinth, suggested that community is only possible through working together with a common purpose. He and Apollos were God's servants, working together for the same goal. Later he talks about the common foundation for Christian community: "For no one can lay any foundation other than the one that has been laid; that foundation is Jesus Christ" (3:11).

Discipleship is more than belief. The real question is, Are we willing to forsake all and follow Christ? Belief and obedience can never be separated. Theology of faith and the life of faith are inextricably bound together for the Christian disciple. We trust and obey!

Paul and Apollos worked together to mobilize the forces of good against the armies of evil. They were God's servants bringing about personal and social holiness, and thus fulfilling the purposes of God to evangelize until the whole world takes on the mind of Christ. We need each other to work side by side, putting aside all differences and forming a great company of witnesses led by Christ. Obedience is joining that great parade.

Prayer: **Lord of faith and life, help me to take hold of another hand, so that we may together be your servants. Amen.**

Sunday, February 11   Read Matthew 5:21-24.

Actions have evident consequences. Attitudes also are equally filled with life-giving power or life-negating potential. Medical personnel testify to disease and pain caused by stress and anxiety—thought processes. Jesus was no helpless victim of fate. Facing opposition and threat of death, he set his feet steadfastly toward Jerusalem. It was a planned obedience. Indeed, his human anguish poured out in the Garden of Gethsemane, "Let this cup pass from me," but his human inclinations were subjected to the higher divine will, "yet not what I want but what you want" (Matt. 26:39). Faithful to his calling and destiny given at his baptism, Jesus was obedient even unto death.

In the Sermon on the Mount Jesus lifted obedience to a level far beyond external observances, for he knew that actions were derived from attitudes. Anger and murder were subject to divine judgment. Likewise, he pleaded that love should be unrestricted in its giving. "If anyone wants to sue you and take your coat, give your cloak as well; and if anyone forces you to go one mile, go also the second mile" (5:40-41). There is no limit to giving. Jesus' words are always filled with generosity: mourn, be merciful, heal, be peacemakers. We are to give, never keeping score of the deeds.

Our baptism grants us participation in the death-resurrection life cycle of Jesus. That life cried over injustice and death. Our tears also can be transformed into acts of overflowing giving, so that others might live with Christ. Obedience is a life-giving choice for each of us and will also bring life to others.

Prayer: **O God of forgiveness and understanding for the world, make my desires and choices hunger and thirst for your reign in my life and in the world. Amen.**

THIS IS MY SON, THE BELOVED

February 12–18, 1996 **Evelyn Laycock✢**
Monday, February 12 Read Psalm 2.

The theme for this week's devotions is "This is my Son, the Beloved," words which Jesus heard from God at his baptism and the Transfiguration. What is meant by these words would depend upon the nature of the One who is speaking. What does it mean to be a "beloved son"?

Psalm 2 vividly describes the nature of God whose constancy, power, and creativity cover the earth; who has decreed that evil does not triumph, but righteousness. In addition, persons who center their lives in God find meaning in the everydayness of life, for "happy are all who take refuge in him."

In Ibillin, Galilee, is a school established by the Palestinian Elias Chacour,* a Melkite Catholic priest. Experiencing the pain of seeing his own boyhood village and home destroyed, feeling the prejudice and power of those who hate the Palestinians and want them out of Israel, Father Chacour has kept his focus on God and God's call on his life. He has spent his life working to achieve peace and reconciliation among Jews, Christians, and Muslims through building schools, libraries, and summer camps for children of all three religious traditions. This has meant physical and mental persecution, rejection, and unbelievable problems because he is Palestinian. His call to be God's beloved son in this mission burns as a consuming fire within him.

Prayer: **I yearn, O God, to be your beloved child. Amen.**

✢Professor, emeritus, Hiwassee College; Director of the Lay Ministry Center for the Southeastern Jurisdictional Administration of The United Methodist Church; Waynesville, North Carolina.
*Elias Chacour received the 1994 World Methodist Peace Award.

Tuesday, February 13   Read Matthew 17:1-5.

There is a tradition which connects the Transfiguration with Mount Tabor, but that is highly unlikely since the top of Mount Tabor was an armed fortress. Another tradition says that the Transfiguration occurred on Mount Hermon, a 9,400-foot-high mountain that can be seen from the Dead Sea, more than a hundred miles away. However, the place and time are not the central focus; the event is. Somewhere and sometime on the slopes of a mountain the Transfiguration took place. It could quite possibly have been at night, for Luke tells us that Peter and his companions were very sleepy (Luke 9:32).

A more important question is, Why did Jesus go there? Luke gives us the clue; he went there to pray (Luke 9:28). Looking at the days preceding the Transfiguration, we see that Jesus had explained to his disciples "that he must go to Jerusalem and suffer many things at the hands of the elders, chief priests and teachers of the law, and that he must be killed and on the third day be raised to life" (Matt. 16:21, NIV). Peter rebukes Jesus for such a statement. The cross did not fit Peter's concept of Jesus being "the Messiah, the Son of the living God" (Matt. 16:16).

In studying the Transfiguration we learn that Jesus went to the mountain to pray in order to know for certain that this was the course God would have him take. What a message! If the Son of God needed to discern the will of God, so do I and so do you. This calls me to reflect on the question, Do I seek God's will in all that I do?

Prayer: **Help me, God, to see beneath the exterior to the interior in order that my spirit may be in communion with your Spirit. Amen.**

56

Wednesday, February 14   Read Matthew 17:1-9.

Seeing the face of Jesus shining as the sun, his clothes a dazzling white, having Moses and Elijah join the group, leaves Peter in awe. In the presence of such an experience Peter feels the reason he is there is to build dwellings for the three so that all can stay on the mountain. Peter's response is interesting, for rather than moving deeper into the experience of what is happening, his interest is in doing something.

While Peter is still speaking, the voice of God interrupts, "This is my Son, the Beloved; with him I am well pleased; listen to him!" That is to say, "Son, you are on the right course. You must go to Jerusalem." Jesus had his answer; his purpose in coming to the mountain was accomplished.

Many of us know the struggle that comes with discerning the will of God. The "pulls" of culture, peers, and our inner selves are strong. But to hear God's affirmation puts to rest the other voices, and we experience peace.

It is fascinating that Moses and Elijah appeared in the vision. Do you think they might have been there to witness to the acts of God on other mountains? Moses and Elijah each had an intimate experience with God on a mountain. Moses received the tablets of law on Mount Sinai (see Exodus 20; Deuteronomy 5); Elijah found God in the still small voice on Mount Horeb (see 1 Kings 19). Further, Jewish belief was that Elijah would appear just before the Messiah's coming. When Elijah came, Moses would accompany him. They, too, are confirmation to Jesus that he is doing God's will and that God is with him. It is further evidence that Jesus is the Messiah and that God's kingdom is present on earth as it is in heaven.

Prayer: **Help us, O God, to remember your faithfulness through the ages. We pray that we may respond to it today through eyes of faith and hearts of love. Amen.**

Thursday, February 15   Read 2 Peter 1:16-18.

Second Peter is one of the last New Testament books to be written. When Jesus had not returned to earth in the form people expected, some in the church began saying Jesus was not the Messiah. Peter combated this heresy by saying, "We did not follow cleverly devised myths when we made known to you the power and coming of our Lord Jesus Christ, but we had been eyewitnesses of his majesty." Peter reminded the people that he saw, heard, and experienced Jesus receiving majestic glory and honor from God at the Transfiguration. He told them that God had said, "This is my Son, the Beloved; with him I am well pleased."

This passage is as relevant as the day in which it was written. One of the current theological discussions centers on the identity of Jesus. Some people say Jesus is only one route among many to God. At a recent meeting, a paper was presented suggesting that Jesus was born following Mary's rape by a Roman soldier. Others profess Jesus is God's Son, but they do not live out his teachings. *Heresy is still alive.*

There is a story about a Utah sheepherder who wrote to a radio station with the following request: "As a shepherd I spend my time with the sheep. I have a radio and listen to your station. I have my violin with me, but it is out of tune. One day, could you stop your programming and play A440* so that I can tune my violin?"

Imagine his joy when he heard, "For the Utah sheepherder, in 15 minutes we will play A440 in order that you can tune your violin."

Peter is saying that Jesus is God's A440, the standard note against which all life is meant to be tuned.

Prayer: Jesus, I bring myself to you for tuning. Amen.

---

*The standard note to which musical instruments are tuned

Friday, February 16   Read 2 Peter 1:19-21.

Again, Peter is talking to persons in the church who say that Jesus is not the Messiah. They are seeing through prejudiced eyes with self-centeredness of heart.

Peter reminds them that no prophecy in scripture permits private interpretation, for the prophets received God's message through the divine revelation of God's spirit; therefore, the message must be interpreted through the Spirit. For the Jews, God's spirit had two primary functions: to bring God's truth to persons and to enable persons to understand this truth.

Peter encourages individuals and the church to allow the Holy Spirit to testify in them to the fact that Jesus is the Light that shines in a dingy place—a metaphor easily understood in a world of no electricity, only small oil lamps. And they were to continue such a focus until the day dawned and the morning star rose *within their hearts*. This is another way of saying to meditate on the Light until the darkness of your life is illuminated by the Christ, the morning star.

As one who appreciates the early morning, I find this imagery deeply meaningful. The morning star will always be the brightest in the heavens at that time of day, dazzling against the dark sky. The brightness, beauty, and constancy of the morning star give hope and assurance that the dawn of a new day is near. The same is true of Jesus the Christ. He was and is the hope, the promise, and the assurance of a new day, the kingdom of God as lived reality now and future.

Prayer: **O God, may my eyes focus on Jesus, the Light of the world. May my life be so yielded to his light that all darkness may be dispelled; that, in his power, I may reflect your light today. Amen.**

Saturday, February 17 Read Exodus 24:12-18.

This text has its closest counterpart in the New Testament in the narrative of the Transfiguration. Some of the similarities are that Jesus and Moses were each on a mountain and the glory of the Lord was on the mountain like a "devouring fire"—visible, consuming, awesome. The voice of God spoke to Moses telling him that tablets of stone containing the law and the commandments would be given him for the instruction of the people. Jesus heard the voice of God say, "This is my Son, the Beloved." The laws God gave Moses, Jesus fulfilled in his life and teaching (see Matthew 5:17). In educational terms, Jesus would be called the "visual aid" of the Law. Experiencing God brings Jesus and Moses face to face with the holiness of God, the core of faith.

God's calling of Moses and Jesus to the mountain shows the self-giving nature of God. The Law, God's gift for instruction and Jesus, God's gift of salvation to humankind, show in an awesome way the very heart and nature of God.

This vision of God is inescapably transformative, for it brings a person from humanness into an awareness of the divine within and the possibility of growing more into the likeness of the holy Creator God.

For those who "enter the cloud," the very presence of God and communion with God's holiness brings transformation. That, in turn, can transform an individual, a church, a community, a society. What a message of hope!

Prayer: **Creator God, may we have the courage to "enter the cloud" of your presence and listen to your word for us. May we leave the cloud to be your word by our lives and in our words. Amen.**

Sunday, February 18   Read Psalm 99.

Psalm 99 is a call to worship. The writer knows God to be the One who is a mighty King, a lover of justice, one who has established equity, executed justice and righteousness. God is holy and worthy of worship. Therefore, the people should worship the Lord, pour forth their praise, their adoration, their confession. In the past God heard the cries of the people and accepted the services of their priests. Moses, Aaron, and Samuel called upon God, and God answered them in the "pillar of cloud."

In verses 8 and 9 the implications for the present are clear: what God has done in the past, God will continue to do in the present. Christians know this to be true. When Jesus told a parable about the pain a father experiences over his two sons (Luke 15:11-32), he is describing the nature of a holy, self-giving, suffering God, one who cares so deeply that he leaves the ninety-nine sheep that are safe to search for the one who is lost. Also, through the beautiful images of lilies and sparrows, Jesus reminds us of the daily care God yearns to give us (see Matthew 6:26-30).

The cross is the ultimate expression of God's love for humanity. Such love is difficult to grasp—God suffering for human evil, even going to a cross for human beings. To grasp this concept brings us to "extol the LORD our God, and worship at his holy mountain; for the LORD our God is holy."

A holy God calls forth a lifestyle of holiness from those who worship God. This lifestyle must be set apart in servanthood and a self-giving love that moves into the pain of individuals and the world. To such a person God can say, "This is my son/my daughter, my beloved."

Prayer: **O God, I yearn to worship you in spirit and in truth. Amen.**

GOD OF MERCY AND FORGIVENESS

February 19–25, 1996   **Perry H. Biddle, Jr.✤**
Monday, February 19   Read Genesis 2:15-17; 3:1-7.

The reality of sin confronts us every day, most blatantly as we read the newspaper or watch the news on television. The news media seem to delight in telling us all the gory details of sinful human actions.

In the lushness of the Garden of Eden, Adam and Eve looked out over trees laden with good produce to eat. All this, God told Adam, was there and free "for the picking." But—*one* tree was off limits, the tree "of the knowledge of good and evil." God said this to warn Adam of the risk of death associated with this tree.

Genesis 3 teaches that when Adam and Eve put forth their hands to take the forbidden fruit, they broke a divine command and thereby committed sin—a rebellious act against God. To know good and evil means to master good and evil, and thus become *like God*. The sin of human beings was the desire to be equal to God—the only privilege humans did not enjoy. This sin, this act of disobedience, severed the particular intimacy of the relationship between God and the human couple. They were sent out of the beautiful, secure garden.

Prayer: **Keep me from sin this day, O God. Amen.**

✤Author; ordained minister, Presbyterian Church (U.S.A.); past president and Fellow of Academy of Parish Clergy, Inc.; Nashville, Tennessee.

Tuesday, February 20   Read Genesis 3:1-7.

We human beings are not immortal. We all have to return to the earth from which we were made. But this earthly condition of human beings was suspended during the time we lived near the tree of life, as Genesis 3 tells us.

This week we focus on sin and on God's gracious work of forgiving sin through Christ. In the past forty years, we have seen a move to downplay sin and its destructive power in the world. The horrors of the Holocaust during the Nazi period continue to remind us that evil is a present reality. Wars continue today in many parts of the world, maiming and killing innocent people.

We find that the question of the origin of sin is linked by some people to the first cause of sin. As we examine the Hebrew scriptures we discover that there is no uniform answer on this; the ills of Job are attributed to Satan, and those of Adam and Eve to the serpent. These approaches are the writers' attempts to explain the origin of evil, which, regardless of the name we give the tempter, is centered in humankind's failure to resist temptation.

In Genesis 2:15-17 God placed human beings in the garden. Their enjoyment of it was a gift of God. Work itself was not evil. The happiness of human beings depended on their obedience to God.

Jesus summed up all the Law and the prophets in the one command to love God and neighbor (Mark 12:29-31). Sin is disobedience to the law of love. What sin has done, God in Christ has worked to undo, breaking the power of evil and offering us the gift of forgiveness.

Prayer: **Holy God, break the vicious cycle of sin in my life and grant me the grace to accept the forgiveness that Christ offers. Amen.**

Ash Wednesday

Wednesday, February 21   Read Psalm 51:1-17.

The Book of Psalms attributes Psalm 51 to David, writing after Nathan the prophet confronted him with his sin of adultery with Bathsheba. It expresses the deep conviction of sin of one who repents and seeks God's forgiveness.

Psalm 51 is an appropriate passage for Ash Wednesday and the beginning of Lent, which is a time of self-examination, repentance, and spiritual growth.

The psalm begins with an affirmation of God's mercy in the face of the psalmist's sin. We can repent of sin only because we have first known the assurance of God's love, mercy, and forgiveness. God comes to us first, as the waiting Father in Jesus' parable offered the prodigal son forgiveness and restoration (Luke 15:11-32).

Too often we think that we have to do something to merit God's mercy. We desperately try to make ourselves acceptable before we turn to God for reconciliation. But the good news of scripture is that God takes the initiative to give mercy and restore us to God's family.

The writer declares, "For I know my transgressions, and my sin is ever before me." Sin and guilt have a haunting, nagging, relentless aspect. We cannot by our own power get sin out of our minds and consciences.

The psalmist acknowledges that he has sinned against God and has done what is evil in God's sight. During Lent we have an opportunity to reflect on our lives, to seek out those things that have offended God, to repent of them, and to accept God's mercy.

Prayer: **Have mercy on us, O God, according to your steadfast love. Create in us clean hearts and put a new and right spirit within us. Amen.**

Thursday, February 22   Read Psalm 32.

Lent should be a happy, not gloomy, time. Someone has said that the purest form of response to God's forgiveness is laughter! The psalmist expressed this when he wrote, "Happy are those whose transgression is forgiven, whose sin is covered." While soul-searching is painful, and repenting of sin demands thought and energy, the result is freedom, joy, and new life in Christ.

While visiting mission stations in Lesotho in southern Africa I met a young woman who worked in a government office. I remember her wonderful smile, which reflected her faith and joy. Missionaries tell us that converts to the Christian faith are joyful because they know there is only one God, and this God has revealed mercy and love in Christ. Therefore, they no longer fear gods who might become angry and do persons harm; no longer fear vengeful gods who can zap persons with illness, pain, or death.

Lent is a time of taking stock, of examining one's whole life, and of taking inventory of one's attitudes and actions. It is a time of prayer, meditation, and devotional reading.

The psalmist says that while he kept silence his body wasted away through his groaning all day long. Repressed emotions—especially resentment, anger, and despair—can destroy body, mind, and spirit. But the psalmist states that when he acknowledged his sin before God and said, "I will confess my transgressions to the LORD," God forgave his sin. Then the psalmist could be glad in the Lord.

Prayer: **God of mercy, remind me, I pray, of your welcoming heart, waiting only for our seeking you. Amen.**

Friday, February 23   Read Romans 5:12-19.

The Apostle Paul juxtaposes Adam and Christ, the new Adam. Sin entered the world through Adam, bringing death; and spread death to all because all have sinned. Even more the grace of God in the one man Jesus Christ abounded for the many.

As we take inventory of our attitudes and actions during Lent, we must balance the judgment of sin with the grace of Jesus Christ. Judgment followed Adam's sin of disobedience, and this judgment brought condemnation. But the free gift of God is righteousness, which is right relationship with God.

One of the most popular hymns in America today is "Amazing Grace." We hear it played and sung in churches as well as secular settings. John Newton, an Anglican clergyman, wrote the hymn after his conversion. He had been the captain of a slave ship. While a slave ship captain, he had even held devotions on the deck of his ship for the crew while slaves suffered and died down below. Yet he came to feel in the depths of his soul that he was a "wretch," saved only by the grace of God. After experiencing the forgiving, transforming, and amazing grace of God in Christ, Newton entered the ministry.

Paul says that even as death exercised dominion through Adam's trespass, surely those who receive the abundance of God's grace will exercise dominion in life through Jesus Christ, the new Adam.

Lent is time to take stock of our sin, not to wallow in guilt. We may claim the amazing grace through which we are forgiven and restored to God's family.

Prayer: **Thank you, loving God, for your amazing grace that saved a wretch like me. Thank you for your free gift of righteousness. Amen.**

Saturday, February 24   Read Matthew 4:1-11.

Jesus was tempted as we are tempted, yet he was sinless. We are not alone when we are tempted; Jesus is with us, giving us strength to resist temptation. The account of Jesus being tempted by the devil in the wilderness shows us how we, too, can resist temptation when it comes our way.

The devil first tempted Jesus to turn stones into bread—the temptation to gain a popular following by meeting the physical needs of people. The devil challenged Jesus with the words, "If you are the Son of God, . . ." Jesus replied with words from scripture, which say humans are not to live by bread alone but by every word that comes from God's mouth.

The devil then challenged Jesus to throw himself from the pinnacle of the Temple in Jerusalem—the temptation to sensationalize in order to dazzle people into following him. Again the devil quoted scripture to assure Jesus that God would rescue him. And again Jesus quoted scripture, "Do not put the LORD your God to the test." We are to trust God's providential care, not to test God.

The third and final temptation the devil put to Jesus was to fall down and worship the devil in exchange for the kingdoms of this world—the temptation to lay hold of political power. But Jesus refused to forsake God who sent him into the world, replying, again in words of scripture, "Away with you, Satan! for it is written 'Worship the LORD your God, and serve only him.'" After this final temptation Satan left Jesus and "angels came and waited on him."

Prayer: **Living Christ, grant me strength to resist temptation this day, in the knowledge that you are ever near me. Amen.**

Sunday, February 25   Read Matthew 6:1-6, 16-21.

In Jesus' estimation, spiritual sins of pride and selfishness are far more destructive of spiritual living than sins of the flesh. Yet we tend to reverse this understanding by condemning the sins of the flesh we don't indulge in and ignoring those spiritual sins that have trapped us.

In the Sermon on the Mount, Jesus warns against practicing one's piety before others in order to be seen by them. He warns that our heavenly Father will not reward such piety on display.

Then Jesus deals with three specific acts of piety: giving alms, praying, and fasting. All are commendable when done in the correct spirit. But when done to gain attention from others, that attention is all the reward one will receive.

During Lent we focus on our spiritual growth, seeking to become more like Christ each day. We can become Christlike only by dying to self and being made alive in Christ by his spirit. We can grow by daily turning from pride in our own spiritual good works and turning in humility to ask God's forgiveness.

In these verses from Matthew, Jesus points us to the way of self-forgetting acts of piety that we do for the glory of God and not for other people to see. As we pray, give our gifts, and practice self-denial by fasting during Lent, let us do these acts in private as Jesus commanded.

Prayer: **As we move through this season of Lent, O God, help us to keep our eyes focused on you and not on what others think of our pious acts. Help us to deny self and glorify you alone. Amen.**

God's Initiative

February 26—March 3, 1996 **Roberto L. Gómez✤**

Monday, February 26 Read Genesis 12:1-4*a*.

At 75 years of age, Abram was frustrated and sad because he and his wife Sarai had no son. For Abram this meant he had no future. God also felt frustrated and sad about the human predicament. God's creation became a nightmare as humankind fell from grace. For God this meant a gloomy and doomed future with humankind.

Genesis 12:1-4*a* relates that God took the initiative to make a difference in the human predicament. Instead of punishment and destruction after Noah's fall from grace, God spoke directly to Abram, blessed him, promised him a future and a great name, and promised to bless all families through him.

To help Abram get to his future, God gave him a mission of faithfulness. Abram obeyed and left his hometown, his family, and his security to follow God. In turn, God made a commitment to be with Abram.

God remains faithful to the promise he made to Abram. God promises a future for those persons, families, and churches willing to listen and to be faithful to God. God blesses the faithful and promises to bless "all the families of the church" through faithful persons, families, and churches.

Prayer: **God, when I experience myself as having no future, bless me with your presence that I may have a vision of the future you have prepared for me. Amen.**

✤Clergy member of the Río Grande Conference of The United Methodist Church; Conference Council Director; San Antonio, Texas.

Tuesday, February 27   Read Psalm 121.

A confessional, liturgical, and dialogic psalm, Psalm 121 provides assurance of God's protection for pilgrims arriving at the Temple in Jerusalem. Psalm 121 undergirds Genesis 12:1-4*a*. The Lord not only promises a future but also sees to it that the recipients of the promise are safe in their journey to that future.

While Abram did not register concern about God's charge to him, there is obvious risk and potential danger in leaving behind one's family, one's home, and one's established economic security to journey into an unknown land and a future only hoped for. Many pilgrims, throughout centuries, have experienced great risks and extreme dangers in their faith journeys when they left behind their support systems.

Recently, two of my friends returned from the country in which they had served as missionaries. They had left behind a successful business, a first-class lifestyle, and a family to become missionaries. After finishing their missionary term, they experienced great danger on their way home. Although they barely escaped with their lives, their love for God was strengthened. Still today they joyfully praise God's holy name for deliverance and sustenance.

Every day God calls people into a faith journey. For some, the faith journey is difficult, filled with risks and danger. In moments of trouble, the pilgrim experiences fear and helplessness. Some will ask where their help will come from.

Psalm 121 is a wonderful and powerful word of hope that the Lord will protect the faithful, even as Abram was protected. The Lord of the living was Abram's protector, and now the Lord of the living is *our* protector!

Prayer: Lord, keep me from evil day and night that I may be faithful to you and move into the future you have promised. Amen.

Wednesday, February 28   Read Romans 4:1-8.

In his Pulitzer Prize–winning book, *Lincoln at Gettysburg*, Garry Wills suggests that President Abraham Lincoln looked for an opportunity to change American political thought about slavery. Lincoln took that opportunity in his words of dedication at the inauguration of the Gettysburg National Cemetery. He profoundly recast American political thought by reaching back to the Declaration of Independence, which uncompromisingly stated that "all men are created equal." In doing so, Lincoln bypassed the Constitution of the United States, which tolerated slavery. Lincoln moved the slavery question from its tie to the Constitution to its basis in freedom as expressed in the Declaration of Independence, the nation's founding document.

Paul looked for an opportunity to share his understanding of God's love for us. He took the opportunity in his letter to the Romans as he interpreted his understanding of what God has done for us and the faith we are to have. Instead of relying on Moses and the concept of law, Paul reached back to the concept of God's grace and Abraham's response.

According to Paul, Abraham was not justified by his works. Rather, God justified Abraham through grace, even *before* Abraham believed in and trusted in God. God reached out to Abraham in love before Abraham responded. As a result, Abraham's faith is a response to God's initiative of grace and blessing.

Paul argued that God's justifying grace is for all. God's love is inclusive, Jew or Gentile, slave or free, male or female. (See Galatians 3:28, NRSV.) Salvation is not tied to the Mosiac Law nor is it dependent on doing the right thing or being the "right person." Salvation is the result of God's unconditional grace for humankind.

Prayer: **O God, remind me that you already love me just as I am. Amen.**

Thursday, February 29   Read Romans 4:9-12.

From the beginning of the Christian faith, Gentiles responded to the gospel. Tension mounted in the early faith communities as the uncircumcised joined in worship and service. Paul himself had been against the new Christian sect and the presence of Gentiles. God touched Paul and changed him so that he understood that God's love and salvation were for all people, including those who were uncircumcised. But how could Paul argue convincingly that the uncircumcised were also reckoned by God to have faith and righteousness?

Paul brilliantly argued that Abraham was uncircumcised when God reckoned faith to him as righteousness. If Abraham was uncircumcised when God accorded him faith through grace, then surely the faith of other uncircumcised people could be "reckoned as righteousness" (Rom. 4:5).

In my hometown, many young people obtain social standing and meaning by joining gangs. The gangs dictate what colors to wear, what style of clothes to wear, whom to associate with, how to greet each other, turf rights, and specific actions to prove loyalty to the gang. Time and time again, young men and women commit violent acts—even murder—to prove their loyalty to the gang and (in their perception) to gain a certain kind of salvation.

According to Romans 4 the gospel has a liberating message for all persons. Paul, inspired by the Holy Spirit, proclaimed that God loves each of us unconditionally. We only need to open our hearts and accept God's love for us.

Prayer: **Open my eyes, dear God, that I may see my cup overflowing with your love for me, for us, for them. Amen.**

Friday, March 1   Read Romans 4:13-17.

Several years ago a friend commented to me and other ordained clergy who were seminary graduates that we were no longer Bible fundamentalists but church law fundamentalists! I was shocked and hurt by his comment, but later I realized how correct my friend was.

My colleagues and I judged others, sometimes severely, according to the law of the church. In essence we were saying to others, "You will find your salvation through the law of the church."

In recent years new believers in Jesus Christ have joined our faith community. They know little or nothing about our church law. As a member of the church for many years and as an ordained minister, I sometimes see new members unknowingly violate our church laws. My reaction is one of frustration and anger over their lack of respect and obedience.

Romans 4:13-17 speaks directly and powerfully to me. It reminds me that God's promises of salvation and new life depend on faith and grace—not on obedience to the law of the church. I am not saying we should forgo church law. However, we must not let church law strangle us and restrict us so we are unable to see God's free and abundant love rushing to and fro outside the walls of our worship place.

Our church laws must not restrict God moving about us and in us. Instead, church laws should point to God and empower our faith so that we, too, may be reckoned as righteous people in the community of Jesus Christ.

Prayer: **O God, help me to obey you by experiencing your love and responding to you with my love. Amen.**

Saturday, March 2   Read John 3:1-10.

I once worked as chaplain in a large county hospital. Since I was the only Spanish-speaking clergy on duty one afternoon, I was asked to baptize a critically ill infant. His parents were young Mexican peasants who were illegal immigrants.

They were Roman Catholics. Because of my biases, I did not want to perform the baptism. I told them emphatically that I was a Protestant preacher and wondered if they wanted me to do the baptism. I wanted them to reject me in favor of the Catholic chaplain who spoke no Spanish.

The short young Mexican mother who wore long braids, a traditional shawl, and sandals looked straight at me and said, *«Usted es un hombre de Dios. Bautice a mi hijo.»* ("You are a man of God. Baptize my son.")

I was stunned by her directive. Suddenly, I realized God was speaking to me through her. What had I done with my ordination, my call to ministry, my love of the sacraments? Was I so bound to my understanding of church law that I was paralyzed for ministry? Would I allow the Spirit from above to free me and empower me for ministry?

My heart broke and I wept for my spiritual blindness, deafness, and paralysis. Immediately I felt peace in my heart. We baptized the child. Later, by the grace of God that little boy got well. By the grace of God, this young mother had given me a new perspective—that my call to ministry and my ordination were of the Spirit that came from above. I was blessed with the presence of the Spirit, and I was born again, this time born of the Spirit.

Prayer: **Lord, remind me that in Christ you make me holy. Fill me with grace to do your ministry. Amen.**

Sunday, March 3   Read John 3:11-17.

A few days ago a colleague presided over the funeral of a 15-year-old who was caught putting graffiti on a store wall. He ran away and was shot. The immediate result was lots of blame. His mother was blamed. The store owner was blamed. The young man's mother blamed the city. On it went.

Many young people are attracted to gangs. They join gangs seeking meaning, self-esteem, and new life. Tragically, most gangs live by the gun and die by the gun.

For many people, families, cities, and even nations, we are living in days of desperation, hopelessness, terror, rising crime and murder rates. Furthermore, some people perceive the Christian faith as outmoded, stagnant, and meaningless. Many young people find it more attractive to join a gang than to belong to a church.

One frequent cry in all these miseries is, "What is God doing about it?" God *has* done something about it.

If we take time to listen to the words of Jesus, if we take time to listen to the spirit of Christ, then we will hear, "For God so loved the world that he gave his only Son, so that everyone who believes in him may not perish but may have eternal life. Indeed, God did not send the Son into the world to condemn the world, but in order that the world might be saved through him."

No condemnation! No punishment! In a spirit of love and hope, Jesus invites us to a new birth and a new life. The promises of Jesus are salvation, love, peace, joy, justice, and eternal life. In Jesus Christ we are blessed!

Prayer: **Thank you, God, for your gracious love and patience. Bless us with your presence and guide us to your kingdom. Amen.**

OUR THIRST FOR GOD

March 4–10, 1996   **Bruce R. Ough**✤
Monday, March 4   Read John 4:5-15.

The history of humankind is marked by intriguing stories of those who sought, always in vain, waters that would insure eternal life. I recall my sixth-grade fascination with Ponce de León's search for the Fountain of Youth in the New World. The thirst for "living water" is universal. Today, this thirst is characterized by our search for the purest bottled water, the healthiest mineral water spa, or the most miraculous holy water.

Every person is created with a deep, persistent thirst for God. This thirst is a gift from God. This thirst propels us to seek God—to seek the "gift of God." Only God can quench our thirst. God is both the source of our thirst and the source of the "living water" that quenches our thirst. Our thirst is for wholeness; the gift of God is healing. Our thirst is for reconciliation; the gift of God is peace. Our thirst is for forgiveness; the gift of God is love. Our thirst is for oneness with God; the gift of God is "a spring of water gushing up to eternal life."

The Samaritan woman at the well is thirsty for healing, for peace, for love, for eternal life. She speaks our prayer: "Sir, give me this water, so that I may never be thirsty." This prayer is awakened within each of us when we enter into dialogue with Jesus. This prayer expresses our deep longing for God. This prayer defines our journey toward God. This prayer is, itself, a "gift of God."

Prayer: **Jesus, give me your living water, that I may never be thirsty. Amen.**

✤Cedar Rapids District Superintendent, Iowa Annual Conference, The United Methodist Church.

Tuesday, March 5

Read Exodus 17:1-3;
Romans 5:1-5.

The Israelites quarreled with Moses and demanded that he give them water to drink. "Why have you brought the assembly of the Lord into this wilderness for us and our livestock to die here?" (Num. 20:4) The whole congregation questioned if the Lord was still among them. Moses had his hands full. He cried out to the Lord, "What shall I do with this people?" (Exod. 17:4)

The isolation of the wilderness heightens our anxiety and feelings of abandonment. Being alone in the desert without any visible means of sustenance makes us quarrelsome, fearful, and rebellious. The deprivation of the desert heightens our senses, particularly our thirst.

If the Israelites had enjoyed freedom in Egypt, Moses could never have persuaded them to attempt the march of liberation. If the desert had been full of alluring oases instead of hunger and thirst, they would never have continued the journey. If the people had not been pushed to the limits of endurance, they would never have learned to depend on God's grace.

Our thirst for God is often born of our wilderness experiences—our times of suffering, our times of despair, our times of resistance, our times of isolation, our times of abandonment. It is our woundedness that shatters the illusion of self-sufficiency. It is in the desert that we learn the blessedness of poverty and our utter dependence on God. It is our pain that enables us to enjoin the journey to salvation. This is the mystery of suffering.

It is in our resistance to God that we experience fully God's unwavering, unconditional yearning for us. It is in our pushing away from God that we feel God's pull. It is in our quarreling with God that we come to know the depth of our thirst for God. This is the mystery of resistance. This is the mystery of the wilderness.

Prayer: **O God of all life, let my wilderness experiences strengthen my thirst for you. Amen.**

Wednesday, March 6　　　　　　　　Read Psalm 95;
　　　　　　　　　　　　　　　　　　　Exodus 17:1-7.

Psalm 95 is a beautiful call to worship. It builds and builds, like an orchestra's crescendo, culminating in a thunderous admonishment to listen to God's voice:

> O come, let us worship and bow down,
> 　let us kneel before the LORD, our Maker!
> For he is our God,
> 　and we are the people of his pasture,
> 　and the sheep of his hand.
> O that today you would listen to his voice!

At Meribah (which means "quarrel" in Hebrew), the Israelites were rebellious, putting God to the test. Still, God demonstrated righteousness. It was in the Waters of Meribah that God's holiness and love were fully revealed. The psalmist reminds us of God's greatness. Then, the psalmist makes it absolutely clear that God prefers a prayerful, listening heart. It is a listening, obedient posture, rather than a quarrelsome posture, that opens us most fully to God's grace. To listen is to acknowledge our thirst for God. Our hunger for God is ultimately expressed in our attentiveness.

Listening, at its fullest, means hearing life through God's ear. It means being "all ears" for God. It is creating the empty, open space within us where we can hear God speak. This is the essence of obedience. Such profound listening leads to an incredible intimacy with the infinite One we call God. Such profound listening positions us to drink deeply from the well of living water. If you thirst for God, if you desire to abide in Christ, "listen to his voice."

Prayer: **Gracious God, grant me an attentive heart that I may drink deeply from your living water. Amen.**

Thursday, March 7   Read John 4:16-29.

Faith is born of our encountering Jesus' unconditional, pervasive love. In this encounter our thirst for God is simultaneously heightened and quenched. This is the mystery of faith. Christ's love both satisfies and awakens a deeper desire to live in God's presence.

As a young boy, I loved the regular trips to and from my grandmother's farm near Alexander, North Dakota. In the center of this little village was a fountain that delivered cool, clean water from a spring that flowed out of a nearby hillside. The spring ran constantly, every season of the year, year after year. The fountain was a regular stop on our trips. I loved the taste of the cool, sweet, refreshing water. I was amazed by the unceasing flow of life-giving water. Each time I drank from this everflowing stream my thirst was quenched. Even though I had faith the spring would always be there, my thirst for the water only grew and my desire to stop at the spring again and again became unquenchable.

Jesus introduces the Samaritan woman to the living water by revealing to her truth about herself and truth about God's forgiveness and love. It is in this moment of truth telling, wrapped in abundant grace, that the Samaritan woman encounters the Messiah; and her faith is born. This is the moment of salvation. Her thirst for living water is satisfied. Her thirst for an abundant life in Christ for herself and others is activated. This is the true worship of which Jesus spoke.

When we drink God's love, when we come to understand that God's love never ceases, we are able to see ourselves for who we are and we are able to see Jesus for who he is—the Christ. When we encounter God's love, we are able to worship in spirit and in truth.

Prayer: **Lord of all life, thank you for the gift of your love and forgiveness. Help me always to worship you in spirit and in truth. Amen.**

Friday, March 8   Read John 4:31-38.

The closer we draw to God, the closer we draw to others. As our thirst for God compels us toward God, it also compels us toward others. Conversely, when we are willing to abandon ourselves in compassion, service, and solidarity with others, we find that we have made room for God in our hearts. Service to others is one of the spiritual disciplines that draws us closer to God. This service, compassion, and love for others feeds our thirst and hunger for God.

When Jesus' disciples urge him to eat something, Jesus takes the opportunity to teach this truth. Jesus said to them, "My food is to do the will of him who sent me and to complete his work." He invites the disciples to enter into this labor—this service, this harvest. Jesus' deep compassion for those who hunger and thirst for a living relationship with God becomes the source of his nourishment.

John Wesley understood this vital connection between our spiritual development and our service to others. For Wesley, unrestrained caring for people was a fruit of a vital relationship with God. To love God necessarily carries with it a love of neighbor. In being attentive to those we encounter in our daily lives—those who comprise the fields ripe for harvest—we create an open space within where we can hear God speak. This reciprocal relationship between our thirst and ministering to the hunger of others is acknowledged by Jesus when he states that the "sower and reaper may rejoice together." As disciples of Christ, we are all invited to enter into the labor of reaping. For in such service lies our nourishment.

Prayer: **Holy God, give me a heart that desires nothing but to serve you and all your children. Feed me with a desire to do your will and to complete your work. Amen.**

Saturday, March 9   Read Romans 5:1-11.

I stood on the bank of a river in northeastern Nigeria. I was there as part of an Iowa United Methodist Volunteers In Mission work team. It was Sunday morning, July 29, 1991. Several hundred worshipers had just walked the two miles from the Jalingo United Methodist Church to the river. I watched as, one by one, seventy-four persons (ages twelve to seventy) waded into the churning, rain-swollen river and were submerged beneath the waters—baptized in the name of the Father, Son, and Holy Spirit.

Following the baptismal service, we all walked back to the church for the Service of Table, Holy Communion. The newly baptized Christians were given seats of honor near the front of the church. Then, to affirm their new life in Christ, they were served their first Communion.

I wrote in my journal for July 29: "This is the most wonderful day I have ever experienced as a Christian." I was simply overwhelmed by the power of that baptismal event. I experienced God's love "pouring" into the hearts of those being baptized and into the hearts of those standing on the river banks bearing witness.

God's desire to respond to our hunger and thirst is dramatically demonstrated in both Eucharist and Baptism. In the eating of the bread and the drinking of the cup, God's love is "poured into our hearts through the Holy Spirit that has been given to us." In Holy Baptism, we are literally flooded by God's grace. Our thirst for God is quenched. It is no accident that our Communion and Baptism liturgies affirm this flood of God's love: "God proves his love for us in that while we still were sinners Christ died for us." It is in this flood, this outpouring, of Christ's love that we find our salvation, our hope, and our joy.

Prayer: **Almighty God, by the power of your Holy Spirit pour out your love on me and all creation so that today I may be a blessing and healing reminder of your living water to all whose lives I touch. Amen.**

Sunday, March 10   Read John 4:27-30, 39-42.

I often reflect on my own faith journey. How did I come to know that Jesus was truly *my* Savior and the "Savior of the world"? I remember when I first invited Christ into my life. I came to that moment, and many subsequent conversions, through the loving witness of many dear friends, family members, and saints of the church. They had drunk deeply of the living water and had brought me to the well.

Most Christians are not converts to the faith because they have been blinded by a light from heaven or because they have successfully but laboriously traversed a maze of doubts, intellectual difficulties, and theological premises. Most Christians affirm Christ as Savior simply because those whom they trust believe in Christ and bear proof of him in their lives. Many villagers believed in Jesus simply because of the Samaritan woman's testimony.

Those who have gone to the well—those who know the source of living water—are the best evangelists. It is those who have recently said yes to Christ and joined the church, the community of faith, who are the most eager and the best able to reach and invite others. It is those who have tasted the living water who want others to "come and see." It is those who have experienced Jesus' love who "know that this is truly the Savior of the world."

For faith to be vital it must be more than glad tidings blown to us from other lives. In the final analysis, faith is not inherited but gained through risking everything on what has not yet been proved in our experience. Like the Samaritan villagers, we ultimately "know" Christ as Savior not because of someone else's witness but because of our own risking, our own experience of Christ, and our own coming to Christ.

Prayer: **O Savior of the world, help me to hear your word and believe. Guide me in leading others to you, the source of living water. Amen.**

March 11–17, 1996   **Henry F. Woodruff✤**
Monday, March 11   Read 1 Samuel 16:1-3*a*, 6-13.

Those called to walk the path

The story of biblical faith is the story of a transcendent God who chooses to become immanent in historical existence. God interrupts human life for a purpose, calls persons to be a part of the purpose, and works through persons to accomplish the purpose. We might not grasp fully the entire scope of God's purposes, but our lack of understanding does not preclude our participation in God's redemptive work.

Such is the superstructure for the biblical narrative of the anointing of David as king. The story reminds us not only of whose agenda is ultimately to be served but also that God can and does penetrate our hearts and minds. God sees what we often cannot: a human life as an instrument for God's redemptive purposes. Surprised by the choice of David, Samuel heard the Lord say, "The LORD does not see as mortals see; they look on the outward appearance, but the LORD looks on the heart." God calls persons—even unlikely persons—to walk the path of God's purposes.

It is a lesson for us to learn as we consider what path God has for us. We may not see the potential we have for God's purposes; our inadequacy, our brokenness may move us to exclaim to the One who calls, "Look elsewhere!" In such moments God can and does speak with clarity, surprising even us, beckoning even us to step forward on the holy path.

Suggestion for meditation: **What—for God's purposes—has God seen in me?**

✤Senior minister, Hudson United Methodist Church, Hudson, Ohio.

Tuesday, March 12   Read 1 Samuel 16:4*a*.

Preparing to tread the path

James Russell Lowell was right: "Time makes ancient good uncouth." It is out of fashion, even insulting, to call "professionals" those called by God to tread the path of God's redemptive purposes. Henri J. M. Nouwen's model of the "wounded healer" will gain assenting nods, but heads hang when priests and prophets are labeled "professional."

Today's text invites us to reclaim the label, even dare to wear it as our own. One nuance of meaning the word *professional* carries is extensive preparation for a specific task. We admire professionals in medicine and law who have endured the rigors of extensive preparation. Should God's world, in desperate need of healing and justice, not be entitled to the same kind of prepared, thoughtful, and dedicated care?

God's word through the writer of First Samuel says yes. Trembling before the one who will be part of God's redemptive purposes, the elders of the city wonder what lies ahead for them. Samuel announces that his intention is for good, that he has come intending to enter into the presence of God. He invites them to join him on the way, but before it can all happen "preparation" must take place: Consecration must precede the sacrifice. God's world waits for those prepared through consecration and sacrifice. Whether laity or clergy, we are called to be ministers who are prepared for a ministry of caring, prepared first by scripture study, by prayer and listening to God, and by a commitment to walk God's path of redemptive purpose.

Suggestion for meditation: **What preparation for God's purposes is mine to make today? What consecration of my life will prepare me for the self-sacrifice God calls me to make?**

Wednesday, March 13   Read Psalm 23:1-4.

The experienced guide

Today's text places in sharp relief the difference between mental abstractions and experienced reality. As any path, any calling, and every purpose are only extensions of the mind until they are lived, obeyed, and walked, so is the shepherding of God a mental "might be" until it is experienced. Love in action, real caring, is like this: We know it is real when we have experienced its creative and re-creative power in our lives.

God's guiding into right paths near peaceful streams of refreshment and to rich places of nourishment is always like this. We know the Guide to be good and caring, strong and protecting because we experience such grace-full caring in treading the path. It is the lived experience of love experienced. It is not a fantasy of wishful thinking but a reality solid and true. The psalmist's words draw their power from such lived experience: God's guiding light of care shone even into the places of deep darkness, and what had been a "might be" became reality—"The Lord *is* my shepherd."

Our experience confirms this reality for us and is the reservoir from which we draw our courage to tread the path of God's redemptive purpose. Only then do we fear no evil, for then what has been an extension of the mind becomes the outreached staff of the experienced Guide.

Suggestion for meditation: **In what moments of my life has God's guiding and protecting care become real for me? Into what paths of rightness and nourishment have I been led, that I might find courage and strength for the journey?**

Thursday, March 14   Read Psalm 23:5-6.

Strength for the middle miles

Hikers refer to them as the "middle miles." These are the most exhausting, challenging miles on the path, when the exhilaration of beginning the journey has evaporated into drudgery and the promise of the path's end has not yet given new energy for the stepping. Experienced hikers know how to triumph over the middle miles; they carry with them high energy foods and plan for moments of rest. Then with a burst of energy and a refreshed mind, the heart is lifted and the steps become lighter.

The psalmist proclaims that God has prepared a table for us, where rest, refreshment, and new energy for the journey can be found. The table is prepared in the midst of all that is an enemy to faithful following: vanished excitement, depleted energy, a fatigued spirit, heavy steps which find the path too long, too hard. In the middle miles God is our host, giving us a super-abundance of all we need to triumph over fatigue and despair. Anointed with a new spirit, steps become lighter. Not only can the journey continue, but the path becomes a joy to tread, a thing of celebration.

Such is the hope for all who have chosen—and *been* chosen—to tread the path of God's redemptive purpose. Regardless of the length of the journey, the power for the treading comes not only from the promised end or from the joy of beginning; the power is from the Host, who gives strength in the middle miles.

Suggestion for meditation: What nourishment for treading the middle miles has God given me? Over what enemies to faithful following has God given me victory through the anointing and sustenance of the Holy Spirit?

Friday, March 15   Read Ephesians 5:8-14.

Stepping in the light

Even smooth, straight, and easy paths become treacherous to tread in the darkness; how much more so when the path is crooked and rough, when the way is shrouded in darkness as deep as death itself! For those called to tread the path of God's redemptive purpose, the hope of a shining light illuminating unsteady steps is the hope that gives courage.

Light does this. Shadows are driven back; illusion is exposed for what it is; truth stands in clear relief, and new confidence for the journey becomes the fruit light produces.

This is the word of hope and courage which the writer of today's text shines on our path. In a society antithetical to the way of Christ, the exhortation is not one of cloistered withdrawal but rather a challenge to "live as children of light" *in* the darkness. Such is the way of authentic witness, for when those who tread God's path step in the light, more than firm footing is found. The text says the "works of darkness" are exposed. Witness to truth is made.

Is there a more urgent challenge or a more courageous word for us? It is not difficult to see the darkness; we, too, are surrounded by the expression of values antithetical to the way of Christ. The difficulty is seeing with clarity the path God offers us and then stepping into it with courage. So it is with hope and joy *we* sing the Epistle's hymn: "Sleeper, awake! Rise from the dead, and Christ will shine on you."

Suggestion for meditation: **Where am I called to walk today, with steps illumined by Christ, for witness to Christ? What "fruit" of God's light can I produce in a world surrounded by darkness?**

Saturday, March 16   Read John 9:1-12.

Reflections on the path

Some journeys are made in solitude, while others demand—even require!—community. Today's directive from the One who leads and gives light is a corporate "we." John affirms that not only has Christ chosen to walk with us, making our steps lighter, but Christ who is the light of the world summons us to reflect the light which has called us out of the darkness.

This is to "work the works" of God, who sent the light into the world. John is clear that even as the man born blind from birth becomes a mirror of Christ's power to give authentic sight, so are the disciples—*all* disciples—instruments with Christ of this creative power: we are those sent, given the power to open the eyes of the blind.

It is in obedience to Christ's directive that light is reflected and the blind see. However, with irony that is typical of John's Gospel, the challenge of faith and obedience is a challenge for all who think they see the path, as well as for all who suffer from blindness. How, then, can we be faithful to the One who says, "Go, wash . . ."? The first step is to recognize our own need for corrected vision. John begins this discourse on blindness by first calling our attention to the disciples' own need: they, who think they can see, are also blind. To reflect light necessitates being washed in it. Other steps follow, but without the light of Christ having touched us, we cannot see to touch others or reflect anything other than our own blindness.

Suggestion for meditation: **What blindness in my life has the light of Christ exposed?**

Sunday, March 17   Read John 9:13-41.

Paths for choosing

No steps are forced on anyone who chooses to tread the path of God's redemptive purpose. Whether to take any step, whether to choose this or that path, is a free and individual decision; else the journey is without meaning. The terror of the choice is that in the choosing we open one possibility and close another. When one path is taken another is excluded, and this choice makes all the difference—as Robert Frost explores in his poem "The Road Not Taken."

The reality of self-judgment by means of personal choice is the reality of the Light in the world. Following the Tabernacles discourse on Jesus as the Light of the world, the Evangelist turns to demonstrating what this means. In the unfolding of the narrative in today's scripture our minds are illumined: The light of Christ makes clear the choice of faith or rejection, seeing or blindness. When Jesus announces, "I came into this world for judgment, that those who do not see may see . . . ," we are confronted with the inescapable decision of obedience or faithlessness. The word John uses for "judgment" can also be translated "crisis," and the crisis is the crisis of choice: Either for or against Jesus, either the path of faith illumined by the Light of the world, or the way of blind darkness. John's word is one of sober reality: By our choosing we judge ourselves.

God's gracious word is that we have before us lighter paths for treading! The poet is quite right: the path taken—or not taken—*will* make all the difference.

Suggestion for meditation: What lighter path is God opening to me today for my choosing, my treading? What redemptive purpose can I choose to reflect the light of Christ?

GOD OF THE LIVING

March 18–24, 1996   **Kenneth L. Gibble**✤
Monday, March 18   Read Ezekiel 37:1-6.

The Killing Fields is a movie I really did not want to see, but knew I must. It tells of the massacre of untold numbers of Cambodians by the Khmer Rouge regime. In an unforgettable scene one of the main characters comes upon the appalling sight of countless human skulls. Ezekiel's vision of the valley of dry bones has come to pass.

Some scenes are so horrifying in their vastness that our minds can hardly comprehend them: the slaughter of millions during the Nazi reign of terror, fire bombs falling on Dresden, an atomic blast incinerating people in Nagasaki and Hiroshima. Our soon-to-end century has witnessed acts of inhumanity on a scale previous generations would have thought impossible.

For Ezekiel, the sight of countless human bones was only a vision. Yet he had lived in a time when war had brought death and captivity to his people. How does one maintain hope in such a time?

For Ezekiel, and for us, hope comes from faith—not faith in human efforts. History has demonstrated over and over again that hatred and cruelty infest the human heart. Only an infusion of divine love and grace can save us. "I will cause breath [spirit] to enter you, and you shall live," says the Lord.

Prayer: **Save us, O God, from the terrors of our own inhumanity. Amen.**

✤Author; teacher; Pastor, Arlington Church of the Brethren, Arlington, Virginia.

Tuesday, March 19   Read Ezekiel 37:7-14.

Ezekiel's prophecy of the dry bones brought to life was given to a people in despair. Jerusalem, the holy city, had fallen to the Babylonian army in 587 B.C.E. Now in exile, Ezekiel and his fellow Israelites are tempted to believe that their life as a people is finished. God sees their despair: "They say, 'Our bones are dried up, and our hope is lost; we are cut off completely.'"

God tells Ezekiel to speak a message of hope to a helpless and hopeless people. The word from the Lord defies the image of death, symbolized by the valley of dry bones. I am going to "open your graves, and bring you up from your graves, O my people. I will put my spirit within you, . . . then you shall know that I, the LORD, have spoken and will act."

One of the central affirmations of Christian faith is that God is more powerful than death. As Jesus put it succinctly: "He is God not of the dead, but of the living" (Luke 20:38). Even though death is a reality, another reality transcends it: God.

One of the most rollicking of all the spirituals is "Dry Bones," a song in which the bones of Ezekiel's vision join together: "De thigh bone connected to de hip bone, hip bone connected to de back bone." Here is the graphic image of God's life-giving power and love. The joy of the song comes not only from the imaginary skeleton's being put together but from the central affirmation that ends each connecting: "Now hear de word of de Lord."

Suggestion for meditation: **Recall as much of the song "Dry Bones" as you can. From time to time throughout the day hum the tune to yourself as an affirmation of the God of the living.**

Wednesday, March 20   Read Psalm 130:1-2.

This psalm begins with a desperate cry for help. "Out of the depths I cry to you, O LORD." The psalmist does not describe his "depths." Is the crisis emotional, financial, physical, or spiritual? We cannot know.

What we *can* know is our own experience of the *depths*. As a youngster, I received no formal swimming lessons. I came to believe, however, that I had taught myself to swim. That belief was tested and badly shaken the first time I swam out well beyond my depth. Turning around to head back to the bank of the creek where my friends and I were spending a carefree afternoon, I suddenly feared that I was sinking. Then I *was* sinking. Terrified, I thrashed around in the water, sure I was about to drown. Older youth eventually pulled me to safety, but the terror of those moments has remained with me. During spiritual crises in my later life, that terror has returned—a feeling of complete helplessness to save myself or those I love.

At such times, our cry to the Lord may be nothing more than a desperate "Help!" What prompts that cry can be fear of a life-threatening illness, despair over the loss of a loved one, or worry that a cherished relationship is falling apart. Whatever the cause of the crisis, the deeply felt reality is, "There is nothing I can do about it." We reach the "depths," in other words, when we become fully aware that our own resources simply will not work. At such times the cry of the psalmist becomes our own.

Suggestion for meditation: **Spend some moments recalling the "depths" of your own life history. What forms have your cries to the Lord taken at such times? What forms have the Lord's answers taken?**

Thursday, March 21   Read Psalm 130:3-8.

In one way or another, all our readings for this week juxtapose death and life. We can speak of many kinds of death—death of a physical body, death of a relationship, even spiritual death. Death is a reality; attempts to deny it are foolish and dishonest.

We often characterize death as the enemy, but that is an inadequate characterization. Some things *need* to die: self-centeredness, hatred, fear.

Verse 3 names the essence of the problem: human sin. "If you, O LORD should mark iniquities, LORD, who could stand?" The answer to that question is obvious—*no one*! Or, as scripture elsewhere puts it, "There is no one who is righteous, not even one" (Rom. 3:10).

Most of us do our moral self-reckoning by comparison. *I may not be perfect*, I whisper to myself, *but at least I'm not as bad as* _____ . And then I fill in the blank with the name of someone whose behavior I deplore.

One of the traditional disciplines of Lent is the discipline of self-examination. Taking the time for an honest self-assessment can be a productive spiritual exercise. Instead of comparing yourself favorably with others, consider where *you* are now in *your* spiritual journey and where *you* could be with God's help.

Suggestion for meditation: **On a sheet of paper, list your answers to this question: What in my life needs to die in order that I may become the person God intends me to become?**

Friday, March 22   Read Romans 8:6-11.

What did Paul mean by his admonition to "set the mind on the Spirit"? Paul believed that only the power of God's spirit can bring about true freedom—the freedom to choose what is good and true and life-giving. Left on our own, we will inevitably choose the safe prison of the world's values, rather than the risky freedom of truth. But when we ask the spirit of God to lead us, we will find true life; we will come to know a peace that only God can give.

All this sounds very grand, but how can we apply it on a day-to-day, practical level? Let me suggest one such application.

To set our minds on the Spirit, rather than on the flesh, means that often we do not go with our first inclination or intuition. What is your first inclination when someone disagrees with you? Most of us are inclined to go on the defensive immediately, to assume that the person in question is being critical of us, maybe even attacking us. This defensiveness occurs in families, on the job, at church.

But what if, when we feel defensive, we were to pray, "Show me your way, O God; let me be controlled by your Spirit"? Might we then be able to give the other person the benefit of the doubt, to allow for the possibility that he or she is seeking the truth sincerely rather than trying to put us down?

Prayer: **Show me your way, O God; let me be controlled not by my first inclination but by your Spirit. Amen.**

Saturday, March 23   Read John 11:1-37.

God, who is "God not of the dead, but of the living" (Matt. 22:32*b*), demonstrates power over death. A faith community that worships God must be able to demonstrate its conviction that death is not the ultimate end. That is why the gathering of the faithful for a funeral or memorial service is not only an occasion for grieving but an opportunity to worship and to celebrate the joy that comes from faith in the God of life.

At funerals, tears are frequently shed. People of faith are not spared the sorrow that follows the death of a loved one. Not even Jesus was spared such pain. Even though Jesus was confident that Lazarus would come forth from the tomb, our Lord expressed his own grief with tears. Death, as we experience it on this side of the grave, means separation from those we love. Expressing our sorrow over such a loss is a natural and good process. Knowing that family and friends share our pain is one of the gifts from God we may receive at such times.

As a pastor I have officiated at many funerals and memorial services. I have seen the power of God's spirit at work when the church gathers to grieve together over the death of a man or woman, boy or girl, whose presence was treasured and whose absence will be hard to bear.

But much more happens at a Christian funeral than shared pain. The scriptures selected for reading reaffirm that not even death can separate us from God's love. Prayers and hymns testify to God's power to comfort, sustain, and bless.

Suggestion for meditation: **Recall a recent funeral or memorial service you have attended. How was God's power over death acknowledged and experienced?**

Sunday, March 24   Read John 11:38-45.

Surely one of the most dramatic of all the events reported in John's Gospel is the raising of Lazarus. On one level, it is the familiar story of a family's grief over the unexpected death of a loved one. On another level, it is a powerful declaration of God's power over death. "This illness," Jesus says, "is for God's glory, so that the Son of God may be glorified through it."

When my brother-in-law died unexpectedly at age 47, the people who attended the funeral were both grief-stricken and shocked. The question we all struggled with was *Why*? I did not envy the minister whose difficult task it was to preach the funeral sermon.

As part of the service a soloist sang one of my brother-in-law's favorite hymns, "It Is Well with My Soul." The words speak about what happens "when sorrows like sea billows roll." It was a testimony of faith that even at such terrible times, faith can declare, "It is well with my soul." By every human reckoning, such a declaration is nonsense. How can it be well with our souls when we have lost the friendship and the love of people we treasure? How, in the midst of overwhelming tragedy, can we receive blessed assurance?

The answer is this: only by the grace of God. Humanly speaking, it is impossible. As impossible as Lazarus coming forth from the tomb. But with God, the impossible becomes possible.

Prayer: **By your grace, O God, help me believe as I say, "It is well with my soul." Amen.**

PILGRIMAGE OF THE PASSION

March 25–31, 1996
Monday, March 25

F. Gates Vrooman✤
Read Matthew 21:1-11;
Zechariah 9:9-10.

We know the itinerary. It leads from Jesus' Palm Sunday entrance into Jerusalem to an upper room, then to a garden, a palace, a fortress, a cross—and a tomb. We also know it does not end there. Through the scripture lessons this week, we also embark on that pilgrimage with Jesus and the disciples.

Matthew gives us the details to ensure we see Jesus' entry into Jerusalem as the fulfillment of Zechariah's prophecy. Some have ridiculed Matthew for his literalistic picture of Jesus, as if describing the Lord's journey into Jerusalem on two donkeys as an exceptionally odd thing. Such criticism is unfair. According to Mark and Luke, the colt is unbroken. It would naturally follow its mother. Jesus did not separate the two animals. He treated even animals with gentleness and compassion. If the colt walked close to its mother, the garments thrown over one animal may have draped over the other. Sitting sidesaddle, as was the custom riding donkeys, Jesus may very well have appeared to ride both animals.

Nevertheless, the key to understanding Jesus' planned demonstration, as most of us know, is that the donkey is a symbol of peace and gentleness. King Jesus chooses not to ride a war horse or gilded chariot. He rides into our lives on a gentle, but sure beast to bring us peace—in our hearts, in our relationships, and in our world.

Suggestion for meditation: **What is the state of my inner peace? How am I a peacemaker? Listen for what God is saying to you.**

✤Senior Pastor, Our Saviour's United Methodist Church, Schaumburg, Illinois.

Tuesday, March 26   Read Psalm 118:1-2, 19-29.

We move in time and space. As we approach Holy Week and Easter, we anticipate holy time. But what about holy space? Holy space seems foreign to many of us until, perhaps, we visit Jerusalem and the Holy Land. Then as our feet press into the rocky soil and we read the scripture related to the places we visit, we are not merely tourists but pilgrims. God employs time and space to reveal God's presence, power, and purpose. What makes it all holy is the activity of our God in the person of Jesus.

The one who comes "in the name of the LORD" is not identified by the psalmist. As the concluding psalm of the Egyptian Hallel, Jewish pilgrims recited it during Passover to thank God for deliverance from slavery in Egypt.

All four Gospels quote Psalm 118 in the story of Jesus' entry into Jerusalem to celebrate the Passover. He enters through the Eastern Gate, sometimes called the Golden Gate. Ezekiel envisioned that gate as the one through which "the glory of the God of Israel" would enter (Eze. 43:1-2). The psalmist proclaims that the righteous shall enter through it (vv. 19-20). It was not the main gate into the city but was the gate used by persons traveling from Bethany. It opened directly into the Temple complex from which Jesus immediately drove out the money changers.

Prayer: **Sovereign of life, enter the gates of my life. Cleanse whatever needs cleansing. Work your salvation in and through me that I may be a holy person living in a holy time and holy place. Amen.**

Wednesday, March 27

Read Isaiah 50:4-9*a*;
Matthew 26:36-46.

We discover in the four Servant Songs in Isaiah a progression from presentation of the servant (42:1-4), to the call of the servant (49:1-6), to insulting of the servant (50:4-9*a*), to—finally—rejection, wounding, and death of the servant (52:13–53:12).

Perhaps the servant is a persecuted expedition leader who is taking or has taken a group of exiles from Babylon back to the Holy Land. Some did not want to make the pilgrimage; they had become satisfied with the foreign culture and foreign god. They opposed the servant and the expedition. Some of the inhabitants around Jerusalem opposed the returning exiles who claimed ownership of the land that the current inhabitants thought was theirs. Perhaps some who wanted to rebuild a pure Jewish identity opposed the servant because the servant called Israel to be "a light to the nations."

Like the servant, we frequently find opposition from one source or another . . . even when we think we are doing God's will. How do we deal with the insults, the rejection, the undercutting of our sense of security and self-worth?

The servant keeps an open ear to God's revelation and does not turn away from God. The servant believes, "The LORD GOD helps me; therefore I have not been disgraced. . . . he who vindicates me is near." The servant is centered in God. This produces courage and rock-solid determination to stride forward on the pilgrimage: "Therefore I have set my face like flint."

Prayer: **O Christ, Servant of God, you set your face toward Jerusalem; you strode forward to certain suffering and death that we might experience divine love and life eternal. Thank you! Abide at the center of my life that I may dare follow in your way. Amen.**

Thursday, March 28   Read Psalm 31:9-16;
                                          Matthew 26:47-56.

At times, most of us have endured put-downs or exclusion. Friends and family may forget our birthday, no longer call or write us, or even speak to us in public. We feel hurt by such treatment.

However, few of us are so thoroughly ostracized, abandoned, and rejected as was the psalmist. Neighbors and adversaries treat the psalmist as junk, broken pottery to be thrown away. Like the psalmist, we may feel utterly drained, but few of us are stalked by killers. Yet, today, some countries so flagrantly violate human rights that Psalm 31 seems an apt description.

For example, Maria Elena Cruz Varela is one of Cuba's most internationally respected, award-winning writers. In 1992 she received a nomination for the Nobel Peace Prize. Maria's writings opposed dictatorship in Cuba. Then one day, government security service men barged into her apartment, demolished the interior, beat her unmercifully, assaulted her guests, and laid siege to her home.

Next, they arrested her and threw her into a small cell with forty hard-core criminals. She became ill. Government doctors operated on her numerous times without using anesthetic. They broke her health but not her spirit. Eventually she was able to leave Cuba. She now lives in Puerto Rico and has begun to write again.*

Psalm 31 seems a fitting commentary on our Lord's pilgrimage to the Passion as well as on the violation of Maria's human rights. Christ understands our hurts and those of political prisoners whose pain and suffering are so great.

Suggestion for prayer: **Pray for prisoners of conscience and those persecuted for their Christian faith. Pray that we may never be among the oppressors of this world.**

---

* "A Lioness in Exile." *Amnesty Action* (Winter 1995): 6-7.

Friday, March 29   Read Philippians 2:5-11.

We want to be faithful Christians. That is one major reason we pray, read scripture, and spend time with devotional materials. But we want more than just an active devotional life. We want to *live* the faith.

How do we live a life "worthy of the gospel of Christ"? (Phil. 1:27) One way is to resolve conflicts which may arise from selfish ambition, conceit, or a "me-first" attitude (2:1-4). How do we do that? We each seek to embody the mind of Christ.

Jesus' life revealed his mind. He humbled himself; he emptied himself of the rank, privilege, and rights due to God, then assumed the role of a servant. In contrast to the Gospel Passion predictions, the servant of this text expects no vindication. Note the two divisions in the hymn. In verse 9 God exalts the self-giving attitude and lifestyle because it does not expect any benefit or reward. It reveals unconditional love. Though Jesus speaks elsewhere about rewards, here we do not discover the servant lifestyle to be a secret entrance into God's kingdom. If we empty ourselves because we think we will win friends in high places, we have perverted self-giving into self-serving.

How differently we think today! We demand our rights. We enroll in assertiveness training. We are quick to sue. Winning is everything—whatever it takes.

God's exaltation of Jesus prompts all creatures everywhere to worship Christ. No place exists where Christ's redemption cannot reach. No person is beyond Christ's redeeming grace.

Prayer: **O God, teach me to be self-giving and humble. Amen.**

Saturday, March 30   Read Matthew 27:11-31.

Pilate releases Barabbas to the mob and after flogging Jesus, hands him over for crucifixion to the soldiers.

Scourging always precedes crucifixion. Soldiers strip Jesus then tie his hands with thongs to the whipping post. The whip is constructed of knotted leather strips studded with small pieces of lead and bits of sharpened bone. Whipping tears away flesh, opens gaping wounds, and raises inflamed welts and large bruises. Under the blows of the whip many victims befoul themselves, many faint, and some die.

After the scourging, the soldiers play the "King's Game" with Jesus by making him their burlesque king. With successive rolls of the dice they inflict him with various forms of abuse. One roll and they drape a warrior's scarlet robe over the torn body of the Prince of Peace. Another roll and they stick into his right hand a flimsy reed for a scepter, thus mocking his powerlessness. Another roll and they spit repeatedly into his face. Another roll and he wins a crown . . . of thorns. Laughing and grinning they kneel before him. Voices dripping with derision, they scoff, "Hail, King of the Jews!"

Today we can travel to Jerusalem and see traces of the game boards scratched by Roman soldiers into the paving stones where Pilate sat on the judge's bench (John 19:13).

Also, today, some magazines, songs, paintings, films, and television programs mock Jesus and what he stands for. But we likewise mock him whenever we fail to pray, trust, or follow the Greatest Commandment (Matt. 22:36-40) and the Great Commission (Matt. 28:18-20).

Prayer: O Lord, I am humbled by your suffering and humiliation for my sake. Fill me with gratitude for your love that I may never mock you but rather bow my knee and confess to all that you are my Lord and Savior. Amen.

Passion/Palm Sunday

Sunday, March 31   Read Matthew 27:32-66.

Picture this: Soldiers push Jesus along the cobblestone streets of Jerusalem. "Keep moving!" the captain commands, slamming the butt of his spear shaft into his prisoner's back. See the grimace on the soldier's face as he swings the hammer down onto the spike. Note the faint smile as he steps back, hands on hips, to observe his work. He gives the command; they raise the cross; its foot falls with a deep "thud" into the hole.

Catch the wink from one soldier to another as the first pours gall, a bitter poison, into the wine and offers it to his prisoner. Jesus spits it out. Soldiers laugh and slap their thighs. See them sitting on their haunches; one raises his arm, shakes his fist, and lets the dice fly. They shout and shove each other as they divide up the prisoner's clothing.

Golgotha rises near the road, just outside a Jerusalem gate. Romans like the site because it is so public; subjects see the high cost of criminal conduct. People passing by shout their taunts at the dying men.

For hours soldiers entertain themselves playing games, telling war stories, and reminiscing about happy times with family back home. They give scant attention to the dying prisoners.

Then darkness. A cry from the cross! Earthquake! Back in the Temple of the Jews, the heavy curtain guarding the holy of holies is torn from top to bottom by the Holy God. That very moment, Gentiles, a centurion, and other soldiers around the cross tremble in fear as they proclaim, "Truly this man was God's Son!"

Suggestion for meditation: **Imagine yourself watching the crucifixion. What are your thoughts, feelings? What do you say to those around you, to Jesus, to the soldiers? What prayer do you utter? Later, are you changed because you were there?**

LAST RITES, BIRTHRIGHTS

April 1–7, 1996　　　　　　　**George Hovaness Donigian✤**
Monday, April 1　　　　　　Read Psalm 36:5-11;
　　　　　　　　　　　　　　　　John 12:1-11.

The anointing

The anointing at Bethany begins Holy Week with a knowledge that seems prescient from this side of the Resurrection. Jesus visited Lazarus's home. Martha served the company. Mary anointed Jesus' feet with a pound of perfume, drying them with her hair. The fragrance of that perfume filled the house, serving as a warning to all that something in this house was different.

Imagine the cloying sweet smell of that pound of nard. Envision the response of the crowd gathered, not to see Jesus but to see Lazarus, who had been raised from the dead. Can the dead be raised in the midst of the sweet smell of funerary perfume?

Priests anointed the kings of Israel as "the Lord's anointed." Anointing remained a ritual act, suitable for festivals and celebrations. Here, though, Jesus refers to a funeral rite.

John portrays Jesus as being aware of his destiny and fully committed in obedience to the journey of faith. The psalmist's words concerning salvation to the upright of heart ring true. The anointing takes place because funeral rituals demanded such and because custom named the Messiah as the Lord's anointed. The anointing prepared Jesus' followers for the little death they would endure, as well as for the inheritance of the great Easter and all the little Easters to come.

Prayer: **Our prayers, O God, rise like the scent of perfume. Our lives are seasoned by ointments of death and resurrection. Living in the surety of your love, may we honor your gifts. Amen.**

✤Clergy, Virginia Annual Conference of The United Methodist Church; managing editor, Upper Room Books; active at East End United Methodist Church, Nashville, Tennessee.

Tuesday, April 2   Read Psalm 71:1-14;
                                              John 12:20-36.

Servant inheritance

The lament and plea of Psalm 71 attributes steadfast qualities to God: the rock, the refuge, the fortress. From within this refuge, the psalmist refers to enemies and those who look for signs of weakness. The psalmist's cry for deliverance strikes an empathetic response out of our own personal trials: "O my God, make haste to help me!"

As Jesus ends his public ministry, the troubling of his soul runs counter to portraits of Jesus as the determined one. We hear Jesus describe the grain that must die in the earth in order to bear fruit. We hear Jesus describe servanthood. We witness Jesus struggling with principalities and powers that would deter him from his own servanthood. We return again to the troubling of Jesus' soul and the voice of God the encourager responding to Jesus' anguish.

We also struggle with anguish and doubt. Our souls are troubled by many things such as the suffering of others, the arrogance of wealth, the inability of institutions to deal with individuals. We grapple with questions concerning the ministry and mission of the church. "What is right?" we ask. "And what is not?"

Discipleship means that we wrestle with such principalities and powers. Birthright means hearing again the attributes of God: God the rock, the refuge, the fortress. Our birthright as servants gives us the assurance and encouragement of God while wrestling with the principalities and powers of discouragement.

Prayer: **A mighty fortress you are, O God. We praise you. In you, O Lord, we take refuge. From you, O Lord, we receive encouragement. Nurture us in the spirit of truth and love. Amen.**

Wednesday, April 3   Read Hebrews 12:1-3;
                                          John 13:21-32.

Bread as birthright

The betrayal of Jesus by Judas remains a mystery worthy of psychology, politics, and biography as well as theology. It is the night of the Passover. Aware of the betrayer's intent, Jesus offers the bread to Judas, daring him to act. "Here, Judas," he says. "Take this bread and remember what you must do." Judas's bread becomes the redemptive bread of remembrance.

Remembrance remains at the core of our own discipleship. Hebrews 12 invites us to remember and to feel the presence of the communion of saints as encouragement along the way. The writer uses imagery worthy of the Psalms to point to perseverance and endurance, especially remembering those attributes of Jesus.

Bread remains a physical sign of our discipleship. We eat the bread and drink from the cup in remembrance of this Last Supper. We eat the bread and drink from the cup in remembrance of God's many acts of salvation. From time to time we need to remember that Judas shared in that loaf of salvation. Like Judas, we, too, face temptations to betray the Christ. The loaf of salvation can point us back to our birthright.

When they leave the service, worshipers in the Armenian Orthodox Church take a small piece of *maz*, an unleavened bread of remembrance. They eat it to remember the servanthood and sacrifice of Jesus. This bread of remembrance becomes a symbol of encouragement. Our own breads of remembrance contain the grains that die and rise again and the leavens of God's reign.

Prayer (adapted from Basil the Great, ca. 330–380): **Have compassion upon me and let these Holies work in me for healing, for cleansing, for enlightenment, for protection, for salvation, for hallowing of soul and body, and for reformation. Amen.**

Maundy Thursday

Thursday, April 4

Read Exodus 12:1-14;
Psalm 116:1-2, 12-19;
John 13:1-17, 31*b*-35.

The cup as birthright

The psalmist refers to the cup of salvation. Before you lift the cup of blessing toward the Lord in thanksgiving for God's mighty deeds, look at what it contains.

Within the cup remain the straw and mud and mortar that the Hebrew people used in Egypt. It contains terrible dregs of the plagues. It holds the feelings of terror related to the first Passover, and it includes the jubilation of freedom from bondage.

This is the cup of salvation, offered in thanksgiving during the Passover. The speaker in Psalm 116 also refers to the vow of servanthood, which is incorporated with the cup.

Jesus looked within the cup offered during the Last Supper and envisioned a new community of servanthood. During the supper, Jesus wrapped a towel around himself and washed the feet of his disciples. He anointed them, not with perfume as Mary used but with a water of blessing. He told his disciples that they also should wash one another's feet and live following his serving example. The cup contained a vision of a servant community, loving and serving one another in joy. By this new servant-love, others would recognize the followers of Jesus and would join the new community of joy.

Lift high the cup of salvation! It contains the tradition of history that began in Egypt. It contains a new inheritance that begins in the present and moves forward in freedom, servanthood, joy, and love.

Prayer (a traditional Armenian table grace): Let us in peace eat this meal which is prepared for us by the Lord. Blessed are the gifts of the Lord. Blessed is the Lord. Amen.

Good Friday

Friday, April 5   Read Isaiah 52:13–53:12;
Psalm 22; John 18:1–19:42.

Servant birthright

Good Friday confronts us with the suffering of the innocent Jesus. Discussions on this day sometimes center on the suffering endured by victims of genocide, such as the Armenians in 1915 and the Jews during World War II.

Yet Psalm 22 and Isaiah 52:13–53:12 bring us in touch with the suffering servant's birthright and legacy. Psalm 22, quoted by Jesus on the cross, appeals to God from the most basic core of the sufferer. The psalm's context is deliverance from a mortal illness, but that cry for deliverance comes from a sickness that touches mind, heart, soul, and body. The anguish grows from griefs and wounds deep in the psalmist; yet, Psalm 22 ends in affirmation and glory and praise to God. It moves from personal agony to corporate justice and righteousness. Out of the agony of the individual comes the vision of future generations who proclaim God's glory.

Isaiah 52 moves in a similar direction. It refers to the servant, despised and rejected, one acquainted with suffering and grief. The innocent servant, proclaims the prophet, receives the punishment intended for all.

Jesus embodied this tradition. Undergirding Jesus' final discourses to the disciples and his actions during the Passover is awareness of the one whose suffering brings restoration to the many. The birthright we have received is grounded in self-giving for the restoration of many others.

Prayer (adaptation of an Armenian benediction): O God of peace, protect and keep your people in peace under the shadow of the cross. Save us from visible and invisible enemies. Move us toward that time when the poor shall eat and be satisfied and your glory shall be proclaimed by future generations. Amen.

Holy Saturday

Saturday, April 6   Read 1 Peter 4:1-8;
                                          Matthew 27:57-61.

Birthright of cultural conflict

The stark confrontation of cultures and values on the cross undergird our discipleship on Holy Saturday. We read how Joseph of Arimathea made the request of Pilate to bury the body of Jesus. No anointing of the dead occurs now, making more poignant the anointing in John 12. Our reading of Matthew causes us to sit with grieving and scared disciples who must wonder what will happen to them in the absence of Jesus.

Jesus and culture have collided. The confrontation between Christ and Caesar pierces us on this day as we look through the lens of crucifixion and resurrection. We experience the confrontation between the proclamation of Christian faith and the proclamations of a culture that elevates frippery.

First Peter pulls us to an awareness that the struggle between Christian discipleship and culture is not new. The writer portrays the larger context of the Christian community as one surrounded by idolatry, licentiousness, and carousing. Then come the words, "They [non-Christians] are surprised that you no longer join them in the same excesses." The letter writer warns the recipients of the end of the age and exhorts them to maintain constant love.

We may not feel the imminence of the apocalypse as did the writer of First Peter, but we are aware on this Saturday-in-between of our need for spiritual disciplines. We need not be worn down by the abrasive qualities of a larger and different culture. Our prayers and almsgiving and service enable love to grow within us, within our community of faith, and within God's reign.

Prayer: **From nothingness came creation, O God. As we ponder Jesus' crucifixion and resurrection, encourage us to live in hope as we face those things visible and invisible that would try to wear away our discipleship. Amen.**

Easter, Day of Resurrection

Sunday, April 7   Read Acts 10:34-43;
John 20:1-18.

Rite of surprise

John's Gospel portrays the resurrection of Jesus as a series of surprises of omission. The rolled-away stone surprises Mary Magdalene. The emptiness of the tomb surprises the disciples who have raced to the scene. The gardener surprises the mourning Mary who cannot recognize the resurrected Jesus. That evening she tells the gathering of disciples, "I have seen the Lord."

We follow that surprise into the church's early history. Peter's sermon in Acts 10 surprises even Peter. He struggles with the relationship of Torah and Gospel, conversion and discipleship. His struggle over, Peter says in effect, "Surprise! God shows no partiality. God's love is for all people. That is the message of Jesus." He testifies to the surprising spread of the gospel through the formation of a new people who follow the teaching of Jesus.

We follow the spread of the Christian movement in our histories. Some periods encourage us, others do not.

And we remain surprised by the outcome of this event and the establishment of a community ruled by God's love, a community of newly created persons. We gather in the public fullness of our churches to celebrate the proclamation of Jesus and God's victory. In our private fullness we stand in awe as we witness to the resurrection in our individual lives and in our communities. The mystery of God's work in our world dwells within us, filling us so that, like Mary, each of us can tell others, "I have seen the Lord."

Prayer: **God of surprises, oils of gladness anoint us today. We thank you for bearing us through times of turmoil and disquiet. Lenten journeys give us time for reformation and renewal. We know that you offer a birthright that cannot be diminished, and we pray that your reign of love will prosper. Amen.**

110

April 8–14, 1996

Anne Marie Drew✤

Daniel Drew†

Monday, April 8

Read John 20:19.

Discerning the presence of the Holy

Through prayer we learn to hear the still small voice of the Spirit. When we are spiritually alive, we can discover God's presence in the smallest wind.

But there are seasons in our lives when only loud thunder can overcome our deafness. Months when only flashing lightning can pierce our blindness. Weeks when only blazing fires will melt our cold indifference to matters of the Spirit. During those seasons, one small phrase in the reading from John provides great hope. Even though the disciples had locked the door, Jesus got through. Breaking through our barriers, the risen Lord becomes the God of thunder and lightning and fire, a God who bursts through the doors we have locked, double-locked, and deadbolted. Sometimes Jesus will patiently wait for us to open the door. Sometimes, he comes in after us.

We need the power of Jesus Christ to push away our stone barriers. In that power lies an Easter promise. Even when we are not listening; even when fear and jealousy and spite and insecurity have us locked within ourselves, our risen Savior will knock down the walls and issue the invitation to new life.

Suggestion for meditation: **What barriers have I erected that keep God from working fully in my life? Why am I holding on to those barriers?**

✤English Professor, U.S. Naval Academy, Annapolis, Maryland; member, St. Elizabeth Catholic Church.

†Saturday and Sunday meditations writer; Pastor, St. Paul and Union United Methodist Churches, Greensboro, Maryland.

Tuesday, April 9   Read Acts 2:14*a*.

God in the midst of our losses

My hospitalized friend was in X-ray when I arrived at her room. Her hospital roommate, a lively, middle-aged woman, began chatting with me. After hitting the mute button on the TV's remote control, she talked cheerfully about a wide range of subjects. When she happened to glance at the TV set, she winced, and tears filled her eyes. Following her glance to the screen, I saw a rerun of the Lawrence Welk Show. Several elegantly-dressed couples waltzed across the dance floor.

"My husband and I used to dance all the time before I got MS," she told me as she clicked off the TV. "It hurts too much to see other people waltzing." Because she had been so friendly, I had not even wondered why she was hospitalized. Never would I have guessed that she had multiple sclerosis.

Today's reading from Acts reminded me of her. When Peter stands up "with the eleven" (NAB), we are reminded that there has been a major shift in those eleven. Judas is gone. And while we may dismiss Judas as a traitor, as one of the Twelve he had been Peter's companion as they traveled together, talked together, laughed together, performed miracles together. Judas's sudden and violent departure must have stunned the apostles. Yet, they had to persevere despite the unthinkable betrayal and loss.

We lose many things. Our seemingly robust health is shaken by a malignant biopsy report. A cherished neighbor moves across the country, leaving us very lonely. The incremental pain of even minor losses can be difficult to bear. But like dear, brave Peter, we can fold the losses into the broader spectrum of our lives, be comforted by God's love, and persevere in God's work.

Suggestion for meditation: Imagine that you are Peter in today's reading. Someone in your audience bears a striking resemblance to Judas. How do you feel?

Wednesday, April 10   Read Psalm 16.

Insomnia

At bedtime, as I smash my head into my pillow and burrow under my down comforter, I say aloud, "Thank you, God, for beds." I love the pleasure of a good night's sleep.

When my sleep is interrupted, though, I get really cranky. A prank phone call. A teenager coming home late from work. The wail of the town siren—any number of things can disturb me. When I can't go back to sleep immediately, I often become frantic.

There is one advantage to insomnia: Praying comes easily in the middle of the night. Without pressures of job or family, there seems to be more room to hear God's voice. The psalmist says, "I bless the LORD who gives me counsel; in the night also my heart instructs me" (NAB). And the night is a prime time for this.

When some prank caller wakes me up at 2 A.M. and I am unable to return to sleep, I pray for anyone at that moment who is near death. When the town siren awakens me as it calls the volunteer firefighters to work, I pray for the family whose lives and property are in danger.

Sometimes, when I am so wide awake that staying in bed is pointless, I randomly open my Bible and listen for God's voice. In the night, when the world is still, solutions to everyday problems often come clear. Solutions present themselves. Unresolved conflicts from the previous day seem to fall into place. In the night God makes clear "the path of life" (NAB).

Suggestion for meditation: **Before you fall asleep, reread Psalm 16. Let the psalmist's words be your last conscious thoughts. Should you awake in the night, return in your mind to the words of the psalm. Or, when you first awaken in the morning, recall the psalmist's words, "I bless the LORD who gives me counsel. . . . I keep the LORD always before me" (NAB).**

Thursday, April 11   Read Acts 2:22-32.

Freed from the tomb

There are tombs all over the Holy Land, among them Rachel's Tomb and the Tomb of King David. The latter, to which Peter refers in Acts 2:29, is one of the most sacred spots in Israel. After the tomb's destruction in 135 A.D., the site on Mount Zion was generally accepted about 1,000 years ago as authentic. The tomb is an elaborate memorial to Israel's greatest king. Velvet and silver enshrine the spot where David's body is entombed.

When Peter reminds the crowd that David's tomb "is with us to this day" (NAB), he touches base with an important symbol. There seems to be a universal human need to know where important people are buried, to know where their physical remains are interred. Think of the grave of John F. Kennedy in our own country. Or the graves of the kings and queens buried in England's Westminster Abbey. Tombs can be eloquent memorials to important lives.

Jesus Christ has no such memorial. Oh, tradition identifies both the Garden Tomb and the Church of the Holy Sepulchre as the site of the tomb of Joseph of Arimathea, where the crucified Jesus was laid to rest. But, while visiting these sites can draw us closer to the human Jesus, they have little to do with the resurrected one—the God incarnate who burst from the grave, leaving behind no physical remains to be revered.

We hear the God of Easter in the whistling wind and in a baby's giggle. We feel God's presence when a long-absent friend wraps us in a hug. Everything from the sweet smell of hyacinths to the yeasty smell of baking bread reminds us of God's creative work in our lives.

Jesus Christ is not interred. No! He is alive.

Suggestion for meditation: **Today, be open to the living Christ's presence. What sights, sounds, and encounters remind you of the life Christ offers you?**

Friday, April 12   Read 1 Peter 1:3-9.

New life in Jesus Christ

The unexpected sound of the public address system had its usual effect on the classroom. My students became alert, grateful for the sudden interruption of routine. However, when the principal's voice came through the speaker, carrying into each classroom of Beaumont School for Girls in Cleveland, silence shrouded all of us. "Sister Dorothy Kazel is one of the four church workers reported missing in El Salvador," the principal told us. "Please pray for the safe return of all four women."

But there would be no safe return. The bullet-ridden bodies of all four women were found buried in shallow graves.

The deaths of these four women, who on December 2, 1980 gave their lives in the service of the church and the people of El Salvador, were acutely felt at Beaumont. Sister Dorothy had been a teacher at our school.

Sister Dorothy's legacy was one of joy. Everyone who knew her spoke of her abiding joy, her great charity.

On the front of the bulletin used for one of Dorothy Kazel's memorial liturgies, there is this familiar quotation from Saint Augustine: "A Christian should be an Alleluia from head to foot." A note in the bulletin explains: "Sister Dorothy expressed the hope that this quotation from Saint Augustine would exemplify her life. She wanted it to be her epitaph."

In First Peter, we are told that there is cause for great rejoicing here even when we are distressed by many trials. The promise of new life in Christ Jesus is always before us. Easter promises that even in the midst of violence and death, there can be resurrected joy.

Suggestion for prayer: Thank God for all those people in the communion of saints whose lives radiate Easter joy. Give special thanks for one who has touched your life in a direct way.

Saturday, April 13   Read John 20:19-23.

Gifts from Jesus

We usually think of the Holy Spirit as first appearing on the Day of Pentecost, but today we read of the Holy Spirit as one of three Easter gifts from Jesus to his disciples. As the disciples gather in fear behind locked doors, Jesus appears, showing them his resurrected body. Then he gives them three gifts.

1) The gift of peace—which they surely need after the horror of the Crucifixion and the frightening confusion of Easter morning.

2) The gift of ambassadorship—the command to go into the world as ambassadors of God's forgiveness. "As the Father has sent me, so I send you." "If you forgive the sins of any, they are forgiven them." Certainly, the betrayals and violence of the past few days must have filled the disciples with bitterness and anger. But Jesus, their master, commands that they offer forgiveness to every person they meet.

3) The gift of the Holy Spirit—the Hebrew for breath, wind, and spirit are the same word, *ruach*. Jesus breathes the Holy Spirit upon the disciples, giving them the strength to go on living.

The Holy Spirit is the instrument of the first two gifts. We best know the peace of Christ in our hearts and lives when we feel the Holy Spirit upon us. Only the Holy Spirit could bring forgiveness into the troubled hearts that had endured the hatred of the Crucifixion. Just as did the disciples, we need these three gifts in order to help bring about God's kingdom on earth.

Prayer: **Resurrected Lord, visit our hearts today, filling us with the Holy Spirit and making us ambassadors of your forgiveness. Amen.**

Sunday, April 14   Read John 20:24-31.

The first Christian creed

Neither the Nicene Creed nor the Apostles' Creed is the first Christian profession of faith. The first creed is Thomas's five words of proclamation on Easter morning.

"Doubting Thomas" has been derided for centuries because he had trouble believing that Jesus arose from the dead and walked through locked doors. However, those miraculous acts require enormous faith on our parts, even now. Certainly, Thomas's doubts are understandable ones.

The very understandable doubts of "Doubting Thomas" should not blind us to "Believing Thomas," the apostle who in five words expresses a volume of faith that we still need to grasp: "My Lord and my God!" The language of Thomas's brief but powerful creed invites close examination.

My Lord. This phrase is Thomas's acknowledgment that Jesus is indeed the same man who was crucified. Not an impostor, not a substitute, not a mirage, or a ghost, but a crucified man now living and standing before him.

And my God! Thomas's expression of faith is one that modern disciples need to express. Thomas acknowledges that this mortal man of flesh, this Jesus, must be more than the sum of his parts. The miracles, the healings, and finally the Resurrection are not the products of human activity or will. Jesus must be God incarnate. In the second phrase of his creed, Thomas indeed claims Jesus Christ as his God.

In this Easter season, we can do no less than join ranks with "Believing Thomas."

Prayer: **Lord, hear me proclaim with Thomas that you are "my Lord and my God!" Amen.**

ON THE ROAD TO EMMAUS

April 15–21, 1996   **Jung Young Lee**✤
Monday, April 15   Read Luke 24:13-14.

When I read the story of two people walking toward Emmaus from Jerusalem, I recall my youth when I used to walk home to my small village from a nearby city. Whenever something happened in the city, my good friend and I always went there to see it. On our way home, we talked a lot about what we had seen and heard. Nowadays, we talk a lot about ball games or other public events in the city.

Important in the Luke passage is not only what happened in Jerusalem but also the intimacy of the two people on the road to their home. Two people are important symbols for mission, for Jesus sent out his disciples two by two. Besides the evangelical significance, the symbol of two has a profound existential meaning. In the Genesis story of creation, two—Adam and Eve— were essential for human existence. The Lord said, "It is not good that the man should be alone" (Gen. 2:18). Human beings always seek companionship. We are relational beings.

Our society stresses individualism and privacy to the extent that we often fail to recognize relationships with other people as an essential element of our existence. Because we stress individualism, we often have difficulty finding a friend with whom we can talk from the heart and share our deepest concerns. We live in a society where true friendship is rare. Christian love nourishes true friendship, for Jesus became our friend. As we read the story of two people on their way to Emmaus, let us open our hearts and minds to those who are lonely and without friends.

Prayer: **Help us, O God, to be true friends to each other, as Jesus became a true friend to us. Amen.**

✤Professor of Systematic Theology, Drew University, Madison, New Jersey.

Tuesday, April 16   Read Luke 24:15-18.

When two people are so deeply engaged in conversation, they do not expect a stranger to join them. First of all, they may not want to pay attention to a stranger, because a stranger would interrupt their intense conversation and break the intimacy of the relationship. If such is the case, their relationship becomes so exclusive that others feel themselves to be—and in fact are—outsiders.

This kind of exclusive relationship also exists in the church. When new people come to the church, we often exclude them from the fellowship of the church. Eventually, they may not return to the church again.

In this story, Jesus was a stranger. The text records no greeting; the first acknowledgment of Jesus' presence comes when he asks a question of the two. Many people in our society become strangers because they are in some way different from the particular dominant group. Many racial minorities, the poor, and women have become strangers in their workplaces and social life. Strangers are also subject to stereotyping. In this story, Jesus was not only a stranger but a stereotyped person. Thus, Cleopas said, "Are you the only stranger in Jerusalem who does not know the things that have taken place there in those days?" Society has a tendency to belittle or be condescending toward those who are uninformed about important public events.

Jesus is present among us today as he was present with the two travelers on the road to Emmaus. But we so often do not recognize his presence. When we are interested only in our own affairs, Christ becomes a stranger, a marginal person in our lives. When we are unable or unwilling to welcome all people in their variety as children of God and, thus, our brothers and sisters, we make Christ a stranger to us.

Prayer: **God, may we open our thoughts to the presence of Christ in our midst and accept his presence in our lives. In Jesus' name. Amen.**

Wednesday, April 17   Read Luke 24:19-21.

Why did Jesus ask them, "What things?" Did he not know what had happened in Jerusalem if he was the same Jesus who suffered and was crucified on the cross? Or did he ask them because he wanted to know their thinking on the event of his crucifixion? Jesus' apparent naiveté and indifference to what had happened to him seems to suggest that he was no longer passionately involved in the past. Was he now transformed into the Christ for all, whose interest was to transform the world?

What had happened to Jesus of Nazareth was the main topic of the conversation of the two people on the road to Emmaus. They were no doubt believers, who ardently wanted to hear eyewitness accounts of the extraordinary things that took place at Jesus' death. Others who had come to the crucifixion were unbelievers, for it was a public event that attracted all kinds of people. Those who were followers, like these two people, had been convinced that Jesus was not just a prophet but was the expected Messiah who would save Israel. However, the events in Jerusalem had shattered their hope.

Their concept of Jesus was not much different from that of most Jews, including Jesus' disciples, who wanted Jesus to be like King David, the mighty deliverer of Israel. They thought that Jesus possessed the power (in an earthly sense) to liberate Israel from the domination of the oppressive Roman Empire. Yet, Jesus was not the same kind of Messiah that they had waited for. Instead, he was a marginalized Jew who appeared in the form of the "suffering servant." His strength was not in military or political power but in his transforming love.

Prayer: **Help us, O God, to remain aware that Jesus is also known to us through our love and service to each other. In Jesus' name. Amen.**

Thursday, April 18   Read Luke 24:22-24.

Matthew's account dramatizes the Resurrection event with vivid symbolism such as the stone being rolled back by an earthquake or the appearance of Jesus like lightning in his white clothing (Matt. 28:1-7). In contrast, Luke describes the Resurrection with the simple picture of an empty tomb and a vision of angels. In other words, Luke as a historian tries to minimize theological interpretations as much as possible.

What seems to be important in this eyewitness account was the women of the group to which these two persons on the road to Emmaus belonged. First of all, we can guess that these two people were not part of the twelve disciples of Jesus but nonetheless were faithful followers of Jesus. They were ordinary persons who shared their conviction with those women who followed Jesus. Another important point that we must pay attention to is that women were the first eyewitnesses to the empty tomb. They also saw the vision of angels, who said that Jesus had risen from dead.

Why were women the first witnesses of the Resurrection? Why did angels first appear to the women rather than to the male disciples? Could it be because women in those days were among the most marginalized of people? Jesus was more closely associated with these women than were other people, including his disciples. These eyewitnesses of the empty tomb, therefore, witness to us that among the closest disciples of Jesus were those women and the poor who were deeply marginalized in society. Christ's love opts for the inclusion of all persons into the kingdom of God.

Suggestion for meditation: **By loving the marginalized people in my community and in my nation, I also show love to Christ. Who are some of these people? In what concrete ways can I show love to them?**

Friday, April 19
Read Luke 24:25-27;
Psalm 116:1-4, 12-19.

The stranger who was seemingly unaware of the things that had happened in Jerusalem becomes a teacher. The two people on the road to Emmaus seem not to have paid attention to what he said. There is no indication that they either responded to his rebuke or appreciated what he attempted to explain as the true meaning of the Messiah through the teachings of the prophets and Moses. Some harsh words like "Oh, how foolish you are" or "How slow of heart to believe" seemed not to bother them at all. They were simply inattentive to what he said, because any remark that came from this stranger, from this "outsider" (because he had not been part of the recent events) had no relevance to them.

The central teaching that the risen Lord attempted to convey to these two people had to do with the real meaning of the Messiah. Their understanding of the Messiah was based on the teaching that one mighty individual especially blessed by God could liberate their people from the oppression of foreign nations. But the real role of the Messiah as taught in the scripture is not as a mighty warrior who uses the power to conquer the world but as the suffering servant who transforms the world through love and service. By suffering and dying on the cross, the Messiah enters into the glory of resurrection. The stranger was the proof of that glory, but the travelers could not understand him.

In our lives, let us remember that many times God speaks to us through unexpected persons.

Prayer: **Help us to recognize all of your children as potential messengers from you. Amen.**

Saturday, April 20   Read Luke 24:28-32;
                                          1 Peter 1:17-23.

The two men might have walked with the stranger more than an hour when the three finally arrived at Emmaus, the small village about seven miles from Jerusalem. As the custom of hospitality indicated, the two invited the stranger to stay with them when evening came. Even when I was living in a small village in Korea more than forty years ago, we always offered a stranger evening meals and a place to stay for the night. Of course, there were no motels or hotels in those days in a small village. In Israel the same kind of courtesy was extended to the stranger when evening came.

The central focus in these verses from Luke is an awakening experience. The evening meal became the catalyst for the two travelers to open their eyes and recognize that the stranger was not, in fact, a stranger. The way the stranger blessed the bread and broke it brought back to them the memory of Jesus, especially the memory of his last supper with his disciples. This seems to indicate that they were either observers of the Last Supper or in the company of disciples who had heard about the supper from the Twelve. When the Emmaus travelers were "awakened," they began to realize the importance of their talk with this stranger on the road. Jesus lived again. He was risen. But then, even as they recognized him, he vanished from their sight.

Likewise, Christ is with us, but only when we awaken to his presence are we able to grow in "genuine mutual love" and be "born anew, not of perishable but of imperishable seed."

Prayer: **Help us to find Christ in the ordinariness of life. Amen.**

Sunday, April 21   Read Luke 24:33-35;
                                        Acts 2:14*a*, 14-24.

We began our week's meditations with the disappointment
and bewilderment of Jesus' followers, especially of those two
traveling the road to Emmaus. Our meditations end with the
confirmation of Jesus' resurrection and sharing that good news
with the disciples of Jesus Christ.

In this passage, we see the sense of urgency. Although it was
evening, the two people traveled the seven miles back to
Jerusalem to meet the eleven disciples. Their encounter with the
risen Jesus was so overwhelming that they could not wait even an
hour. The sense of urgency to share the good news drove them to
meet the disciples in Jerusalem. Because of the joy that they
experienced, distance did not matter to them, and darkness did not
cause them to hesitate. This urgency to share the good news is the
foundation of our evangelism and the church's mission. Nothing
can stop us from sharing the awakening experience of meeting
our risen Lord.

When the two arrived, they found the eleven disciples gathered
in one place. They, too, had experienced the resurrection of Christ:
"The Lord has risen indeed, and he has appeared to Simon!" We
do not know whether Jesus appeared to Simon before he appeared
to the two people on the road to Emmaus. The time of appearance
was not important. What most mattered to them was the confirmation of Jesus' resurrection. He was truly dead on the cross but
was truly risen as he had promised and as scripture had foretold.
Sharing their experience of encountering the risen Christ on the
road to Emmaus becomes the model of the church's life, and the
awakening experience at the breaking of the bread gives added
meaning to the Lord's Supper in the life of our church.

Prayer: **Give us the sense of urgency to share our experience of
the living Christ with other people. In Jesus' name, Amen.**

April 22–28, 1996　　　　　　　　**Frederick J. Streets**✣
Monday, April 22　　　　　　　　Read Acts 2:42-47.

Living with others

There is nothing more empowering than the feeling that we are living with a sense of integrity and wholeness. These come to us when we discover the true meaning of our lives—what it is we are called to be and do. Those who are mentioned in today's text are often referred to as the "first converts." In communion with God and in community with one another they discovered who they were and what was to be their life's mission.

So many people feel that they do not belong to a community or a place. Others grow increasingly so self-centered that they come to belong only to themselves. It is sad to see anyone living in either of these conditions. They remind me of the idea expressed by Howard Thurman in *Jesus and the Disinherited* that some people live in contact with others but without real fellowship with anyone. It is "contact that is devoid of any of the primary overtures of warmth and fellow-feeling and genuineness."

The gift of God's spirit enables us to foster a sense of community among those whose faith and commitment reflect our own. Within such community we live out the Christ example of being a servant in the larger world. We receive strength for living our own lives from those whose journey is also in and with Christ.

Prayer: **Gracious God, help me through my relationships to serve you, and strengthen my Christian servanthood to others. Amen.**

✣Yale University Chaplain and Pastor of the Church of Christ (UCC) in Yale, New Haven, Connecticut.

125

Tuesday, April 23   Read Psalm 23.

Assurance

Our sense of God's presence and care for us can be shattered by so many things. Those experiences represent the "darkest valleys" of our lives. We are often hurt in life and must undergo changes. Change can be a difficult experience for us to have regardless of its nature and origin. However, as human beings we have a great capacity to endure the changes that we face. In this beloved Twenty-third Psalm, the author shares with us the sense that God leads and cares about us through all of the changes and experiences we undergo.

This psalm also reminds us that there is much in life that enhances our awareness of God and the strength that God gives to us. These are the moments when we are led into "green pastures," alongside "still waters," and invited to sit at "prepared tables." These refreshing pauses can come in any form and at any time. God presents them to us daily. We can have these experiences more often if we strive to take advantage of the opportunities God gives us to enjoy them. We must look for them each day.

This psalm uses the concept of a place as metaphor for a faith perspective of life. It is an attitude of reverence for life that helps us to be thankful and joyful for life and open to its surprises. A faith perspective acknowledges the reality of evil, but it does not give evil ultimate authority over us. It is our trust in God that makes God our shepherd.

Prayer: **Dear God, no matter how many experiences we have had or what our age is, we are young in our relationship with you. Lead and guide us as our shepherd, friend, and Savior. Amen.**

Wednesday, April 24　　　　　　　Read Psalm 23.

A prayer meditation on a personal relationship

Gracious God:

I thank you for being my guide and shepherd
who at times causes me to lie down in
　　healthy places
and leads me beside waters
that praise you
and gives me a sense of peace.

Because I am yours
you will not lead me away from your truth.
When I am shadowed by things
that carry me to the depth of anxiety,
you bring me comfort in ways unimaginable
and undetermined by me.

I am grateful for the way you feed me
when I am undernourished
and for bringing my tired body and troubled
　　spirit a balm
that causes my very being to shout for joy
and with relief.

Help me to remember that you are
　　with me always.
Take the stuff of my life
and create a resting place in you
until we are together forever.
Amen.

Thursday, April 25   Read 1 Peter 2:19-25.

The value of it all

Life is not lived without consequences. A question that we associate with suffering of any kind is, What meaning and value does it have for us? Can any suffering be justified? These are questions also raised by those who care about and tend to our needs as we go through our ordeals. There are many causes, known and unknown, and numerous forms of suffering. The way we interpret the meaning of our suffering may not give us a perspective sufficient for us to accept what has happened to us, but we endure.

Many of the early faith communities, which eventually evolved into the Christian church of today, often faced political, social, and religious oppression. Individuals were punished because of their social status or what they believed.

The writer of our text for today offers us the example of Christ's suffering as a guide for dealing with our own. Christ as our exemplar shows us that suffering is not to be glorified. Suffering as a result of living by what you believe may be inevitable. However, the negative consequences of denying our values are greater than those we encounter when we are true to ourselves. It is difficult for some of us to imagine a loss greater than our own or the death of those whom we love. However, the greater destruction comes from living a lie because, as a result of doing so, we lose ourselves. We cannot relate to a person who is not really there! Ultimately the most important gift we can give to one another is the gift of ourselves. In it lies the power to enhance the life of another human being.

Prayer: **Dear God, when I face suffering, help me to endure it gracefully. May the integrity of my life be reflected in my suffering but never compromised because of it. Grant in all my being that I be a gift to others. Amen.**

Friday, April 26   Read John 10:1-10.

Hearing voices

Learning to recognize, cultivate, and listen to our "inner voice" is a common theme in popular self-help literature. This emphasis is a variant of the ancient encouragement to "know thyself." The passage for today characterizes the relationship we are to have with God through Jesus Christ by using the metaphor of "voice" to make its point.

Each person's voice is a distinct feature of us as human beings. We learn how to speak with the voice we are given at birth. The sound of our voice is a natural physical attribute. People recognize us by our voice, and we react to theirs. Our relationship to other people causes us to respond to their voice according to what they mean to us.

A good relationship between two people is the result of both of them working to make it so. We learn to distinguish the voice of a person who wishes us well from that of one who signals the possibility of harming us.

The nurture of our daily relationship with God through Jesus Christ includes praying, meditating, and studying God's word and serving others. We learn to recognize the voice of God in us and who we are as Christians through activities such as these. The self we become and the voice we acquire in Christ enables us to associate the voice of God with our own good. We seek to be empowered by our self-awareness and by becoming more conscious of ourselves in Christ. It is a relationship that sharpens our ability to listen for the many ways God speaks to us about being fulfilled and living a meaningful life while serving the common good.

Prayer: Creator God, you speak in many ways but as one voice. Help me to know your voice more and more so that I may live my life in relation to your desire—and that I may do so with honest devotion to you and in service to others. Amen.

Saturday, April 27   Read John 10:10.

Something more

The Gospel of John expresses a common theme of the Bible—the relationship between God and humans. John, more than any of the other New Testament writers, describes this relationship with a deep sense and mixture of individualism, spirituality, intimacy, and mysticism. We are not surprised then by his reference to his idea of what God in Christ considers as an abundant life.

Most of life has nothing to do with our acquisition of things. It is about discerning what really matters to us throughout our lives. What gives us our deepest sense of this and the great meaning our lives have is the answer to the question, What is an abundant life? Experiencing pleasure, having the resources to meet our basic needs, and being happy may be secondary gains of an abundant life; but they are not its primary objective. Discovering what more there is to life than these can lead us to God's abundant life.

Jesus understood the scarcity and values of those whom he addressed. He offered them abundance of life by a new perspective based upon their relationship to God through him. The values they derived from this relationship motivated them to think differently about themselves and their life situation and to act in a new way toward others.

This interpretation of John's understanding of what Jesus meant by giving life more abundantly may be considered too limited by those of us concerned about the oppressed and the need for social reform. All individual liberation and social change have roots in the transformation of people. Jesus understood this. Our desire for an abundant life is a spiritual quest and hunger that finds its fulfillment in Christ.

Suggestion for meditation: **Consider what really matters to you and how these values reflect your faith in Christ and bring to you a sense of God's peace.**

Sunday, April 28　　　　　Read Acts 2:42-47; Psalm 23;
　　　　　　　　　　　　　　1 Peter 2:19-25; John 10:1-10.

A common theme

The four texts we have used for our meditations throughout this week share a common theme: Jesus Christ as our shepherd leads us into a new relationship with him that changes how we see ourselves, our world, and how we relate to other people. It is a relationship that protects and strengthens the integrity of our lives and guides our spirits.

It is important from time to time to ask yourself, What is the common theme of my life, and how am I living it out in the world? What is it that I want my life to express? To what does my life consent? To live seriously and mindfully is to live with intention. This is the invitation and the kinds of challenging questions Jesus presents us with in the Gospels and is implied in our particular readings for this week.

Howard Thurman speaks to this issue in *The Inward Journey*. "There is nothing more exhausting for the person than the constant awareness that his life is being lived at cross-purposes," he writes. He further asserts that energy is found when we isolate our deepest desire and dedicate our lives toward a single goal.

We can discover in Christ our deepest desire and devote ourselves to its end, trusting that Christ can help us to free ourselves from whatever distracts us from our peace in him. It is hard, difficult, and sometimes painful work to do so, but we are assured by the risen Christ of his presence and strength.

Prayer: **Gracious God, bridge my desires with the intent of my will. May the results of my actions be pleasing in your sight. Amen.**

131

OUR TIMES ARE IN GOD'S HANDS

April 29—May 5, 1996   **Charles D. Whittle**✤
Monday, April 29   Read 1 Peter 2:4-10.

When we need a point of reference . . .

When the North American colonies became independent, weights and measures were different from place to place. Statesman John Quincy Adams realized that one country should have one set of standards for everyone. In 1813 his mother wrote about his room where there were "no less than eighteen large packages, addressed to all the Governours in the United States." These were inquiries about weights and measures in the various states.

In 1821, while Secretary of State, Adams submitted to Congress an impressive document about his findings. It was widely praised for its excellence, but no legislation was adopted. While he was president from 1825 to 1829, he continued to press for standards. Then in 1830 he became a member of Congress and still pressed for standards and equality for all citizens. Finally in 1836 Congress passed the resolution which included most of his recommendations. Then a duplicate set of official weights and measures was given to each state government. At last the country was truly united.

We also need a standard in our moral and spiritual lives. That is one of the reasons God sent Jesus into the world—to be the standard by which we are to live and love, to act and react . . . the "cornerstone" by which all of life is measured and aligned.

Prayer: **Help me, heavenly Father, in my attitudes, my actions, and my reactions, to live in the spirit of Jesus. Amen.**

✤Superintendent, Big Spring District, Northwest Texas Conference of The United Methodist Church; Big Spring, Texas.

Tuesday, April 30   Read John 14:6-9.

When we need direction . . .

A young man said to me, "I understand God, and I think I understand the Holy Spirit, but where does Jesus fit in?"

A good question.

Jesus demonstrated for us the way to relate to God, to ourselves, to other persons, and to society. He seeks to bring out the potential in every person.

If we follow Jesus, where will we go? What will we do?

• We will go to the place of prayer. Jesus took time to pray. He sought the will of God daily.

• We will discover what God is like. God is like Jesus.

• We will discover one another as brothers and sisters. If God is Father, then we are family and will relate to one another as brothers and sisters.

• We will go to the institutional church and participate. The first thing Jesus did after his baptism and wilderness journey was to go to the synagogue and participate in the worship and learning service. (See Luke 4:14-21.)

• We will go to the place of total commitment. Jesus said, "Thy will be done." We pray this regularly as a part of the Lord's Prayer.

• We will love our enemies. "Do good to those who hate you, bless those who curse you, pray for those who abuse you" (Luke 6:27-28).

• We will help people in need.

• We will seek the lost and tell them about Christ.

Prayer: **Heavenly Father, help me to follow Jesus in all things today—and every day. In his name I pray. Amen.**

Wednesday, May 1   Read 1 Peter 2:2-3.

In times of growing up . . .

For over 200 years every minister who has been ordained in my denomination has been asked the question, "Are you going on to perfection?" Sometimes I wonder if we might paraphrase that today as, "Are you planning to grow up?"

Growing depends on proper nourishment. Just as newborn infants require pure milk for physical development, so we need "pure, spiritual milk" for spiritual development. And when we taste pure, spiritual food we discover "that the Lord is good."

Note the words *pure, spiritual milk*. Less than 100 years ago, Louis Pasteur discovered that most disease-producing micro-organisms could be destroyed by sterilization. From his name we call the process *pasteurization.*

The "pure milk" we need is sound teaching, through the reading and understanding of scripture, learning from those who are interested in our welfare, listening to conscience, and practicing the principles of the Christian faith through translating what we learn into how we live.

God so wants us to realize our fullest potential in this life that God sent Jesus to reveal divine love and to show us how to live and love. Then God came in the Holy Spirit to develop in us our best self.

The Christian life is one of continuing growth with new discoveries and developing potential. Yes, indeed, we "taste and see that the LORD is good."

Prayer: **Help me, heavenly Father, to grow more like Jesus, in whose name I pray. Amen.**

Thursday, May 2 Read Psalm 31:1-5; John 14:1-10.

When we need assurance . . .

Douglas MacArthur said, "Only those are fit to live who are not afraid to die."

One of our basic needs is assurance. Assurance comes from confidence. Confidence comes from knowing that God is caring for us.

John Wesley, founder of Methodism, received inner assurance as he listened to the reading of Luther's preface to the Epistle to the Romans. Wesley recorded his experience:

> About a quarter before nine, while he was describing the change which God works in the heart through faith in Christ, I felt my heart strangely warmed. I felt I did trust in Christ, Christ alone, for salvation: and an assurance was given me that He had taken away my sins, even mine, and saved me from the law of sin and death.*

Among the first recorded words of humankind to God were "I was afraid" (Gen. 3:1). All through the scriptures we read how God comes to fearful men and women with the message, "Fear not." In a time of fearful transition, Jesus spoke to his disciples, "Do not let your hearts be troubled. Believe in God, believe also in me."

In all things our times are in God's hands (See Psalm 31:15.) God's assurance gives us reassurance that nothing can happen to us that we cannot face with God's help.

Suggestion for meditation: **What are my fears? Do I believe God cares? Do I believe that my times are in God's hands? I will remember that Jesus said, "Believe . . . ," the first step toward assurance.**

---

*Wesley's Journal, Wednesday, May 24, 1738.

Friday, May 3   Read Acts 7:54-60.

In times of opposition . . .

Stephen was one of seven chosen to administer assistance to Greek-speaking widows. "Full of the Spirit and of wisdom" (Acts 6:3), Stephen was having an effective ministry. Opposition arose from members of one of the synagogues who began to argue with Stephen, but they could not stand up against his "wisdom and the Spirit with which he spoke" (6:10).

Secretly they persuaded some men to say, "We have heard him speak blasphemous words against Moses and God" (6:11).

Stephen was seized and brought before the council. False witnesses testified, "This man never stops saying things against this holy place and the law" (6:13). The high priest asked him, "Are these things so?" (7:1)

Stephen began a long recitation of the history of Israel, beginning with God's call to Abraham, the journey to a new land, the sojourn in and deliverance from Egypt, and the history of Israel's rebellion against God. His accusers became enraged by his words. They dragged him out of the city and began to stone him.

Here we learn how Christians react to opposition. "While they were stoning Stephen, he prayed, 'Lord Jesus, receive my spirit. . . . Lord, do not hold this sin against them.' "

How we react to other people's actions may be our most effective witness. Stephen loved his enemies and prayed for them. With God's help, we can too.

Prayer: **Help me today, Father, to witness with my reactions as well as my actions. In Jesus' name. Amen.**

Saturday, May 4   Read Psalm 31:1-5, 15-16.

In times of distress . . .

At some time in our lives, each of us experiences distress. For many persons every day is a day of quiet desperation, a daily struggle for survival. Often the most common prayer is, "Lord, help me."

David was blessed of God. He was a leader of his people as well as a king and mighty warrior. He was not, however, immune from trouble. His troubles came from political enemies, from his own moral failure, and even from his own beloved son Absalom's betrayal.

In times like these he turned to the Lord and prayed, "O LORD, . . . deliver me, . . . lead me and guide me, take me out of the net."

David committed himself to the Lord, declaring, "Into your hand I commit my spirit," and "My times are in your hand." He affirmed his faith, "You have redeemed me."

Active faith produces contact with God. Contact with God produces confidence and security, even in the midst of distress. God does not automatically immunize us against the pressures of daily living or cause us to be unaffected by the problems of the world. Through our faith, God can help us to adjust, to move with purpose, and to find calmness in the midst of life's ups and downs.

***Prayer:* Heavenly Father, I do not ask to be delivered from trouble today but to be delivered from fear, anxiety, and distress. Use redemptively whatever happens to me. In Jesus' name. Amen.**

Sunday, May 5   Read John 14:12-14.

When we face an impossible mission . . .

For many years I had difficulty understanding the prediction of Jesus, "Very truly, I tell you, the one who believes in me will also do the works that I do and, in fact, will do greater works than these, because I am going to the Father."

How, I thought, *can I even do the works that Jesus did, much less do even greater works?* Then it occurred to me: One way I can do these things is connectionally.

As I connect with other Christians in a local congregation who connect with hundreds of thousands of other Christians I can: build and maintain great hospitals and clinics of healing; teach hundreds of thousands of children in schools, colleges, and universities around the world; provide homes for children and for adults in need of secure places; be present with assistance for victims of floods, earthquakes, wars, famines, and abuse.

As I connect with other Christians, I can counsel and minister to persons in crisis; maintain centers of day care for children of working parents; sustain myriad other ministries; and best of all, I can preach the gospel of grace to people in every nation.

Yes, I can do these things . . . connectionally.

Prayer: **Dear Jesus, help me gladly to join hearts and hands and resources with Christians everywhere to do your works of loving care. Amen.**

COME AND HEAR

May 6–12, 1996
Monday, May 6

Mary Lou Santillán Baert✤
Read Psalm 66:8-20.

The psalmist offers an invitation: "Come and hear, all you who fear God." What was in the psalmist's heart and mind? What vow was the pilgrim fulfilling? Why the extravagant offering of fatlings, rams, bulls, goats? Has there ever been a time in your life so hopeless that you pleaded with God and vowed to give God everything in exchange for a favor?

The psalmist was aware of how Israel had been saved from difficult situations: the yoke of slavery in Egypt, the wilderness pilgrimage toward the promised land, the struggles to settle the land. It was all God's doing, and the psalmist recognized this.

That the psalmist could acknowledge the goodness of God while being refined and tested is awesome. Is this also our experience? God's goodness and intervention on behalf of God's people need to be told. The psalmist was ready to witness.

The one who senses the healing touch is anxious to extol the One experienced—unknown to some but known to the psalmist, who counted on God's faithfulness.

Remember *your* story. Through what trials and tests has God brought you? Whom have you invited to "come and hear"?

Prayer: **Thank you, O God, for listening and for keeping me close in your steadfast love. Amen.**

✤United Methodist clergy, member of the Río Grande Conference; Pastor of St. Luke's United Methodist Church (Love Field), Dallas, Texas.

Tuesday, May 7   Read Acts 17:17-21.

Paul, Silas, and Timothy had traveled through Philippi, Thessalonica, and Beroea. They had had some successes, but there had also been some agitators along the way. So Paul was sent to Athens, a city full of idols.

What must have gone through his mind—this man who had experienced the saving grace of the one, true, living God, the God not made with hands, the God not formed in humankind's image?

How do we react when we see the idols people have created around them? Are we provoked enough, as Paul was, to go to church, to places of business, to supermarkets and proclaim: "Come and hear!"

Paul talked with those around him in the synagogue and marketplace. He even went with them to the Areopagus, not to argue but to proclaim.

The Athenians were hungry and thirsty for new knowledge. Here was this stranger with a new teaching. They were curious and wanted to know what his words meant. What an opportunity to witness!

Have we taken advantage of those times when friends or strangers have asked us questions about our religious experience? How eager have we been to declare that Jesus Christ is our Lord and Savior, raised from the dead to give us life? And what does all that really mean? Are these just words we repeat because we have heard them from time to time? Can we explain them?

Success is not the target; faithfulness is. Eloquence of speech is not a requirement; speaking from the heart is. Crowds are not a necessity; one listening heart deserves to hear.

Pause to reflect on what you really know and truly believe. To what would you witness?

Prayer: **Help me, O God, to proclaim joyously what my mind has known and my heart has felt about the resurrected Lord. Amen.**

Wednesday, May 8   Read Acts 17:22-31.

On top of the Areopagus Paul observed that indeed these Athenians were a religious people. An altar "to an unknown god" was evidence of this. The apostle began where the people were and tried to lead them from ignorance to true worship.

God is proclaimed as Creator, the One "who made the world and all things in it," the One who is Lord of heaven and earth. God is also declared the Sustainer, the One who gives life and breath to all.

In 1970, just past mid-May, my oldest sister was hospitalized. She died the next day on the eve of my mother's birthday. She was buried on Saturday. On Sunday my father, as was his custom, went to church and taught the adult Sunday school class. The lesson that morning was based on Acts 17 and Paul's experience in Athens. What would my father say? He had just lost a daughter, the first child, the one born fourteen months after my parents arrived in the U.S.A.; the one who called them every day.

The scripture was read. Looking at the adults in the classroom, my father stated firmly, "This unknown God is no stranger to me. Even now in the midst of my grief, I know in whom I have believed. I can only praise God for loving me so much. God blessed me with the gift of being father to her for those few years. How good God was to grant me such a daughter to love and such a daughter to love me. This is no unknown God! Come and hear me tell you about the God I know."

I had expected a Bible lesson. Instead I discovered again the power of the God who dwelled within my father. And I heard again my father's reassurance that he *knew* he lived and moved and existed in God.

Prayer: **Come and dwell within me, O Lord, as I yield myself to live and move and exist in you. Amen.**

Thursday, May 9   Read 1 Peter 3:13-17.

"Who will harm you if you are eager to do what is good?" asks the author of First Peter. Many of us would immediately respond, "But we've seen and know that bad things do happen to good people—again and again. We could even make a list of sufferers and include our names."

But the writer continues, saying that there is a promise of blessing even in suffering. How can suffering be a blessing? Many of us would give anything not to suffer or experience pain.

The suffering intensifies when we dwell on the anguish that accompanies it. We are not to be intimidated by any of these things. We are not to fear what others fear; rather, we are to sanctify Christ as Lord in our hearts. This will enable us to say, "Come and hear!" What an opportunity to declare the hope that is within us!

I lived in Mexico City several years ago. A particular seminary professor there was greatly admired, respected, and loved. His teachings were profound and powerfully inspiring, yet understandable. Unfortunately, he had a stroke. But when he began to recover and could communicate again, his students asked if they could meet in his home. They were still eager to learn from him and wanted in some way to demonstrate their love and concern for him. They would not abandon him.

They continued this practice for some time. When he died, there was great sorrow. When his body lay in state at the seminary, it was his widow who, with gentleness and reverence, consoled the students. The hope of Jesus Christ within her sparkled in her face even in the midst of sorrow.

Prayer: **I believe, O God. Help my unbelief when I do not understand suffering or pain. Amen.**

Friday, May 10   Read 1 Peter 3:17-22.

Whether suffering is just or unjust, most of us would rather not see or hear anyone in agony or pain. We have lived through enough wars. We have seen the newsreels of victims, of violence, of Holocaust survivors, of hunger casualties. Time and again we have exclaimed, "No more!"

We want answers. We look for them wherever we can in order to gain some peace of mind. One expert will give us a medical or scientific reason, another may place blame, others may urge us to accept suffering as God's will. How can we know if suffering is for good or evil? Whose criteria determine this?

Jesus, who was without sin, suffered once and for all. The righteous one was put to death in the flesh for the unrighteous ones. He who was without sin became sin for our sake "so we might become the righteousness of God" (2 Cor. 5:21).

Death could not keep Jesus in the grave. God raised him, and he is made alive in the Spirit. He went on to make a proclamation to the spirits in prison. "Come and hear!" he was saying. "You're not going to believe this, but it's true! It happened to me."

Out of suffering came reconciliation, peace, and salvation. God used the pain of the Innocent One to bless the sinners. The Almighty destroyed evil—reversed the letters and said, "Live!"

The news is good, fantastic! Celebrate! Invite *everyone* to come to the party.

Now is the time of salvation!

Prayer: O God, help me to celebrate, for the good news of Jesus Christ is too good to keep to myself. Amen.

Saturday, May 11   Read John 14:15-17.

Who has had the greatest influence in your faith journey? Was it a compelling preacher? A knowledgeable and resourceful Sunday school teacher? A gifted music director? A charismatic adult leader? All these and others may have helped you along the way, but perhaps the one who inspired you the most was someone who loved you in a way that no one else before had cared for you.

Love is more than just a warm, fuzzy feeling. It is more than "a many-splendored thing," more than "what makes the world go 'round," much more than "never having to say you're sorry."

Jesus demonstrated with his words and life that to love is to desire and to work for the good and benefit of the other, including the enemy. To love means obedience to Jesus' commandment even if obedience implies sacrifice.

God is love. We are created in God's image and thus we should also be the incarnation of love.

The time was drawing near. Soon Jesus would be facing death. He had tried to prepare his disciples, who seemed to have difficulty hearing and understanding what he really meant. For three years he had said, "Come and hear!" Yet Philip still (and perhaps others too) was asking about the way—even though the way, the truth, and the life had dwelt *with* them! Had they not seen or learned anything during their time together? Had they lived intimately with Jesus and not really known him?

It seemed that Jesus wanted his disciples to know one basic thing. If they truly loved him, they would obey his commandment to love. To love was to obey.

Jesus knew that they could not do it alone and he addressed this concern. The Holy Spirit will be our helper as the Spirit was the helper of the disciples.

Prayer: **O Lord of life, bless me and enable me to obey Jesus' commandment to love—whatever the cost. Amen.**

Sunday, May 12   Read John 14:18-21.

Jesus will not abandon his disciples. Even as he makes his farewell speech, he is thinking of them. He will ask God to send the Holy Spirit to dwell in them. The Spirit will come as a comforter, counselor, companion, helper, guide. The Spirit will remain with them forever.

John Wesley wrote, "Among the many difficulties of our early ministry, my brother Charles often said, 'If the Lord would give me wings, I'd fly.' I used to answer, 'If God bids me fly, I will trust Him for the wings.'"

The disciples would soon be responsible for continuing the ministry begun by Jesus. They had relied so much on him. Who would guide them now? Were they fearful? Were they self-confident? Were they excited? Were they perplexed? Would they be up to the challenge before them? Did they ever wonder why they had not paid closer attention?

Jesus had been a unique storyteller, a charismatic teacher, a sensitive healer, a devout man of prayer, a forgiving friend, a compassionate listener. He had loved children and lepers, widows and rich young rulers, Jews and Gentiles, men and women. Had the disciples developed any other talents besides fishing and tax collecting during those three years with Jesus?

A promise was made to the disciples. The Holy Spirit would come—with power! When God lays upon us a difficult responsibility, God supplies what we need to fulfill it.

The Gospel writer seems to say in conclusion, "Come and hear again: 'Whoever keeps God's commandments is the one who loves me.'"

How much do we love God? Can we count the ways?

***Prayer:* Come, Holy Spirit, exchange our hearts of stone for hearts of love. Lead us to obedience. Amen.**

145

GOD'S EMPOWERMENT

May 13–19, 1996   **Elaine M. Prevallet, S.L.**✤
Monday, May 13   Read Acts 1:6-14.

This week we look forward to the Feast of the Ascension. Matthew's Gospel, and the earliest ending to Mark's Gospel, carry no account of the ascension of Jesus. John's Gospel seems to presuppose its inclusion in the Resurrection events. Only Luke, in the Gospel and in Acts, tells of Jesus' ascending to heaven.

Until the fourth century, Jesus' ascension was not celebrated as a separate feast. Yet, the impulse of faith is to cherish every moment and ponder every episode of the sacred story of God's presence among us in Jesus. Jesus came to earth, his life proclaiming the power of God's love; but he died the death of a common criminal. The Resurrection proclaims his vindication, while the Ascension celebrates his exaltation in power at God's right hand. Thus, on Pentecost, he sends the Spirit to the disciples, his body the church.

We need to view the Ascension as a moment within this cycle. If we celebrate the Ascension without reference to the Resurrection and Pentecost, we can only imagine a Christ who has come and gone, leaving us orphaned and powerless. But Jesus' body bears the marks of his death, and his exaltation allows him to intercede for us always and empowers him to send the Spirit. Though the Ascension seems to separate Jesus from us, it focuses on the moment in the paschal cycle that affirms the empowerment of Jesus as Messiah transcending the limitations of space and time. His empowerment becomes our own.

Prayer: **Risen Savior, fill our hearts with joy in your ascension and empowerment at God's right hand. Open us to experience the power of your resurrection in our lives this day. Amen.**

✤Roman Catholic sister; Director of Knob Haven Retreat Center at the Motherhouse of the Sisters of Loretto; Nerinx, Kentucky.

Tuesday, May 14   Read Psalm 68:1-10, 32-36.

The psalm as a whole lacks cohesion, but the lines of our reading celebrate the power of God who gives power and strength to the people. They prod us to meditate on what power means and how God's power works. Maybe we have internalized an image of God as Lord of hosts, leading armies to battle. Maybe we have feared that God's power would explode upon us in wrath or punishment.

The epidemic of violence in our own society makes us stop and think: could a God of power and might legitimate our violence to one another? Does the power that God "gives . . . to his people" give them (us) a right to dominate and control, even through violent means? We need to ask ourselves whether we do in fact think of power—even God's power—in terms of force, violence, and control.

But does not our experience teach us that love, and not force, carries the *real* power for lasting change, for life-giving transformation? Not forcing, but gently evoking—that is how the power of love works. We need to notice how often in scripture God's power expresses itself in compassion: the mighty God who "rides upon the clouds" is parent to orphans, protector of society's victims, home to the homeless, liberator of prisoners. Perhaps we need to meditate not on God's might but on how God's power showed itself in the life, death, and resurrection of Jesus. Power and strength for truth-telling, healing, reconciling, for enhancing life: that is the love-power God shares with us. God's power and the power God gives to us rises out of the ground of divine love.

Suggestion for prayer: **Think of an instance when love effected a real change in your life, and ask for the grace to be a channel for that kind of power this day.**

Wednesday, May 15   Read John 17:1-11.

These words of Jesus at prayer with his disciples during the Last Supper are spoken in deepest intimacy. Sensing that his life on earth is reaching its end, Jesus reflects that he has given his all: he has accomplished the work God gave him to do. He has lived faithful to the mission God entrusted to him; he has taught the disciples everything he could. As he prepares to leave, the desire of his heart is simple: "That they may be one, as we are one."

We can read these words as if we are present, for in truth we are the disciples who feel left behind in the world as Jesus prepares to ascend to the Father. We have received the words God gave Jesus. We have believed that Jesus was sent by God to reveal God's deepest identity: God's most intimate name of Love. Jesus, the embodiment of God, expresses his deepest prayer in the longing for communion: that all may be one.

Jesus' ascension empowers him to share with us the Spirit of truth and love. What a gift if, as our own lives draw to a close, we could say as Jesus did, "I have accomplished the work you gave me to do!" What is that work? Jesus' hope is that our *lives* will be a work of communion. We can begin now, simply with our heart's readiness to approach and do each day's tasks in love, knowing that our life comes to us each moment as a loving gift from the hand of God. Each evening, we can return the day to God with those same words: *I have accomplished the work you gave me to do*. It is nothing esoteric, no heroic ministry. Only love. It is that simple. Can we believe that?

Prayer: **Loving God, grant me the grace to do with love the tasks of this day, in full trust that this is the work *you* have given me to do. Amen.**

Ascension Day

Thursday, May 16

Read Psalm 47;
Ephesians 1:15-23.

The empowerment of Christ, on this Feast of Ascension, means that he can, and does, now share with us his very spirit, his life, his heart, his eyes. Paul prays for the community at Ephesus, that they may have the eyes of their hearts enlightened, that they may know "the immeasurable greatness of [God's] power for us who believe."

The words tell us something about the kind of power that is God's gift to us in Jesus. It is the power to be the heart and the eyes of Christ in our own lives. We, the church, are now the body of Christ, "the fullness of him who fills all in all." Our hearts see the world with Christ's eyes, see its poor, see its suffering. We have the heart of Christ with which to love our world into peace and justice for all people. When we watch the news, when we encounter suffering, poverty, deception, injustice, violence—we can see with Christ's eyes. The compassion we feel is Christ's compassion. What an honor and privilege!

But like the disciples, we cannot stand looking up to heaven admiring the gift. We gather into the community of faith that knows its mission to enter into the suffering of the world as Christ did, and to bring the love of Christ's own heart for its healing. Christ's empowerment is our empowerment, but like his, ours is won through the daily dying and rising that is the fabric of our lives. Christ dies and rises in and with us; Christ's spirit reaches the world through us.

Prayer: **Spirit of the Risen Christ, give me the faith and the courage to be a true disciple of Jesus. Amen.**

149

Friday, May 17   Read 1 Peter 4:12-13; 5:6-11.

Today's reading places us squarely in the life-death-life cycle that is at the heart of God's revelation to us in Jesus. Do not be surprised, says Peter, do not think it is strange that you have to suffer. Like it or not, suffering is integral to the life that God shares with us in Christ.

We would like to think that God's calling will immunize us against suffering. But what God promises in Jesus is not immunity but presence and power: the God of all grace will be with us, empowering us in the struggle.

What is the struggle? The text points to persecutions: the early Christians knew themselves to be "outsiders"; they were a threat to the Roman status quo because they would not engage in the idolatry of emperor worship. Our idols are not our rulers, our presidents, our governors. But maybe power itself has become a national idol. We in the U.S.A. believe that to be secure our country must always be number one, that we must maintain ourselves as the richest and most powerful nation in the world regardless of the exploitation involved. Most nations trust in military power as the source of security and strength. Are not these idolatrous beliefs symptoms of a lack of trust in God?

We may not be publicly persecuted if we try to live by Jesus' commandment of love. But we will have to suffer if we go against the mainstream, if we choose to stand with those who are poor, those who do not have power in our society. Compassion means *suffering-with*. We will have to struggle, to keep our vision clear and our hearts loving. We will not think this strange if we are followers of Jesus.

Prayer: **Loving Spirit of Jesus, be with me this day so that my love may truly be united with your own love for the world. Amen.**

Saturday, May 18   Read Acts 1:6, 8.

The disciples are relishing the marvel of the presence of Jesus among them after the Resurrection. They are on the winning side. They are imagining the important roles they are going to have in the new kingdom Jesus will now establish. They will receive the glory of having been smart enough to see Jesus' potential and be his followers. But Jesus knows a different scenario. The power he promises is not what they imagine. It is *God's* power through the Holy Spirit. The disciples cannot make it happen. They have to receive it as a gift.

But the power is given through Jesus; it is for them to be witnesses of Jesus. The power will therefore be a power that involves both death and resurrection, a transforming power that brings life out of death.

Once again we have to distinguish the kind of power Jesus promises from our cultural notion of power. For us, power too often means force, violence, and domination. But the power of violence only spreads more violence and death. It does not issue in life. We need to see where the violence is and where the death that results from the violence is. Then we need to bring to that place a different power, the power of the Holy Spirit, the power of truth and of love.

Am I willing to be a power of reconciliation in the midst of strife, of love in the midst of hatred, of truth-telling in the midst of lies and deception? This will mean struggle, for it is always easier to turn aside; it will mean accepting the risk of suffering. Jesus promises us the power of God's spirit to bring life out of death, but that means we must *confront* the places in our society—and in our own lives—where the power of death prevails.

Prayer: **Spirit of Jesus, empower me so that I may be an agent of love, truth, and gentleness. Amen.**

Sunday, May 19   Read Acts 1:11.

Angels have a way of getting to the heart of the matter. Like the angels at the tomb after Jesus' resurrection, who pointedly ask the women, "Why are you seeking the living among the dead?" (Luke 24:5) these angels, too, send us right back to earth. Jesus has risen and ascended, but we cannot stand with our mouths open marveling at the wonder of it. We have a job to do, and the meaning of the death-resurrection-ascension of Jesus is not complete until we are doing it. Ascension means Jesus' empowerment; the gift of the Holy Spirit at Pentecost, our empowerment, completes the cycle.

How do we await the Spirit promised by Jesus; where do we anticipate the Spirit's coming? The disciples gathered, men and women together, into a community of prayer. Ordinarily, the Holy Spirit does not reach us as detached individuals. We have our individual roles to play, of course, each one a specific manifestation of the Spirit destined for a specific context. That is essential. But we are a *community* of believers. Our culture makes it difficult to think straight about power. We need the community to sustain us in the revolution the Spirit inspires—transforming the world in God's love.

Each of us has a role in keeping the community of the church faithful to the teaching of Jesus, being honest ourselves so that we can keep others honest, being loving in order to create an atmosphere of love. Praying together, pondering the words of scripture in the context of the needs of our world and our society provide the space in which the Spirit can move us, can empower us. The Spirit draws us together. We cannot do it alone.

Suggestion for meditation: **How faithful am I to helping create a true community of faith? O Spirit of God, open my heart to your nudgings. Amen.**

May 20–26, 1996   **Joe A. Harding**✣
Monday, May 20   Read Numbers 11:4-17.

When have you experienced spiritual burnout? Overwhelming demands and expectations? How often do you remind yourself that you are in good company?

Moses was clearly on the edge of leadership burnout. He needed help. After the Exodus, the people constantly complained. They got tired of eating manna. They wanted meat! They spoke of mouth-watering fish, cucumbers, melons, leeks, garlic, and onions. They cried out with angry voices, "Now our strength is dried up, and there is nothing at all but this manna to look at." They cried out for variety. In the desert they wanted gourmet food.

In desperation Moses prayed, "I am not able to carry all this people alone, the burden is too heavy for me." God then gave Moses a very simple suggestion: Get some help. "Gather for me seventy men of the elders of Israel . . . let them take their stand there with you" (RSV). In other words, go to the same people who are complaining and say to them, "I need your help." They gathered together in worship and prayer and an amazing thing happened—God's spirit came to rest on seventy of them.

God wants those in the community of faith to share in leadership and ministry. In shared ministry persons can experience the reality of God's work not just as casual spectators but as energized co-workers, offering help to hurting and receptive persons.

Prayer: **Loving God, bring before my mind the people that you want enlisted for this great cause. Thank you for letting me know your help is already on the way. In Jesus' name. Amen.**

✣Director of Growth Plus and Vision 2,000, General Board of Discipleship of The United Methodist Church; clergy, Pacific–Northwest Conference; Richland, Washington.

Tuesday, May 21   Read Numbers 11:24-30.

We continue toward Pentecost with a second basic insight learned from the Book of Numbers. Moses recruited the help of seventy elders to listen to complaints of the people and to give leadership in the long journey. Like Moses, it is difficult for some of us to admit that we need help.

Jesus asked for help. He sent out the twelve apostles to witness. He also gathered seventy others whom he sent out two by two (Luke 10:1). Perhaps the apostles had reservations about this larger group's being included in this strategic ministry. They certainly had not received the training that the twelve received. Notice, however, what happened when the seventy returned. Were Peter, Andrew, James, and John really happy when those not in the innermost circle came back saying, "Lord, in your name even the demons submit to us!" (Luke 10:17)

Joshua, truly a great leader, actually resented the success of two men, Eldad and Medad. The Spirit came upon them, and they were prophesying. Joshua said, "My lord Moses, forbid them" (RSV). Moses' response was immediate and direct: "Are you jealous for my sake? Would that all the LORD'S people were prophets, and that the LORD would put his spirit on them!" The effective leader must not only ask for help but also teach people to rejoice. Success in ministry comes from unlikely places.

The question is, Who controls the Spirit? Not religious leaders but the Giver of the Spirit. "Would that all God's people were prophets" is a wish anticipating lay ministry and empowerment of God's Spirit for effective, committed ministry for all persons.

Prayer: **Spirit of the living God, deliver us from our desire to control you. Give us freedom to rejoice when you use different sisters and brothers in different churches for your ministry of salvation and restoration. In Jesus' name. Amen.**

Wednesday, May 22 Read Psalm 104:24-34, 35*b*.

Christians of tomorrow's church will be joyous and enthusiastic in their praise of God. They will share the wonder of God's abundant creation. The psalmist gives us a powerful example in these words, "O LORD how manifold are thy works! In wisdom hast thou made them all" (RSV). Perhaps our youth might say, "Lord, your creation is awesome—it is really *totally awesome!*" In verse 26 the psalmist invites us to stand by the sea to look across it as he says, "There go the ships, and Leviathan that you formed to sport in it."

The psalmist understands God's spirit as the active agent in creation. "When you send forth your spirit, they are created; and you renew the face of the ground." The psalmist is clearly a visionary leader in commitment to praise. "I will sing to the LORD as long as I live; I will sing praise to my God while I have being. May my meditation be pleasing to him, for I will rejoice in the LORD."

Faithfulness to God's vision moves us beyond dry doctrine or theological orthodoxy to a Spirit-inspired and Spirit-released praise. Is there a dimension of praise, gratitude, and wonder that we have not yet experienced? Often leaders, lay and clergy, have sought to control the direction of worship and praise by their organization and planning of worship experiences. The Spirit confronts our inner darkness and chaos to create radical receptivity to wonder. The word of God speaks light, and there *is* light!

Let us join with the psalmist in enthusiastically proclaiming, "Bless the LORD, O my soul! Praise the LORD!"

Prayer: **Holy Spirit, grant us a childlike joy in your gifts of creation. Release us to move beyond words to authentic praise. In Jesus' name. Amen.**

Thursday, May 23   Read John 7:37-39.

How is the Christian, especially the Christian leader, to sustain vision when the hot sun of resistance and apathy saps strength and brings all hope into question? At times the vision that inspired the spiritual journey disappears just as we discover that the shimmering water in a hot desert is only a mirage. What then?

The author of the Gospel of John has a word for us from Jesus. The setting was one of the Temple courts. The occasion was the last day of one of the great feasts. "While Jesus was standing there, he cried out, 'Let anyone who is thirsty come to me, and let the one who believes in me drink.' As the scripture has said, 'Out of the believer's heart shall flow rivers of living water.' "

The images of fresh, cool water flowing in the desert is a familiar vision in Hebrew scriptures. (See Isaiah 41:17-19 and Isaiah 44:3-4.) The phrase "out of the believer's heart" now locates the place of the renewing stream. In other words, the source of renewal is not external but is internal. Renewal is available to all believers in Jesus Christ. At this point, Jesus shares his interpretation and meaning of living water. "Now he said this about the Spirit, which believers in him were to receive; for as yet there was no Spirit, because Jesus was not yet glorified."

In other words, the Spirit brings into the present reality Jesus' promised transformation. The "as yet" refers to Jesus' crucifixion, resurrection, and ascension. Through these events, God glorified Jesus. All were necessary before the Spirit's outpouring.

In Ezekiel 47, a river flowing from the Temple transforms the Dead Sea; the stagnant water becomes fresh. What stagnant places within you need to be made fresh by the transforming power of God's Spirit?

Prayer: **Spirit of the living God, let your living presence flow through me. Let me receive your renewal from within. In Jesus' name. Amen.**

Friday, May 24   Read John 20:19-23.

The person who is receptive to God's vision for the future will find that other visions also present themselves—visions born of doubt, uncertainty, and fear of failure. When we become discouraged and doubt God's promises, it is tempting to seek safety and security behind locked doors of skepticism and bitterness.

The disciples who were meeting behind closed doors after Jesus' resurrection were seeking safety and security. Jesus had assured them that he would return to them. Several had actually seen the risen Christ. The words of the women and Cleopas added to the climate of hope. Still the disciples needed more than words.

On the evening of the first day of the week, Jesus appeared to his followers and spoke words of peace to them. He showed them his hands and his side. He told them about their mission: "As the Father has sent me, so I send you." Then he breathed on them and said, "Receive the Holy Spirit."

The author of the fourth Gospel wants us to understand that the Holy Spirit is not some alien reality. The Spirit is nothing less than the breath (authentic inner life) of Jesus. Breath is that which gives life. In the account of Creation (Gen. 2:1), the breath (*ruach*) of God is life-giving.

In the upper room is the beginning of the second creation as Jesus breathes upon his followers and speaks, "Receive the Holy Spirit." The Spirit is the reality of the Creator God and of the victorious Son, sharing God's transforming power and presence. The Spirit is not abstract doctrine but living reality. The breath of Jesus Christ restores and energizes with victorious confidence.

Prayer: **"Breathe on me, Breath of God, fill me with life anew, that I may love what thou dost love, and do what thou wouldst do." Amen.***

---

*From the hymn "Breathe on Me, Breath of God" by Edwin Hatch (1878).

Saturday, May 25   Read Acts 2:1-5 (6-13).

Christian living in the future tense requires receptivity and risk. An encounter with the living God is risky. God is full of surprises and does not always follow our agendas or plans. The word *suddenly* in Acts 2:1 suggests such a dramatic surprise and interruption. This God is beyond our schedules, bulletins, preconference handbooks, and controlled worship services. Efforts to organize the Holy Spirit vanish before the activity of this God.

"Suddenly" a sound came from heaven like the rush of a mighty wind. The powerful sound certainly announced, "Something is *really* happening"! The appearance of tongues as of fire that rested on each one of them suggested that the God of the past—perceived in blinding light or in flaming mountains, cloaked in clouds or even in a brilliant burning bush—was truly present for every person.

God was now empowering each disciple. No longer was God a past or remote being. What a candlelight service that was! The disciples began to speak in other tongues as the Spirit gave them utterance. Jesus' promise for power to witness was fulfilled! (See Acts 1:8.) The witnesses were heard. The response was life changing. The speakers' effectiveness was not born of their personal eloquence but in the mighty act of God's speaking in and through them. Such an explosion of joyous witness was truly the birthday of the church. The event ranked in significance with the birth and resurrection of Jesus Christ. His personal presence with the church in power enabled their enthusiastic proclamation.

Christians and Christian leaders for the future have room for God's surprises. They are willing to receive and respond. Cynicism or put-downs do not disable Christians living in God's future. "They are filled with new wine" (Acts 2:13).

Prayer: **Creator God, thank you for coming to us personally and powerfully through your Spirit. Create within us a passionate receptivity. Amen.**

Pentecost

Sunday, May 26   Read Acts 2:13-21.

The Holy Spirit enables persons to break down barriers. Christians living into the future church can face cynical laughter with bold, positive affirmation by the Spirit's power. Peter refused to allow those in Jerusalem to dismiss the Pentecost event.

Peter's stance shows God at work, fulfilling God's promise. This forthright posture and speaking out evidence the pouring out of God's Spirit. Yet the Spirit's anointing is not limited to male religious leaders; the Spirit is inclusive ("upon all flesh"). Peter breaks down barriers of male dominance as he proclaims the prophet Joel's visionary announcement of the worthiness of daughters and sons to receive the Spirit and to prophesy (proclaim) the word of God. Judgments of too young or too old are obsolete in the age of the Spirit. Status in God's kingdom is unrelated to society's standards.

Visionary Christians affirm the ministry of all. They are radiant proclaimers of a new reality—the reign of God. We find the central message of Pentecost here: "Then everyone who calls on the name of the Lord shall be saved."

"Save" is one of the great biblical words. Often in the Hebrew scriptures the word meant victory in battle. The threatened or oppressed needed deliverance from tyranny and peril. Many New Testament references to salvation denote deliverance from specific ills. We are unable to save ourselves. The Holy Spirit empowers the proclamation of Jesus Christ, which when received in faith leads to new creation, deliverance, and victory. Such hope is the great message of Pentecost.

Prayer: **Thank you, loving God, for Jesus, who told us that we need only to ask to receive the fullness of your Holy Spirit in our lives. Come, Holy Spirit, and transform us from within. Amen.**

May 27—June 2, 1996   **Bob Holmes✣**
Monday, May 27   Read Matthew 28:16-20.

This passage of scripture is known as the Great Commission, Jesus' final assignment to his disciples. As disciples, followers of Christ, in our own time, we are included in this commission: to "make disciples of all nations."

That sounds so overwhelming that most of us do not take it personally. Yet that is how it is meant to be taken. It is our task no less than it was the task of the first disciples. But that does not necessarily mean we have to hop a plane to a country halfway around the world. The task is ours right where we are. It does not require preaching on a street corner or teaching a Bible class, although some of us may do both.

To "make disciples of all nations" can be done by the manner of our lives, by the style of our responses to people, by the values we uphold, by the opinions we express, by our sincere caring for the poor, the oppressed, or other disadvantaged people—or by suggesting a reconciling strategy for dealing with a conflict. We may do more to communicate the love of God by listening to the distress of another than by anything we might say. Sometimes we may call attention to the words and spirit of Jesus, but we need not baptize someone in order to acquaint them with Jesus. We may do no more than behave in such a way that a person will want to find out more about the faith that makes us who we are.

Discipleship is meant to be daily and local, that is, we are to be disciples wherever we find ourselves.

Suggestion for prayer: **Think of a commonplace way to "witness" for Christ. Ask the Holy Spirit to assist you in doing this.**

✣Clergy member, retired, of the Yellowstone Annual Conference of The United Methodist Church; police chaplain; Helena, Montana.

Tuesday, May 28   Read Genesis 1:1–2:4*a*.

It is fitting that the opening chapter of the Bible is an expression of praise and celebration of creation and all that it contains. Some people familiar with scientific theories concerning the physical processes of creation stumble on this poetic biblical story. They apparently believe that one must choose between two opposite theories of creation. Thus, in this mode of thinking, to accept scientific discoveries necessitates turning one's back on scripture and, therefore, on faith.

Such a choice is unnecessary, for both accounts are true. The scientist suggests theories of *how* creation took place and *when*. The Bible, on the other hand, addresses different and even more important questions, such as "*Who* ordered creation and *why*?"

As long as science and religion appreciate each other's field of inquiry, there is no need for conflict between them. The community of faith, which includes a great many scientists, holds that creation is not the result of pure chance but results from an intentionality characterized by intelligence, artistry, and imagination of infinite proportions. Creation exhibits superhuman planning which has eventuated in what we believe to be a particular interest in the human creature. Thus, it appears that the Source of creation is personal as well as infinitely creative. As Christians we stake our lives on that faith. The more impressed we become with the sheer marvel and beauty of creation, culminating in the miracle of the noblest of human spirits, Jesus of Nazareth, the more grateful we are that God's amazing creative enterprise includes us.

Prayer: O God, we believe that you are the Author and Architect and Life-giver of all creation. How amazing that even in this greatness of yours, you care for each of us! We thank you for Jesus Christ, whose life on earth showed us so explicitly this deep personal concern of you for us. Amen.

Wednesday, May 29   Read Psalm 8.

Just as we celebrated the fact and beauty of creation yesterday, so did the psalmist centuries ago. It is as if the psalmist looked about him and was utterly awed by what he saw and the intention behind it. He must have thought, *As if it weren't enough that God made this splendid universe and the earth in particular, God went on to create human beings like us.*

God must have known what a risk it was to give us the freedom either to care for or carelessly misuse creation, either to be stewards or simply consumers of God's gifts. That choice confronts us constantly. We are dependent upon the resources of creation for our lives, but we are called to be responsible in our use of those gifts so that future generations will have them just as we do. As children of a generous parent-like God, we are called to protect the beauty as well as the productivity of creation on which we and our descendents depend.

"What is man?" the psalmist asks (RSV, NIV), and answers the question in the remaining verses of the psalm. The answer is akin to saying, "Given mastery over all that God made, people surely are capable of using creation without using it up. Human beings can work together to enhance creation's capacity to feed the entire human race. We can use God's gifts to improve life in ways that will not diminish it for those who follow us."

If we consider ourselves God's children, we will so live as to justify God's faith in us that we will share our magnificent inheritance with our children and our children's children.

Suggestion for meditation: **My praise of God and my thanksgiving for God's creation can best be expressed by the care I show for every part of it I touch.**

Thursday, May 30   Read Psalm 8.

It might seem as though for the psalmist to consider human beings as "little lower than God" is to express an insufferable arrogance. A glance at the history of human behavior discloses that we are a long way from being like God. To be sure, the purpose of the psalmist is not to glorify humans, but to glorify God. Nevertheless, what God has created in the human creature warrants our wonder and amazement.

It has been said that there is something of Adolf Hitler and of Mother Teresa in all of us. Thus it is easy to conclude that we are, at heart, as evil as we are good. But Jesus sought to clear our thinking about that. Jesus showed that we are not dualistic creatures with equal parts of good and evil or evil creatures who sometimes do good things. Rather, he proclaimed that we are children of God and are meant to behave as such. His message was that there is in each of us an ever-ready spark of the divine, and that our frequent selfish, sinful behavior is an aberration, a betrayal of our true selves. We are not, in other words, just a little above the devil; our true nature is to be only a little lower than angels. We may choose not to fulfill that true identity, but it is a potential that always lies before us, to the day we die. The life and teachings, death and resurrection of Jesus Christ are all directed at our seeing this potential in ourselves.

Prayer: **Our gracious God, help me to know that I am created with a spark of the divine in me. Help me to fan that spark into an ember and that ember into a flame, that I may become the person you created me to be, rather than the counterfeit it would be easy to be. Amen.**

Friday, May 31   Read 2 Corinthians 13:11-13.

As we see the divisions and separations within the Christian fellowship today, it is easy to conclude that we have strayed from the single-minded unity of the earliest church. The truth is that there was not much unity even in the earliest church, as Paul's letters clearly reveal. And that is precisely why he concludes his letter to the church in Corinth as he does.

Human beings being what we are, given minds to think independently, it is unlikely that we will agree with one another in all things—even things theological. Paul's own experience protected him from that naiveté. And it may sometimes be just as well that we do not all think alike. A woman said to a friend, "Isn't it good that we don't all think alike about things? If everyone felt about my husband as I do, everyone would want to marry him." "Yes," her friend responded, "and if everyone felt as I do about your husband, nobody would want to marry him."

Differences can be healthy. It is from our differences that we often learn. Our thinking always needs challenging, and it will be challenged most by those who differ from us. There is almost always some part of truth that we can glean from those with whom we differ.

Perhaps what Paul meant when he admonished Christians to "agree with one another (and) live in peace" is what guided John Wesley to write to a Catholic friend, "If your heart is as my heart, give me your hand."

Prayer: **God, give me the courage of my convictions. But grant me also the humility to recognize that I can learn from those whose thoughts are different from mine. Amen.**

Saturday, June 1   Read 2 Corinthians 13:11-13.

There is a phrase in Paul's closing admonition that is easy to pass over: "Put things in order." I have wondered a lot about what Paul meant by that and why he included it along with his directions to find agreement, to live in peace, and to express love for one another.

If anyone needs to hear that instruction, I do—to put things in order, for in many ways my life is out of order. My priorities have gotten out of order. Sometimes there seems to be no order at all. I find myself moving from one responsibility to the next without any overarching purpose.

Putting things in order means to stop and take stock, to reconsider, to reevaluate. Our lives may need rearrangement, some things dropped out, new things added. The proper order is not likely to become clear in the midst of turmoil, but in moments of reflection, it may.

Putting things in order means to prioritize. Which things that take our time are most important; which are nonnegotiable? Among these may be some chores having to do with taking care of ourselves so that we can better care for others. Those things often get left to last. Some activities are really a waste of our time and life. On the other hand, it might be well to "waste" more time by flexing some different muscles, by catching up on our sleep, or by taking time to "Be still, and know that I am God!" (Psalm 46:10)

It is when we have a sense of order—not rigid, but confident— that peace will be with us.

Suggestion for meditation: **Begin listing the things that occupy your time and attention. See if they need reordering. As you review your list, leave some spaces for being still and knowing who God is.**

Sunday, June 2   Read Matthew 28:16-20.

We end this week with the same scripture passage with which we began. To me, the most important sentence in the Great Commission is the final sentence: "And remember, I am with you always, to the end of the age."

There are times when the challenges set before us, when the decisions that confront us, when the tragedies that befall us seem too much to bear. We forget that we are not alone, that there is more strength available to us than just our own. We know the words, but we have forgotten to trust. Much as we need it, we just cannot believe in God's grace.

It is difficult for me to visualize God; there is so much more to God than I can imagine. But I can visualize Jesus, and I often do—Jesus walking with me, riding with me in the car, listening to me, sometimes with his hand on my shoulder. When I am alone I sometimes speak aloud to him, listening for his responses. I have a very real sense of Jesus' presence. That helps me feel God's presence in ways I can know even though I cannot explain.

It comes down to this: If I am to know God's presence with me, I must be present with God. I must be intentional about choosing to be with God. And I must listen to what God is trying to communicate to me.

It is God's presence that gives me comfort, confidence, courage, new ideas, and the assurance that even though I may displease God sometimes, I can never fall outside the orbit of God's grace-full love. And that is enough.

Suggestion for meditation: **What is a new way that today I can follow Brother Lawrence's example to "practice the presence of God"?**

A JOURNEY WITH GOD

June 3–9, 1996   **Brandon I. Cho**✢
Monday, June 3   Read Genesis 12:1-9.

Is rearranging the furniture of our lives God's favorite hobby? God's call to Abram had such an effect. After the death of his father, Terah, Abram decided to carry on his father's business and family tradition in Haran. God, however, had a different idea for him. God called him out of the blue, "Go from your country and your kindred and your father's house to the land that I will show you." Here, *Go* meant *Get thee out!*

What did this call mean to Abram? It meant changing the course of life. It meant going from familiarity and security to risk and uncertainty. It meant changing from a settled, established way of life to a life of sojourning. It meant changing from the worship of pagan gods to following the one true God.

Abram could have said, "Lord God, I am too old for this. Leave it to the younger ones." But, instead, he followed God's command. "By faith Abraham obeyed when he was called to set out for a place that he was to receive as an inheritance" (Heb. 11:8).

This marvelous story helps me redefine the term *retirement*: "Retirement means putting on a new set of tires for 60,000 more miles and journeying with God." The ultimate goal of faith is not settling down in our comfort zone but moving on with God, who offers us vast possibilities and opportunities.

Prayer: **O God, who calls us to a journey of faith, free us from the entrapment of comfort zones and stagnating faith. Give us the courage to embark on a new adventure of faith with you today and always. Amen.**

✢District Superintendent, Santa Barbara District; California–Pacific Annual Conference of The United Methodist Church; Chatsworth, California.

Tuesday, June 4   Read Psalm 33:11-12.

The earlier portion of this psalm focuses on praising the God of creation, and then it shifts to human history and God's direct involvement in it. We now see the God of all creation interacting with all generations and "charting the course" for them. Here we experience not only the cosmic God who creates but the God who cares for human beings and their course of history.

The word translated "counsel" in verse 11 is the same word as that for God's creative wisdom. This passage thus can be rephrased: "The eternal creative wisdom of God and the thoughts of God's heart are revealed to all human generations. And the nation that receives this God as the Lord and the people whom God has chosen to inherit God's creative wisdom are blessed."

In the midst of great changes and challenges in its national and global life, our country needs to constantly seek God's counsel, God's creative wisdom, as its ultimate guiding light. This nation needs to keep its focus on the thoughts of God's heart that calls for unity, healing, harmony, equality, justice, and compassion instead of divisiveness, brokenness, fingerpointing, scapegoating, exclusion, and judgment. With God's creative wisdom we can help set the tone and policies of our nation in harmony with God's will.

Whether or not we agree with our leaders, can we agree to pray for this nation and our leaders, seeking God's counsel, God's creative wisdom, for this generation and the generations to come?

Prayer: **God, help us to seek your counsel, your creative wisdom, for our individual lives and the life of this nation so that we can live in harmony with your will. Amen.**

Wednesday, June 5   Read Romans 4:13-17.

How does one develop the right relationship with God and inherit God's promise? In his letter to the Christians in Rome, Paul suggested two ways: 1) through human efforts to obey and keep the Law; or 2) through one's complete dependence on God's grace by faith.

There are two Greek words for promise. *Huposchesis* is a conditional promise which is similar to contracts or agreements people sign. "I'll scratch your back if you'll scratch mine" is a guideline for such working relationships. The other word is *epaggelia*, which calls forth an unconditional promise made out of one's goodness and mercy. It coincides with the meaning of *agape*, God's unconditional love, which is a free gift with no strings attached.

Abraham's journey of faith and his response to God's call stemmed from his complete dependence on God's *epaggelia*, God's unconditional promise. God promised that Abraham would become a great nation and that in and through him all families of the earth would be blessed (see Genesis 12:2-3).

Faith is a matter of both grace and merit. Faith begins with receiving God's grace-filled *epaggelia*. Our merit then reflects our gratitude-filled response to that gift. It is through our daily renewal of receiving God's grace and gratitude-filled living that we can become the children of God's promise and the Abrahams and Sarahs of this generation.

Prayer: **O God, renew my heart to receive your grace once again and to live a life of promise in your Spirit today. In Jesus' name. Amen.**

Thursday, June 6   Read Romans 4:18-25.

Can we believe in the God who makes the impossible possible? The Apostle Paul recounted Abraham's belief in God's promise that he would become the father of many nations. This promise came to him when he was one hundred years old and his wife Sarah was ninety. They had no child of their own. Just as they were ready to accept their "sunset" stage of life and must have been resigned to the fate of childlessness, God presented Abraham with a seemingly impossible promise. Certainly, it was powerful enough to shake his whole being. Should he doubt the promise with human reason or believe it in hope? Although he could have been perceived as a fool in the eyes of visible realism, he chose to believe that God can and will make the impossible possible. He did not in unfaith waver at the promise of God. Instead, Abraham's faith was revitalized.

The Apostle Paul stressed that the account of Abraham's experience and blessing was written not only for his sake but for our sakes as well. We, too, can experience the God who makes the impossible possible in our lives and ministries.

Too often we let our vision and ministries be restricted by our human realism. In response, Paul reminds us that we need to let our faith push us to look beyond human realism and under-standing to God the Creator, who makes all things possible. Faith in God challenges us to maximize possibilities in God, to tap God's infinite creative and resourceful power. Isn't it time that we give God room to work and fulfill God's promise for us? Ask yourself, *What is possible in God's realism for me and my ministry today?*

Prayer: **O God of Abraham and Sarah, we accept your challenge to believe in your infinite creative power and promise. Help us to follow you today with a more daring faith than was ours yesterday. Amen.**

Friday, June 7   Read Matthew 9:9-13.

Matthew was a toll gatherer or a customs officer who collected duty fees on all goods and commodities of the people who entered and left the territory of Galilee. He probably engaged in illegal extortion to collect extra money for himself. Because of his abuse of power, he was despised and rejected as an outcast by his fellow Jews. He was considered unpatriotic, selfish, and greedy. Although he had a comfortable life with many material goods, he lived with guilt, pain, rejection, and isolation. He had no community where he could have a sense of belonging.

Jesus, a man of concern for others, saw Matthew and called him. Jesus saw in him not a person of greed and selfishness but a person in pain, in dire need to be loved and transformed. Out of his compassion and grace Jesus invited Matthew to follow him. And Matthew did. We also learn that Jesus "broke bread" with Matthew and his fellow tax collectors. Through this sacramental act of grace, he enveloped them with love and gave them a community of transformed discipleship.

I have one basic philosophy of ministry that says, "If you want to open someone's heart, feed 'em good first with love." Jesus' economy of love was always based on grace, not on rules, regulations, and judgment. When the Pharisees criticized him for eating with tax collectors and sinners—the unrighteous outcasts—Jesus simply said, "It is mercy I wish, and not sacrifice. For I did not come to invite the righteous, but sinners" (AP).

We are called to the ministry of God's grace which begins with confessing our sins and receiving God's grace that makes us whole again and again and again. Thanks be to God!

Prayer: **Make us your people of grace, O God, and renew our commitment to serve the world by your grace. Amen.**

Saturday, June 8   Read Matthew 9:20-22.

Have you ever run into a desperate moment or dangerous situation in which you were moved to reexamine your prayer life? I have had plenty of those, such as when flying through bad weather, when involved in a bad auto accident, and with our rude awakening by the January 1994 earthquake in Northridge where my family and I live.

The Gospel writer shares a story about a desperate woman who had a hemorrhage for twelve years with no cure! This was a most terrible and humiliating ailment for a woman of Jesus' time. She had been shut off by and from people as an unclean woman with a contaminating disease. At a point of sheer desperation, she was willing to do anything to find a cure for her physical illness and social condemnation. She slipped up behind Jesus and touched the tassel on his robe. She knew she was not supposed to be in a crowd with her condition. Her hope to receive healing from Jesus by touching his tassel unnoticed was stronger than social restrictions.

Even in the midst of the multitude, Jesus noticed this woman. In his sight, she was no longer a poor, sick nobody lost in the crowd but a person in need who deserved to receive his whole attention, to be made whole, and to become a wholesome child of God. Jesus knew what it means to under-stand her (meaning, *standing under*) and to lift her up with healing.

I am like this woman at times, standing in need of God's presence and healing. There are many others who need God too. Our churches, communities, nation, and the world need to touch the tassel of God's healing and wholeness. God help us!

Prayer: **O Jesus, may your healing power encircle this earth and all living creatures. Amen.**

Sunday, June 9   Read Matthew 9:18-19, 23-26.

The ruler of the synagogue, who was chosen from among the elders, came to Jesus and asked him to touch his dead daughter and make her live again. How unusual for a chief administrator of the synagogue to step out of his strict orthodox practice and ask a commoner—a dangerous heretic—like Jesus to perform an act of infinite compassion and power.

We note that when it is a matter of life and death, human-made institutional rules and regulations become a secondary concern. The order of the day becomes a life from, of, and in God. And Jesus' main goal was to bring God's life to humanity.

It is a matter of priority. As servants and leaders of our Christian community, we need to transcend ourselves from concern over our institutional survival and maintenance. Instead of domesticating our church ministry and culture, we need to step out of our comfort zone and meet Jesus in his mission-field, which is often found outside our institutionalism and denominationalism.

The ruler of the synagogue did just that. He freed himself from being the guardian and administrator of the Law and the order of the synagogue. He met Jesus in his mission-field and asked him to rescue his daughter from the grasp of death. May we be touched anew and transformed by the life-regenerating spirit of Jesus for the mission and ministry of this generation.

Prayer: **O Jesus, give us your new life as we seek to be faithful in witnessing to you in word and deed. Amen.**

SURPRISE!

June 10–16, 1996   **Fern M. Underwood✤**
Monday, June 10   Read Genesis 18:1-15.

Who can know what a new day may bring? God's word to Isaiah includes both present and future, "Behold, I am doing a new thing" (Isa. 43:19, RSV).

Abraham and Sarah rose one particular morning as they had for about a hundred years. It probably seemed like any other day. Then as Abraham was sitting at the entrance to his tent he saw three men standing nearby. The hospitality he showed to the three prepared the way for the confirmation by one of the visitors that Abraham and Sarah would indeed have a son in their old age. He opened his life to one of God's "new things." The author of Hebrews advises, "Do not neglect to show hospitality to strangers, for thereby some have entertained angels unawares" (Heb. 13:2). The writer has this incident in mind because this is what happened to Abraham. He welcomed the men and provided refreshment.

The men delivered a message. Surprise! The time God had promised years ago was to be fulfilled! Abraham and Sarah were to have a child! Sarah's laughter is but one of many possible reactions to divine action.

God still surprises. The Lord is faithful and "will strengthen you and guard you from evil" (2 Thess. 3:3, RSV). God "is not far from each one of us" (Acts 17:27). God "cares for you" (1 Pet. 5:7). God's world is full of surprises for those who are alert.

Prayer: **Help me, Creator God, to live this day in awareness and expectation of the surprises you have in store for me. Amen.**

✤Retired businesswoman; member, World Methodist Council; certified lay speaker, United Methodist Church, Osceola, Iowa.

Tuesday, June 11   Read Genesis 18:13-14.

"Is anything too wonderful for the LORD?" The Bible is filled with situations that appeared hopeless but were answered by one of God's surprises.

In Exodus God caused Pharaoh to release over 600,000 slaves on whom he depended to build his cities.

In Judges a multitude of combined enemy forces came against God's people. Through Gideon, the least of the smallest tribe, God defeated them with three hundred men (Judg. 7:4-7).

About 500 years before Jesus, the people of Judah were exiles in Babylon for 70 years. God inspired Cyrus, king of Persia, to release them to their homeland so they could rebuild the Temple and walls of Jerusalem.

When "the ruler of this world" seemed to have mastery over God's people, God came in Jesus. How unbelievable for those who behold Jesus on the cross that God would reveal the greatest of all surprises—death does not have the final word!

Throughout the Bible the history of God's people is retold, a reminder that God did not and does not intend that beloved humankind be victims—but victors! God rescues by giving power to the weak and strength to the powerless (Isa. 40:29). God's answer to Paul's prayers regarding his thorn in the flesh was, "My grace is sufficient for you, for my power is made perfect in weakness" (2 Cor. 12:9).

Evil often seems to have the upper hand. Personal and world problems appear to have no solution. But the Bible assures that God is the same yesterday, today, and tomorrow. Let go the problem. Allow God to take charge. Be surprised by what happens!

Prayer: **God, teach me to trust you. Help me see beyond my problems to the largeness of your promises for me and for all people. Amen.**

Wednesday, June 12   Read Matthew 9:35–10:8.

Have you ever played a game for which you chose sides? Designated captains surveyed potential team members and made a selection. To be chosen was exciting, to step out of the crowd and line up with the captain who chose you.

Throughout the Bible are accounts of God's chosen. In the Gospel of Luke the writer says that after Jesus spent the night in prayer he called his disciples and from them chose twelve.*

It must have been exciting to be part of that inner circle when crowds came to hear Jesus proclaiming the good news of the kingdom, to watch him curing every disease and infirmity.

But one day—surprise! Jesus began to illustrate the meaning of "do the works that I do and . . . greater works than these" (John 14:12). Suddenly the disciples learned that they were not receptacles into which all the teaching and experiences would be poured, but channels through which to pass them along to others. There is an obligation to bear fruit. (See John 15:1-8.) Without benefit of the physical presence of Jesus the disciples were to go out to do what Jesus had done.

The good news is that Jesus never sends anyone out unequipped. He who had been given all authority in heaven and earth gave the disciples authority to accomplish their mission—and through his spirit continued to do so in the early church.

What if those who now comprise his body would realize the import of this message? Not only we but the whole world would be surprised!

Prayer: **Holy Spirit, teach us anew what it means to be God's chosen race, God's holy nation,† and equip us for the work you would have us do. Amen.**

---

*See Luke 6:12-16.
† 1 Peter 2:9

Thursday, June 13   Read Matthew 10:1-4.

God's choices are always surprising. This is true because "My thoughts are not your thoughts, nor are your ways my ways, says the LORD" (Isa. 55:8).

God's "I choose you" comes at unexpected times to unexpecting people: Moses, a murderer in exile in Midian, and Aaron, his brother in slavery in Egypt, chosen to lead God's people out of Egypt; barren Hannah giving birth to the prophet Samuel; the shepherd boy David bringing down the giant Philistine; ordinary men chosen to be Jesus' disciples.

Who can anticipate God's actions or revelations? To prophets throughout the Hebrew scriptures God had spoken of an anointed one, the Messiah, whom God would send. The Messiah could have come in any way or ways, even in a manner inconceivable to the human mind. Surprise! God sent Jesus in the way all of us come into the world—as a tiny baby.

But many people did not realize what had happened. Jesus was in the world yet the world did not know him. His own people did not accept him. Even the disciples were slow to perceive his identity. Even as Jesus prepared to leave, Philip said, "Show us the Father." Jesus replied, "Whoever has seen me has seen the Father" (John 14:8-9). He further said that his physical departure from the world would not end his presence with them, for the Holy Spirit would come to them.

What a delightful surprise when God's chosen discover the true identity of Jesus, when they experience God's recreative, guiding, directing Spirit in their lives!

Prayer: **Jesus, help me this day and every day to see you more clearly, to love you more dearly, and to follow you more nearly.* And may I understand more nearly how to love others as you have loved me. Amen.**

---

*"Three Things We Pray," Richard of Chichester, 13th century.

Friday, June 14   Read Romans 5:1-9.

Surprise! While we were yet sinners, Christ died for us! When we were deeply in debt, with nothing to our credit, Jesus gave his life for us. We have been bought with a price, and the price was the life of our Lord.

A foundation for the event of the Cross is in Exodus 12. To persuade Pharaoh to let God's people go, God sent a series of plagues. In what would be the final blow, God sent the angel of death to strike the firstborn of all families in Egypt.

To spare God's people, the Hebrews were to sacrifice a lamb and smear the blood on the lintel and doorposts of their houses. The angel of death would see it and pass over. This instituted the Passover that has remained a memorial.

The details of the climactic end of Jesus' physical life are strikingly similar. John the Baptist identified Jesus as "the Lamb of God who takes away the sins of the world" (John 1:29). It was at Passover time that Jesus became the ultimate sacrifice. His blood was shed in order that everyone who believes in him may not experience spiritual death but may have eternal life (John 3:16).

What a surprise awaits us when we appear before God's throne and discover that the world's rules do not apply. Jesus has already paid our entry fee. What a Savior!

Prayer: **Dear God, I stand in awe! What you have prepared is indeed beyond what my eyes can see or my ears can hear or my heart can imagine.* I can only accept. Thank you. Amen.**

---

*See 1 Corinthians 2:9.

Saturday, June 15   Read Romans 5:1.

A young man of India grew up exposed to the variety of religions of that country. In time he desired to find truth and the meaning of life. He read the books that purported to be the path to the Supreme Being and to peace.

While reading the Bible he came upon Romans 5:1. In these words he recognized the uniqueness and treasure of the Christian faith, "Since we are justified by faith, we have peace with God through our Lord Jesus Christ."

How tragic if we who have grown up in the church and who have heard the gospel story all our lives are unmoved by the import of these words! We have been justified—cleared of all sin just as though our sins never happened. In the words of the Lord, "I will forgive their iniquity and remember their sin no more" (Jer. 31:34, RSV).

This was why Jesus gave his life. He was not *put* to death. He said, "No one takes [my life] from me. . . . I lay it down of my own accord" (John 10:18, RSV)—for you! for me! We have not earned such a favor. We cannot be worthy of such a sacrifice. It has been done for us! When Jesus was asked what constituted the work of God, he answered that the work of God is to believe in him whom God has sent.

Accept with joy what has been done. Be surprised anew by the value Jesus has placed on your life.

Prayer: **Jesus, you said, "I came that they may have life, and have it abundantly."* You taught the way, you demonstrated the life; you sent the Spirit of truth to help us attain it. Thank you, Jesus! Amen.**

---

*John 10:10

Sunday, June 16   Read Psalm 116:1-2, 12-19.

To love the Lord is a response to God, who first loved us and created within us the capacity to love. By the example of God, in whose image we are made, the first impulse of *agape* love is giving. In the beginning God created a world and attended to every facet of its function and beauty. God pronounced it good and gave it to humankind to tend and care for.

Humanity, characterized by Adam and Eve, determined to live by their own egocentric desires rather than by God's will. Yet God closed the chapter by wrapping them in cloaks of forgiveness (see Genesis 3:21).

In Ezekiel 16 the visionary prophet described the lavish adornings the Lord gave and gives the beloved—embroidered cloth, fine leather, gold and silver jewelry. In spiritual terms we know these are "love, joy, peace, patience, kindness, generosity, faithfulness, gentleness, and self-control" (Gal. 5:22-23).

How appropriate that during the worship service designed to express love for our Lord, time is allotted for bringing an offering! "I will pay my vows to the LORD in the presence of all his people," sang the psalmist.

The one who loves God continually asks, "What can I give my beloved? With what surprise can I brighten his (her) day?" Likewise is our excitement and eagerness in expressing love for the Beloved—God. The woman who came to the house where Jesus was a dinner guest surprised those present by bringing a jar of costly ointment and pouring it on Jesus' head. Even the disciples regarded it as an extravagance, but love makes such gestures and does not count the cost (John 12:1-8). The greater the gift, the greater the surprise, the greater the joy.

Prayer: **God, help me live my love for you with an open hand of love for you and my neighbor, returning in kind what you have first given me. Amen.**

UNLIKELY VESSELS, TRYING CIRCUMSTANCES

June 17–23, 1996   **Bruce C. Birch**✚
Monday, June 17   Read Genesis 21:8-14.

It is comforting to read stories of faith ancestors who are examples of righteousness and justice. Today's reading from Genesis is not one of those stories. It is a story of mean and petty family conflict, yet it is also a story of God's presence and divine purpose even when we act sinfully.

When Sarah grew old and was still childless, she gave Hagar, her Egyptian slave, to Abraham for the purpose of conceiving a child who could be Abraham's heir (Gen. 16:1-4). Hagar had no choice in this matter; but she did give birth to a son, Ishmael, in whom she delighted. Abraham regarded Ishmael as his son and heir; but after Isaac's birth, Sarah declared that she wanted Abraham's entire inheritance for him. She demanded that Hagar and Ishmael be cast out into the desert. Abraham passively agreed and sorrowfully sent them out with only a skin of water and some bread—surely a death sentence for this mother and child.

But God spoke to Abraham and revealed that divine purpose encompasses even this moment. Although Isaac was the heir through whom God would raise up Israel, God had a purpose for Ishmael as well. From him, too, would come a great people. What unlikely vessels for God's purposes—a jealous mother, an Egyptian slave woman, a condemned boy! Yet, God was at work.

Prayer: O gracious God, you know our worst moments as well as our best, and we are humble. Remind us that you can redeem our sinful failings as well as our gifts. Amen.

✚Professor of Old Testament, Wesley Theological Seminary, Washington, D.C.; clergy, Baltimore–Washington Annual Conference of The United Methodist Church.

Tuesday, June 18   Read Genesis 21:15-21.

At times in the biblical story we are reminded that God's story is always larger than our own story. In Genesis we are usually concerned with the stories of Israel's ancestors—the beginning of our own faith story. But the conclusion of the story of Hagar and Ishmael reminds us that God is at work in the whole of creation and in the history of all peoples.

Hagar exhausts her food and water in the wilderness. Weeping bitterly, she lays Ishmael by a bush to die. But God hears the voice of the child and speaks to her. God gives a divine promise also to Hagar and Ishmael. From them will come a great nation. God then shows them a well of water and their lives are saved. This is the second time God has spoken to Hagar and affirmed a promise for the future of her son, Ishmael (compare Genesis 16:7-14). How remarkable that the first person in the Bible to be visited by a divine messenger is an Egyptian slave woman, and it is not once but twice!

The story tells us that God was with Ishmael, and he became a great desert nation. Today, Jews and Christians think of themselves as the seed of Abraham, through Isaac. But Muslims believe they, too, are the seed of Abraham, through Ishmael. In a world where religious differences have often meant conflict, perhaps we need to rediscover our common beginnings in the providence of God.

Prayer: **God of all creation and Lord of all history, let us never believe that we hold you as a possession. Remind us that relationship with you comes as a gift and that we are part of a larger plan to redeem your whole world. Amen.**

Wednesday, June 19   Read Psalm 69:7-12.

We all hope that life lived in faithful relationship to God will be joyous and fulfilling, but human life is not just a succession of pleasant and happy moments. All our texts this week are reminders of God's presence in the difficult moments of life's journey.

This psalm reminds us that sometimes those difficult moments come because of our faith. The psalmist has become an object of scorn, has suffered alienation from his family, and has been ridiculed for his piety. Faith is not always an acceptable matter; the practices of faithful living are not always fashionable. This is certainly true in our increasingly secularized world. Even the most faithful and active church members find it difficult to be consciously identified as people of faith in the world beyond the church walls—in schools, workplaces, businesses, and homes.

When we are ridiculed or dismissed for our faith, we naturally feel personally wounded; but the psalmist has a perspective that we need in such moments. The psalmist understands that such reproach is directed not at us but at God: "It is for *your* sake that I have borne reproach. . . . It is zeal for *your* house that has consumed me; the insults of those who insult *you* have fallen upon me" *(italics added)*. Whatever in our world is self-serving, unjust, manipulative, and lacking in compassion will be threatened by the very notion of a loving, just, and righteous God. Rejection by such elements in the world is a measure of the success of our attempts to live so that others may see God through us.

Prayer: O Judge of all the world, give us courage to let your love show through our lives. Make us living testimony to your grace even in the midst of those who feel most threatened by your love and justice. Amen.

Thursday, June 20   Read Psalm 69:13-18.

The psalms of distress that cry out for help are wonderful in their ability to describe our distresses in the most honest, straightforward way but then to move immediately to expressions of trust and confidence that God is with us in the midst of our distress. The psalmist, who has just shared a severe picture of the ridicule and alienation that he has experienced in his community for God's sake (vv. 7-12), turns to express confidence that in God there is aid and comfort. He prays urgently yet confidently for God's help: "My help comes from the LORD" (Psalm 121:2). Even in the midst of painful experiences and the need for help, the psalmist can affirm, "For your steadfast love is good." This is one of the perspectives that distinguish people of faith. We know that ultimate reality rests in God and never in our immediate surroundings. Thus, we can trust in God's goodness even when the immediate circumstances of our lives are not good. This ability to trust God's goodness is what makes us capable of hope even in a world often given to hopelessness.

The Gospel writers knew this psalm and saw its truth reflected in the life of Jesus. When his enemies began to plot his death, the disciples knew it was the God who was seen through Jesus that threatened many. "His disciples remembered that it was written, 'Zeal for your house will consume me'" (John 2:17). But even when such plotting ended in death on the cross, God's goodness had a further word of life to speak. It is this resurrection word that Christians trust as the ultimate reality out of which we live. Like the psalmist, we know and trust that even in the most difficult circumstances God's "steadfast love is good."

Prayer: **O Source of all goodness, in a world marked by so little trust, embolden us to live in confidence of your goodness, even when persons and circumstances around us ridicule such confidence as naive and foolish. Amen.**

Friday, June 21   Read Romans 6:1-11.

"Should we continue in sin in order that grace may abound?" What a strange question! In his letter to the church at Rome, Paul has just said that "where sin increased, grace abounded all the more." Now he is anxious lest some take this as license to do what they please, assuming that God's grace will make it all right.

A man recently confessed in a group setting that he often felt closest to God when he was most conscious of his own sinful and unworthy practices. This man has confused the need for God with the grace of God. In our knowledge of our own sin, the ways in which we fail to practice the love of God, we often have moments where we recognize and acknowledge our need for grace. But Paul tells us that when we open ourselves to God's grace in those moments, "we are no longer enslaved to sin." Our old self is crucified with Christ so that with his resurrection we might be raised to new life. We are "dead to sin and alive to God in Christ Jesus."

Even in the church, many people have heard the word of life and grace which comes in Christ Jesus but have refused to lay down the burden of sin. They bear guilt over personal or societal brokenness as if it were the admission price to God's grace. Nothing could be further from the truth! God in Christ has lifted those burdens. To hold on to our sin and guilt is to refuse the gift of new life that God offers.

Prayer: **O God of grace, forgive us our fondness for our own sins, our ostentatious parading of our own guilt, our faithless suspicion that we must earn the gift of grace. Lift our burden of sin and grant us new life. Amen.**

Saturday, June 22   Read Matthew 10:26-33.

The life of discipleship is not a series of mountaintop experiences lived by saints of God. It is a life often lived through trying circumstances by those who seem unlikely vessels for God's grace. In this reading, Jesus is speaking to the disciples to prepare them for their mission. The mission will at times be difficult, and they will often feel unworthy and inadequate to the task.

In this brief passage Jesus tells them three times that they need not be afraid (vv. 26, 28, 31). Nothing will be covered up or kept secret or in the dark. They need not fear the truth of God. Those who would oppose them, even to the point of killing the body, cannot kill the soul. The disciples need not fear the enemies of God. God's caring regard is so all-encompassing that it includes every hair of our head and every sparrow that falls to the ground. The disciples need not fear the disregard of God.

The task of being disciples for the gospel in the world is a challenging and often fearful task. We fear being discredited or opposed or dismissed. The mission to be disciples in the world could not be successfully completed on the strength of our own resources alone, but in God even the most unlikely vessels of grace will be sufficient, even in the most trying circumstances.

Prayer: **O Lord, we confess our fearfulness in the face of the world's many obstacles to our discipleship. Remove our fear and open us as messengers and bearers of your grace in a broken world. Amen.**

Sunday, June 23   Read Matthew 10:34-39.

What a difficult passage this is! Jesus is reminding his disciples and us of the cost of discipleship. We don't really want to hear this. Discipleship on behalf of the gospel will not always bring harmony (peace); it can also divide (sword). And these divisions for the sake of the gospel can be in relationships with those we most cherish: our parents, our children, our spouses, our close friends.

It is customary when discussing this Gospel reading to remember what a radical minority the early Christians were in the Roman world. To become a Christian was often to break with one's own family and community. It is also common to remember that our world still includes many places where Christians have heroically embraced the faith in spite of opposition from family and culture. But sometimes the truth of a passage comes clear in simpler truths closer to home:

My phone rang, and it was a teenager from our church youth group. He had just read this passage for a teen Bible study he was attending, and he wanted to talk about it. Did it really mean that we had to love God more than our families or friends? We talked awhile about how harsh this seemed. Then he said he thought he had experienced this while trying to be a Christian at the high school. It divided him from some of his friends who either did not understand or rejected his decision. But loving God made lots of other relationships more meaningful and important, including his relationship with his parents. At first, he had lost his life (with some friends, and with old ways of relating to parents and others), but in new ways he had found life through God. I think he knows what Jesus was talking about.

Prayer: *O God of life, we confess our desire to serve you without cost. Help us to understand that all other relationships find new meaning when placed within our relationship to you. Amen.*

RESPONDING IN FAITH TO GOD'S FAITHFULNESS

June 24–30, 1996
Anna H. Bedford✜

Monday, June 24
Read Genesis 22:1-11.

"Here I am," says Abraham in answer to God's voice. Perhaps he feels guilty over his shameful treatment of Ishmael and his shabby behavior toward Abimelech (see Genesis 21). Anyway, this time he is attentive to God's incomprehensible demand, "Take your son, your only son, Isaac, whom you love, and go." He obeys without question. Sometimes to be fully present to the Spirit's prompt leads to shouldering an onerous task.

"Here I am," responds Abraham to his beloved son, walking trustfully beside him through the lonely desert. Perhaps his heart is full of turmoil at the terrible contract he has made with God. The bewildered boy confronts him, "Where is the lamb for a burnt offering?" His heart tearing, the father remains firm. Sometimes to be fully present to another person means choosing between a loved one and a cherished commitment.

"Here I am," replies Abraham to God's messenger, his fingers numbly grasping the fatal knife. Did his heart beat with anguished hope that God's valid claim on his firstborn would not be realized; that Isaac, the child of promise, would live? Or did he resign himself to believing that God could yet choose some other means to fulfill the covenant promise of land and descendants? Or did he abandon himself to despair because God had forsaken him? Sometimes to be fully present to what God is doing in the world is to experience the pain of judgment, the test of obedience.

Prayer: **Into my silent, waiting heart pour your presence, Holy One. May I be fully present to everyone I meet today. I trust you for strength to face whatever the day may bring. Amen.**

✜Associate editor, *Horizons*, the magazine and Bible study of Presbyterian women, Presbyterian Church (U.S.A.); Louisville, Kentucky.

Tuesday, June 25   Read Genesis 22:12-14.

In the Metropolitan Museum of Art in New York City hangs a painting by the 18th century Italian painter Giandomenico Tiepolo. In "The Sacrifice of Isaac," with bold strokes and thickly layered paint, the artist portrays Abraham, one arm upraised, a hand clutching the death-dealing blade, the other grasping a cloth that mercifully blinds the young man, Isaac.

Abraham's eyes are rheumy, his expression glazed, as a shadowy, grey-robed angel appears on his right, pointing to heaven. Abraham has not yet seen the ram crouching in the thicket behind him.

But Isaac holds the picture's focus. Loosely bound, muscular, evidently he is complicit in this act of destruction. Indeed, Tiepolo underlines Isaac's innocence by the white cloth cinched around his waist and his complicity by the scarlet robe falling behind him, symbolic of martyred saints. God has provided Abraham with a son willing to fill whatever role God commands.

This particular moment frozen on canvas explicitly captures the contradictions between love and obedience, innocence and complicity. The potential power of such a moment is to expand our capacity to embrace contradictions.

Unlike a painting, we are always in the process of unfolding, shifting, and reinventing ourselves. Our lives are a constant dialogue between pain and joy. So stop the action for a moment. Freeze the frame. Wait for God's reconciling word to break through. God provided a ram for Abraham. God has one for you.

Prayer: **Lord, today I will face many conflicting demands and dilemmas. Make all my moments calm and bright. Grant me the assurance that, always, you will provide. Amen.**

Wednesday, June 26   Read Psalm 13:1-4.

The results of the biopsy are in. She has a rare, incurable liver disease. Unknown to us, she has had it since childhood, and it is now in an advanced stage. She will need a liver transplant within a few years.

I am angry; I am sad. I cannot pray. All I can manage is a selfish complaint: "Oh, Lord, why did this have to happen to us? Our family has already been through so much. How much more can we take?"

Whining at the Almighty? David did it! Lacking Abraham's unwavering faith (Rom. 4:20), four times he wrings his hands and wails, "How long . . .?" He begs God for enlightenment before a melancholy inertia sets in, uprooting the centeredness of his being. He dreads becoming a pathetic laughingstock.

The psalmist's troubles are all-encompassing. They are theological (v. 1); personal (v. 2*a*); and social (v. 2*b*). He is anxious, not for his enemies but for his loss of faith. Believing himself forgotten, he feels far from God.

I think of how I can be a credible witness for the Lord when I am caught in this sinking-in-the-swamp feeling of depression. And I recall that even the Lord Jesus experienced feelings of abandonment (Mark 15:34). Like David, I cry out to the Lord, for to whom else shall I turn? I will not center my trust on circumstance but on the character of God.

Prayer: **Lord Jesus, hear my cry of absence and bless me with your presence. Use my pain to make me more sensitive to the silent desperation of others around me. Use it also to draw me closer to you. Amen.**

Thursday, June 27   Read Psalm 13:5-6.

Quit brooding and count your blessings! A blunt message, but effective. David's psalm holds a succinct problem-solution motif. Darkness is real; nevertheless, we can move through it to dawn. How? Through remembering God's faithfulness and responding with prayer and praise.

Long ago, one of the desert fathers said that remembrance of God is a profound form of prayer that eventually transforms us and all our relationships. The lives of those who belong to God matter to God. Testifying to the ways in which God has been faithful in the past provides a basis for hope for the future.

But this is something we cannot do by ourselves. We need to encounter others who care about us and who have walked where we walk. Healing comes when an intentional community affirms us as lovable and capable persons, of value to God. Such a community helps us see that we need not allow our sorrow, sickness, or failings to define us. In return, the testimony of healing we offer the community encourages and enriches it for ever deepening ministry.

The church provides the richest example of intentional community. Its scripture, tradition, and experience all point to the faithfulness of God. Not surprisingly, David promises to give formal thanks to God in the Temple (v. 6), possibly in fulfillment of a vow (compare Psalm 7:17). For him as for us, restoration to the gathered community is crucial to the healing process.

Prayer: **Compassionate God, I see your love reflected in the faces of your faithful people throughout time and in every place. Assured of that love, I can live through the present and face the future with hope. Amen.**

Friday, June 28   Read Romans 6:12-15.

The multitalented TV personality Steve Allen once did a series in which he brought great figures from different periods of history together around a dinner table for an evening of conversation. If I could, I would get together King David, the poet warrior, for a tête-à-tête over tea with the Apostle Paul, the Christian theologian and missionary.

What a fascinating conversation this would be! David writes of his wide-ranging emotions, from the depths of despair to heady flights of feeling. Paul, on the other hand, uses reasoned discourse, occasionally laced with patches of purple prose, to state his arguments. David beats his breast and cries, "Do as I say, not as I do!" while Paul boldly uses himself as an example of how to live the Christian life.

On one thing they would agree, however. Of themselves, the good works any of us does have no saving power. Law makes us aware of sinfulness, but only grace saves a nation or an individual. Yet Paul, writing a general letter to the church in Rome, suggests that transformation is also a choice. God's saving work in Christ is ours, but we must choose to live in its light. We can offer ourselves to God as those reborn, or we can let old habits rule. The decision to be among those who are working with God to fulfill God's ultimate purpose in the world is a conscious one.

God wants us to be persons who live our lives in covenant with God through Jesus Christ. Bringing our lives into accordance with this expectation is a daily discipline. Once we have done that, however, because we are not bound by law, we have a wide array of life options with which God will be pleased. That is what grace is all about.

Prayer: **Thank you, God, for allowing me to share in your creative and redemptive work. Guide me this day. Show me how to exercise my freedom responsibly. I pray in Jesus' name. Amen.**

Saturday, June 29   Read Romans 6:16-23.

Everyone is under the power of some force—either sin or grace. Is freedom an illusion then? Are we just caged birds? "No!" says Paul, resoundingly. Sin and death no longer have dominion over us. We are free not to sin. Forgiven and freed, we respond in faith to a faithful God.

Even so, Paul knows that the Christian life is one of unremitting struggle. Daily we make the choice to be self-centered or Christ-centered. The whole trend of our lives either affirms or denies that choice.

The story goes that once in ancient times a wise man's donkey was stolen. The old man went crying through the streets of the town, "Whoever returns my donkey, to him I will make a present of it!" "But, teacher, this makes no sense!" said his neighbors. "Indeed it does," said the wise man. "In so doing, I will receive double—the joy of a treasure restored and the pleasure of giving a gift!"

The Christian life has the same kind of paradox. Emancipation from the power of evil leads to enslavement to the holiness of God. Deliverance from sin means entrance into service. The joy of being alive in Christ leads to the pleasure of passing on the gift. Day by day, in the ordinary events of our lives, we work out the ethical implications of being set apart to serve the One who never fails us.

Prayer: **Faithful God, for this day, may your glory be the sole measure of everything I do at home, at work, at play. May I seek to do your will with all my heart. Amen.**

Sunday, June 30   Read Matthew 10:40-42.

It was late. The weary travelers knocked heavily on the door of a medieval monastery. Through the locked door sounded the porter's gracious response, "Your blessing, please!" Hearing it, the strangers knew at once the Benedictine brothers would welcome them in.

Matthew provides a similar image as he writes with the early church in mind. To offer hospitality to prophets (itinerant missionaries), the righteous (teachers knowledgeable in scripture and the law), and disciples (sent out by Jesus, as vv. 1-5 declare) was to participate in their ministry. To welcome the servants of Christ was to welcome Christ himself.

It still is. Then and now, the response of faith to God's faithfulness is strictly practical: open your heart and home to those who are spreading the good news of Jesus Christ. Early disciples were true "little ones"—humble artisans, tradespeople, slaves. Today, hospitality seekers may come as global ecumenical church leaders or as new neighbors seated in the next pew. We are to make a personal connection.

Sharing material goods and table fellowship with other Christians is a concrete expression of the love that binds us to God and to one another. Hospitality spills over the borders of an ordered life. It means giving time; being open to the unexpected; being willing to be interrupted, inconvenienced even. To do it joyfully, one must be able not only to give but also to receive, to be a guest. The reward of both host and guest is a new sense of being alive in Christ.

Prayer: **Welcome, Lord! I open the door of my heart to you this day. Make me truly at home to others and to all creation. Your blessing, please! Amen.**

GOD'S FAITHFULNESS, OUR RESPONSES

July 1–7, 1996   **Thomas R. Fletcher**✤
Monday, July 1   Read Genesis 24:34-38.

Eliezer, Abraham's servant, was loyal and faithful to his master. From a strictly human standpoint, he had a difficult task set before him. It would involve a long and arduous journey. This journey would take him from his comfortable life in Canaan to the upper reaches of the Euphrates River. He came to the city of Nahor close to Haran. Physically, the journey would be exhausting. His mission: to find a wife for Isaac. Abraham was very specific in his instructions. He did not want his son marrying one of the Canaanites who surrounded them.

Eliezer's task would also carry a mental burden. You see, until Isaac's birth, Eliezer had stood to be Abraham's heir (Gen. 15:2). Now his task was to find a suitable wife for the one who had replaced him as heir. Did jealousy spring up? Could he have been tempted to take a shortcut, to approach the first available woman who crossed his path? Nothing in our text would indicate anything of the sort. Eliezer was a faithful servant, unquestioningly and dutifully performing the task before him. Why? This servant had a trust in God. Eliezer's name means "God helps" or "God of help." Eliezer was not concerned with what he might have inherited had the circumstances been different. His trust was in God, and he demonstrated this trust by faithful service to his master, Abraham.

If my trust is truly in God, I will not concern myself with what might have been. I will faithfully perform my duty as a Christian, trusting that the "God of help" will meet my every need.

Prayer: **Lord, help me to see the example of Eliezer. Help me, like Eliezer, remain your faithful servant this day. Amen.**

✤Youth Pastor of New Life Baptist Church, Cowen, West Virginia; professional photographer of nature and travel.

Tuesday, July 2   Read Genesis 24:42-49.

God of help

Eliezer had completed the rigorous journey across the desert. He now stood in Abraham's hometown. How would he find a suitable wife for his master's son? Would he simply ask the first young available maiden he saw if she would like to become the wife of a rich young bachelor who lived far away?

It would be obvious to any casual observer that this traveler came from wealth. The appearance of wealth has been known to incline many to become marriage-minded. Eliezer could not trust his selection to circumstances. He needed to know his selection was of the Lord. He had labored through his desert journey and thus had accomplished the physical part of his task. Now he needed spiritual insight for the completion of his mission.

Eliezer knew that he could not possibly know what person would make Isaac a faithful and true wife. These matters cannot be judged by outward appearances. However, he knew the One who knows the hearts of all persons. He knew he could trust the "God of help" to guide him, and he laid the matter before the Lord in prayer. He asked the Lord to give him a sign, to direct him to the one the Lord had chosen to be Isaac's wife.

We face many situations in which we cannot possibly know all the factors involved. We want to make correct decisions in following the Lord's will. We do all that we know to do, yet we may still be unsure of the choice to make. We can, though, follow Eliezer's example. We can lay the matter before the Lord and trust that the Lord will direct our steps.

Prayer: **Lord, although I like to know how my decisions will play out, only you have that knowledge in all circumstances. I pray for wisdom as I seek your will. Help me wait expectantly for evidences of your guidance. Amen.**

Wednesday, July 3   Read Genesis 24:58-67.

Time with God

Isaac was well aware of the mission on which his father's servant had set out. Eliezer had wasted no time on the journey. He had prayed for God's direction, made arrangements for Rebekah to become Isaac's wife, and immediately set out for the return trip to Canaan.

Most of us are uncomfortable with the thought of arranged marriages. However, in many societies that is the way marriages have been contracted. I wonder if Isaac may have felt some concern as well. What did he do about those concerns? What could he do? He took the matter before the Lord.

As Eliezer and the procession returned, Isaac was out in the field. He was not going out to meet the caravan. He had no way of knowing which day or at what time it would return. Isaac was going out to "meditate" (v. 63, NIV). It would appear that this was his custom daily: walking, meditating, praying. The day of the caravan's return was no different. Isaac was in the field for his quiet time. He was probably laying before the Lord the matter of his impending marriage. I am sure that he, too, had been praying for the Lord's hand in the selection process. Isaac was facing major changes in his life. In the face of those changes, he kept his appointment in the fields with the Lord.

As we face changes in life, we, too, may be comforted if we have a routine with the Lord that we follow during those periods. We need the solidity that a daily quiet time with the Lord brings to our lives. As we follow that routine, we, too, may look up to see the answer to our prayers appear on the horizon.

Prayer: Lord, help me to daily have my quiet time with you, seeking your guidance and answers. Amen.

Thursday, July 4   Read Psalm 45:10-17.

The bride

This psalm speaks of a royal wedding, with instructions for both the king and the bride. The beautiful language celebrating a royal marriage is sometimes considered a messianic psalm. The king is interpreted as the Messiah and the bride as Israel. This psalm is quoted in the New Testament (Hebrews 1) as referring to Jesus.

Thus the bride has been seen by some Christians as a metaphor for the church, the bride of Christ. Humanly speaking, as Christians we have some things which must be left behind in our espousal to Christ. We must forsake worldly pursuits and fascinations. Our attention is to be focused on our Lord. Our loyalties belong to him alone. In return, the king will clothe his bride. The bride is clothed in the most perfect of vestures: the righteousness of Christ. We must give careful consideration, as verse 10 implores us; we must realize the ramifications of the position in which we have now been placed. We have a new focus. Old things must be left behind. We must unreservedly give ourselves to our Lord, who cares for us beyond our imagining.

Prayer: **Lord, draw me closer to you. May my only concern be, "How can I please you?" You have clothed me in your righteousness; I will praise you forever. Amen.**

Friday, July 5   Read Romans 7:15-25*a*.

The only hope

In this text is the Apostle Paul speaking of a pre-conversion or post-conversion state? Is the person Paul describes a Christian or not? Paul's repeated use of "I" and the present tense of the verbs indicate he was speaking of a present reality.

Paul strongly felt the tension every earnest believer has felt. It is when we decide to follow the Lord without reservation that sin erupts against us. If we choose to placate the flesh, to justify "mistakes," to not be "too serious" about our faith, there is no battle. When we decide to be "sold out" for Jesus Christ, the war is on! Sin rages; and the more determined we become, the fiercer the battle. But the more determined we are to gain victory through our willpower, the more crushing will be our defeat.

I spent many years of my Christian life as a determined, dedicated, and *defeated* legalist. Why? The same reason we all meet with defeat. We cannot gain spiritual victory through the means of the flesh. God will not allow it. God knows we would claim all the glory for ourselves. The gravitational pull of sin is too great. We may seem to be doing well for a while, but failure is coming.

Our only hope is that which Paul declares in verse 25—Jesus Christ. It is only as we fully rely upon the Lord that we gain victory. It is only as we surrender to the Lord and allow the divine to work in us, that true, lasting victory can be ours. The moment we take up the gauntlet to do it ourselves, we doom ourselves to failure.

Prayer: **Father, the only true victory is in Christ alone.** *I* **cannot do it. I surrender completely to you. Amen.**

Saturday, July 6   Read Matthew 11:16-19.

Closed minds

There is no pleasing some people. There is a quirk in human nature that causes people to want to believe they are just a little better than those around them.

Jesus and John the Baptist had to deal with that attitude in the religious leaders of their day. Those leaders saw themselves as being in charge. They believed themselves to be the only stewards of religious knowledge. They would call the tune. It was up to others to dance. Neither John nor Jesus would join in their childish games. John was serious in his asceticism. He was paving the way for the Messiah. Jesus was serious in his spiritual freedom. He had come to set humanity free: free from sin, free from dead religion.

God had directed the conduct of both John and Jesus. Their conduct was to point people to God and to elicit a response from them. God used (and uses) different methods, not expecting that every person would be exactly like every other person.

Do we judge others by our own religious ideas? If they refuse to dance to our tune, do we write them off? In our attitudes and behavior are we like those religious leaders of long ago?

Prayer: **Lord, help me to see you in others. Forgive my criticism. Remind me often that others need not meet my standards, but yours. Amen.**

Sunday, July 7   Read Matthew 11:25-30.

True knowledge

The most difficult person to teach is the one who assumes that he or she already possesses the knowledge being taught. All knowledge comes from an admitted ignorance. When we admit that we do not know, that is when we are ready to learn.

The religious leaders of Jesus' day assumed they knew exactly what God expected and exactly how God should behave. After all, they had the training. Shouldn't they be the experts?

The sad fact is that sometimes much learning can build a barrier between a person and God. This passage is not against intellectualism; it is against pride. God is the one who has given us the capacity to retain knowledge. I believe God expects us to use that capacity to the fullest extent possible. It is when we begin to take pride in the knowledge itself—in *our* knowledge—forgetting God, that problems arise.

Jesus gives thanks for the knowledge revealed to the "infants." It was revealed to those who realized they did not have all the answers. Such may have had education, but they realized that "education" did not give them all the answers. I am reminded of Nicodemus, a trained religious leader who came to Jesus. The Apostle Paul was well trained in the Jewish law and knowledgeable in the dominant culture. No, today's lection is not against learning. Rather, it warns against arrogance arising out of that learning and against a self-sufficiency based on academic knowledge alone. It warns against placing our intellect above God's revelation.

Prayer: **Father, all true knowledge comes from you. Remind me, Lord, that I am truly dependent upon you. Amen.**

THE DIVINE-HUMAN INTERACTION

July 8–14, 1996   **Robert L. Reddig✤**
Monday, July 8   Read Genesis 25:19-23.

Rebekah's pregnancy was an answer to her husband Isaac's prayer, for she had been barren. Isaac's prayer was answered beyond his expectation or knowing. As twins struggled together within her, Rebekah uttered the sort of lament familiar to us all, "If it is to be this way, why do I live?" Why the aggravation? When Rebekah turned to the Lord for an answer, she heard more than she could comprehend. She was told that she had more than an uncomfortable pregnancy—she had rival nations within her, a powerful history was about to unfold. She was a full participant in God's purposeful plan. Her discomfort was not just an incidental nuisance.

God often grants us more deliverance and discovery than we can absorb. How hard it is to trust the unfolding of God's purpose! How hard it is to trust the unfailing nature of God's care! The sort of physical and spiritual discomfort that Rebekah experienced is later echoed in the Psalms. Again and again the psalmist ponders, *What's going on here? Why me? What's the point?* With full knowledge of God's abiding love for us in the past, we nevertheless clamor to know, "*Now* what are you up to, God?" It's just twins, Rebekah, just twins.

Prayer: **Loving God, in the tumult within and around us, may we discern your guiding hand and eternal purpose. Amen.**

✤Psychotherapist and director of a mental health clinic; elder in the Hillsboro Presbyterian Church (U.S.A.), Nashville, Tennessee.

Tuesday, July 9   Read Genesis 25:24-34.

Esau was a skillful hunter, a vigorous man of the fields. He liked action and red meat, and he had a hearty appetite. But this man so cunning as a hunter, so full of vitality, was bested by his quiet, tent-dwelling brother, Jacob, who also had an appetite. Esau had a very literal and concrete logic, swapping promise for pottage. "I am about to die; of what use is a birthright to me?" Between his shortsightedness and his brother's deceit, we have little to admire. Were we to have the benefit of exit interviews with each of the brothers, we would probably learn that each came away from this encounter satisfied.

As we repeatedly learn from scripture, many of our hungers and satisfactions are unreliable guides for conduct. Adam and Eve all too easily set aside the admonition of God and the promise of blessing for a brief exercise of will and a lean satisfaction. Esau had an appetite for red pottage; Jacob, an appetite for privilege. Both hold mirrors to us all. They represent two of our most popular strategies in life—having our fill and getting ahead. These are our appetites; these are our guides.

We are called to wait for and cherish our blessings. We are called to accept that we have siblings whom God loves. Our appetites for anything less than God's will can only lead to deeper hunger.

Prayer: **Gracious God, may we turn our deepest longings to you. Amen.**

Wednesday, July 10   Read Psalm 119:105-112.

Those who know something of my fondness for backpacking and adventure would say, among other things, that I never saw a flashlight that I did not like. I have always been fascinated by the physics of light energy, and I admire the ingenious engineering in a good all-weather flashlight. On a long and difficult hike, this simple hand-held tool can often mean the difference between safety and disaster, between confidence and dread. A good light can, to a limited degree, command and part the darkness, predict the immediate future of a path, and invite me to go on. Even in the midst of the bright splash of morning, the small pack-bulge of a flashlight reassures me that the coming night will be just fine too.

The psalmist declares, "Your word is a lamp to my feet and a light to my path." These words of devotion and comfort reflect one of God's most important intentions for our lives. They tell us how our journey is to be: We are not given command of the sun, and we are encouraged to keep moving. We have in God's word a lamp for our feet and a light for our path. How often we want to floodlight the countryside, to make a highway of our path. How often we are tempted to pitch camp and settle down in comfort, to sink a well and build a barn. How quickly thereafter we go, so to speak, to the movies. We are entertained by light focused on the paths and journeys of others. God wishes to illuminate *our* feet, *our* path, and usually urges us to keep moving.

Prayer: **Gracious God, may the light of your love, the lamp of your word, draw me closer to you. Amen.**

Thursday, July 11 Read Romans 8:1-8.

"The law of the Spirit of life in Christ Jesus has set me free from the law of sin and death" (RSV). In this brief verse Paul identifies his spiritual center and its implications for his life. And embedded in this verse is a deep psychological truth. The core of Christ's teaching and the central elements of our faith are often best expressed in paradoxical form. The innocent Lamb of God is punished for our sin. The last shall be first and the first shall be last. The meek shall inherit the earth. He that loses his life will save it. There are many more such paradoxical sayings.

Paul presents an arresting paradox as well in saying that the law of the Spirit sets him free from the law of sin and death. He highlights not just the important distinction between obedience to the law and covenant of the Hebrew scriptures and life in grace through Jesus Christ. Paul expresses this truth as well: if you must have a boss (and we must), choose a good one. If you require constraints (and we do), choose those that give you freedom.

The parable of the prodigal son illustrates this point very well. A young man exuberantly and mistakenly assumes that freedom and the full life are the natural result of declaring independence (see Luke 15:11-24). Paul reminds us that our choice is never between devotion to God and the unfettered and boundless enjoyment of our wills. He reminds us that we are creatures with but one clear path to freedom—life in Christ Jesus.

Prayer. **Dear God, bind us with your love so that we may be free of our reckless and often ruthless wills. Amen.**

Friday, July 12   Read Romans 8:9-11.

Standing in the checkout line at the supermarket on a Friday night, I am left with few illusions of my importance. Regardless of how effective or pivotal I may have been during the day, I need groceries like everyone else, and to get them I must humbly and patiently stand in line. Not only that, anyone who cares to notice will have some idea of my diet, the state of my over-the-counter health, and a hint or two about the way my mind and body are working. I cannot rise above this. I cannot for long postpone this shopping or replace it with something more elegant or high-minded. I cannot pretend I do not need the things in my grocery cart. I have this body to care for, and for the time being, I am wedded to it.

During any given day we probably have more than a few reminders that we are tethered to human nature; that we have a body that seems regularly to keep us from gaining spiritual altitude. Paul reminds us that despite the pull of our human nature, God's spirit can flourish within us. The Spirit can infuse the daily drabness of routine with the significance of an eternal unfolding. "But you are not in the flesh; you are in the Spirit, since the Spirit of God dwells in you."

We all know well the myriad ways we are pulled to attend to our physical needs. In the call of the flesh we each hear and recognize our own voices. God's spirit within us represents a deeper longing, one which puts all mundane things, including our shopping, in proper perspective. I am in the Friday grocery line not because I love my cart and the things in it, or because I plan to dwell in the store. The line is an unavoidable stop before heading home, and it is home where the loves and yearnings are best expressed, given, and received.

Prayer: **Spirit of God, infuse the ordinary things around us with your purpose. Amen.**

Saturday, July 13   Read Matthew 13:1-9.

It did not start out to be a feud, but it ended in one. Years ago near my father's farm, two neighbors had adjoining fields, separated by a broad strip of prairie grass. The grass was a path for both neighbors. As it grew tall and thick it sheltered grouse, pheasant, gophers, rabbits, and mice. The neighboring farmers could drive on the grass and inspect their growing grain, idle and fuel their tractors, and often at lunchtime they would find sanctuary and conversation on this luxurious green carpet. It is a matter of dispute as to who started encroaching on the strip with spring plowing. Despite having broad and abundant fields on either side of the grassy path, each farmer felt the urge to add a bit more to his harvest by cultivating this mutually held treasure.

Over time, the path became a thin and irregular green line, then a dark furrow, favoring the neighbor who plowed last. The wildlife moved on, and the conversation stopped as the grudge set in. The feud was sustained as each farmer surreptitiously deposited large rocks, unearthed during vigorous cultivation, on his neighbor's field. Harvests, always good, got better.

Over the years the abundance of grain in our community and many others like it drove the price of wheat and other grains down. Farms have gotten larger and more efficient, and grassy paths, the peace they brought, and the two neighbors are gone.

In the parable of the sower, some of the seeds fall along the path, not a receptive place for grain. A path is for something else, perhaps for someone else. If we hear and understand the word, we are soil. That is enough for us to know. We have all we need for a harvest.

Prayer: **Creator of the earth, in our striving for the abundant life may we be respectful of the paths of others. Amen.**

Sunday, July 14 Read Matthew 13:18-23.

With the parable of the sower, Jesus speaks to a great crowd of listeners, listeners as varied as the soil described in the parable. His message is quite straightforward, and later in the thirteenth chapter (vv. 36-43) we have Jesus' own clarification of his meaning.

Nevertheless, we bring modern understandings to this parable. We bring modern intentions, as if this were simply a story of unsophisticated agriculture waiting for our proud and scientific improvements. We might, for example, advise the sower to construct a scarecrow, to harrow and add peat moss to the path, to deep-till and remove the rocks, to apply herbicide to the thorns, and finally to fertilize the entire field. But the sower of the parable is not naive. He is both fascinating and faithful. His eye and his effort are on the good soil, not on the path or the rocks or the thorns. His sowing leads to a harvest of a hundredfold, sixtyfold, and thirtyfold. Presumably, this harvest makes all the effort worthwhile.

What are we to make of birds, rocks, and thorns, realities in ourselves and in the field of life around us? Jesus delivers this admonition: "Let anyone with ears listen!" (v. 9) Jesus spoke to multitudes but commissioned only a small circle of disciples. God's efficiency is not ours. God's holy economy may be quite beyond our understanding. What we do not see in the parable of the sower is good soil lying fallow. There is great obligation in hearing, greater obligation in believing. As always, we are called to account not so much for our given nature as for our willingness to receive and magnify the goodness that grace has placed within us.

Prayer: **Gracious God, grant us ears that hear and hearts that forgive. Amen.**

GOD'S PRESENCE WITH US

July 15–21, 1996 **Anne Broyles**✤
Monday, July 15 Read Romans 8:12-17.

One of the most meaningful aspects of becoming part of a Christian faith community is one's immediate acceptance into a *family*. A person can be connected to a biological or adopted family, can be living alone or in a multi-person household, be part of a tightly knit family grouping, or even be estranged from those once called "family." Yet none of these facts makes a difference in terms of our acceptance into the family of God.

In Jesus Christ, we are adopted if we are "led by the Spirit of God." Any previous pedigree or genetic lineage is unimportant. "Now if we are children, then we are heirs—heirs of God and co-heirs with Christ" (NIV).

Claiming Christ as Savior opens up to us a connectedness to all others who similarly live in kinship to the Risen One. We may have felt lonely in the past; now we are included in a great circle of caring that extends worldwide—past national boundaries, language differences, ethnic distinctions, or the variety of barriers humans construct between persons.

The gift we receive in Christ is bountiful: a new spirit that will sustain us no matter what events occur in our earthly pilgrimage, and a community of love and acceptance to undergird us as well.

Suggestion for meditation: **As you look on those you have called "family," reflect on how the Christian community is different from and similar to your previous experience. Take a moment to give thanks to God for the different manifestations of family in your life so far.**

✤Author; co-pastor of Malibu United Methodist Church; retreat leader in Christian spiritual life and in family spirituality; Malibu, California.

Tuesday, July 16   Read Romans 8:18-25.

If we measured the present world only by what we read in the newspapers or hear on the evening news, the forecast for the future would be bleak indeed. Wars, famine, personal and institutional violence, acts of cruelty, environmental murder, and on and on. We can almost *hear* creation groaning.

The headlines and news stories remind us that our world is no longer the perfect place God created long ago. What we do not encounter in the news, however, is the fact that God is still active in the world in ways we do not begin to recognize or understand.

This passage from Romans reminds us that the agony of today is the seedbed of the new world that is to come. As Christians, we are called to hope—to see beyond the violence and pain of today and to work toward and in expectation of the reign of God.

"For in this hope we were saved" (NIV). Because we hope, we refuse to accept a blanket condemnation of our world. Instead, we work toward a bright future. We volunteer at a shelter for the homeless, we donate money for AIDS research, we march for peace. We seek to share the stories of those who represent all the good in our world rather than focus on tales of inhumanity, corruption, and cruelty. We look for the good we can do and we *do it*, living in the hope that comes to us from Jesus Christ.

Prayer: **Gracious God, let hope so infuse my life that all I am and all I do is testimony to your power in my life. Let me face the world's problems with vision, energy, and the perspective of one who knows the One who is the hope of the world. In his name I pray. Amen.**

Wednesday, July 17 Read Genesis 28:10-15.

When Jacob wearily laid his head upon a stone and fell into a deep sleep, the dream came quickly. Given Jacob's recent history, it would have made sense for his dreams to have been haunted by guilt, remorse, or concern for the future. Ambitiously, this younger brother had tricked his father, Isaac, into giving him the birthright that rightfully belonged to his older brother, Esau. Esau was furious at this betrayal. Mother Rebekah cautiously sent her beloved Jacob away while Esau's anger cooled down.

So, with a stone for a pillow, Jacob slept, and suddenly a dream came that did not haunt him with past deeds but rather allowed him a glimpse of a ladder between heaven and earth. Jacob was privileged not only to view angels travelling between heaven and earth but also to see the Lord in splendor.

God spoke directly to the wayward dreamer, reminding him of the promise made earlier to Jacob's grandfather, Abraham. God's ancient promise will hold true despite Jacob's lying and cheating ways. (See Genesis 12:2-3; 13:16.)

Think of Jacob, his eyes wide as he gazed on the heavenly scene, amazed at what his ears tell him: the Almighty One speaking words not of condemnation but of hope for the future. Think of Jacob, his heart healed as he hears God say, "Know that I am with you and will keep you wherever you go."

Like Jacob, we have made mistakes. How have we betrayed those who love us? When were we unable to speak the truth? Were there times when our own need to be #1 got in the way of our relationships?

To us, God speaks the same word: "Know that I am with you and will keep you wherever you go." The errors of our past are forgiven. God frees us for the new future that awaits us.

Suggestion for meditation: **What word of forgiveness do you need to hear from God? How is God pointing you to the future?**

211

Thursday, July 18   Read Genesis 28:15-19*a*.

On the road from Beersheba to Haran, Jacob found a resting place. Given the landscape of that area, it was probably barren and rocky—nothing that spoke of wonder or holiness.

Yet, after his dream of a ladder to heaven in which God spoke directly to him, Jacob awoke and said, "Surely the LORD is in this place—and I did not know it."

Suddenly afraid, Jacob looks at his surroundings, realizing, "How awesome is this place!" What the day before had simply been a convenient stopping place on his journey was now "the house of God . . . the gate of heaven."

The dream, the angels, the words from the Almighty had transformed a barren landscape into *Bethel*: House of God. Even so, the barrenness of Jacob's life encountered a living God who met him where he was and showed him that each place could be sacred, all moments holy.

Overcome with the clear sense of God in his life, Jacob felt the need to respond. He took the stone which had pillowed his head during the night and set it up as a pillar. Pouring oil on the stone, Jacob consecrated the place where he had met God.

Have you felt the power of God's presence in a specific time or space? Take a few minutes to answer the following questions, being mindful of some of the ways that the living God comes to you:

How have I seen God?

In what ways has God spoken to me?

What are my holy places?

Have I ever, in my own way, consecrated a place, marking it as a place where God lives?

Prayer: **Merciful God, thank you for the different ways you enter my life. Keep me open to hear your voice and see your face in the people and places of my everyday life. Amen.**

Friday, July 19   Read Matthew 13:24-30, 36-43.

Even if we do not know the intricacies of farming, we do know that we would rather be considered "good seed" than be known as a "weed," especially if it is God's garden we are talking about.

In the parable of weeds among the wheat, Jesus used everyday farming images to focus on the reality of good and evil coexisting in the world just as wheat (the good seed) and weeds grew together in the same field. At certain points in the growing season, the farmer could not distinguish between wheat and weeds; it was only at harvest time that the profitable wheat could be clearly separated from the useless weeds.

The image of harvest reminds us that God will take an accounting of the good and evil "at the end of the age." "The Son of Man will send his angels, and they will collect out of his kingdom all causes of sin and all evildoers. . . . Then the righteous will shine like the sun in the kingdom of their Father."

Daily, each of us makes choices that call for our discernment: if I take this action, will I be "sowing good seed" or adding to the "weeds"? In other words, do I give my energy to that which will make the world more positive or do I contribute to that which is negative? The consequences of many choices we make are not immediately clear. Then discernment must come into play: how do I so live that I allow God's spirit to work in me for the good? How do I shine like the sun in God's kingdom?

Prayer: **Loving God, be with me in all my decision-making so that I may choose for the good, the right, the positive. Keep uppermost in my mind the example of Jesus so that I, too, may be an example of good seed sown and growing productively. Let me live as one with "ears to hear." In the name of Jesus I pray. Amen.**

Saturday, July 20   Read Psalm 139:1-6.

Most of us will have at least moments in our lives when we feel alone, misunderstood, left out. This psalm reminds us that no matter what our situation, God not only walks with us but knows us better than we can even begin to know ourselves.

God, the psalmist tells us, knows us through and through: every thought, every action, our past and present. "You hem me in, behind and before, and lay your hand upon me. Such knowledge is too wonderful for me." God's incredible knowledge of each person is not stifling or frightening but gives a sense of security because there is the strong implication that God loves and accepts as well as knows us. With God, we have no need to pretend to be other than who we are at our core.

Suggestion for meditation: **Read the following meditatively and as a reminder that God's great love surrounds you every moment of your life:**

> I may be high; I may be low;
> I may be fast; I may be slow,
> But all I am is God's.
> I may feel dull; I may feel bright;
> I may feel like an oversight,
> But all I am is God's.
> No need to play the social game.
> I'm good enough. I bear God's name.
> And all I am is God's.
> Poor, indigent; rich, on a throne;
> With company, or all alone;
> All I am is God's.
> And God, with me my whole life through
> Is right beside me, and with you.
> We, God's creations, shine anew
> For all we are is God's.

214

Sunday, July 21   Read Psalm 139:7-12, 23-24.

The children's book *The Runaway Bunny* by Margaret Wise Brown chronicles a conversation between a young rabbit and his mother. Anxious for independence, the bunny tells his mother all the places to which he will run away. For every exotic incarnation he imagines for himself, the mother has a response that includes an affirmation of her love: no matter where he may roam, she will be there for him.

The psalmist reflects that God's power goes far beyond geographical boundaries; God's love sustains us no matter where we roam.

God is not like "Big Brother," some alien force that seeks to trip us up and find out our mistakes. God is not keeping a scorecard on which we will always come out the loser. God participates in our lives to encourage us to be our best selves. God is on *our* side. God is *in* us. God surrounds us with love and power until we cannot help but want to "do the right thing" and live in God's spirit.

The psalmist prays, "Search me, O God, and know my heart; test me and know my thoughts. See if there is any wicked way in me, and lead me in the way everlasting." But we do not get a sense of someone afraid of heavenly judgment. We see a person who wants to work with God in order to walk "in the way everlasting."

Most of us need some time every day to reflect on our lives: Did our words hurt someone? Were our actions less than loving? Can we learn from our experiences?

Prayer: **Search me, O God, and know my heart. Test me and know my thoughts. Lead me in the way everlasting and help me accept your faithful love in my life. Amen.**

THE SURPRISING GRACE OF GOD

July 22–28, 1996   **Paul L. Escamilla✛**
Monday, July 22   Read Genesis 29:15-28.

The opening sentence of this reading should give us a clue that Laban is an individual for whom self-interest wears the mask of magnanimity. First of all, we have no indication that Jacob had planned to place himself in the service of Laban. He has come to find a wife, not employment (see Genesis 28:2). Secondly, we know from an earlier account that Laban tends to ask leading questions, which open like doors to deals made on his own terms (Gen. 24:31). Jacob names his wages; Laban appears to agree, but never gives him his word, only words

Jacob, schemer, dreamer, and restless soul that he is, is yet strangely bridled by the subtle power of his love for Rachel, his chosen. His seven years of serving seem to him but a few days. Seven more are exacted of him by the machinations of Laban, but neither are they more than scarcely mentioned. Fourteen years pass virtually unnoticed because of one person's sense of devotion to another. Thus while Rachel and Leah appear to be mere objects in a transaction, they prove here and later to be far more.

Having succeeded in outwitting both his brother and his father, Jacob truly meets his match in Laban. All the more remarkable that through this biblical period in which deceit often lies with trickery, the good promise of God will yet find its way.

Suggestion for meditation: **Meditate on the many ways in which God works through earthen vessels.**

✛Pastor, Munger Place United Methodist Church, Dallas, Texas.

Tuesday, July 23   Read Psalm 105:1-6.

The Psalms are, of course, the songbook of the scriptures. Here are songs of lament and despair as well as songs of joyful celebration. Before (and after) studying this psalm as a text of scripture, we would do well to enjoy it as song—not Israel's song only, but ours as well.

There is the pleasure of praying a prayer-song written ages ago and ample enough to be spoken and sung meaningfully ever since. Beyond this we can derive important lessons about the life of faith from looking closely at the words we are singing. In this case, we see in the first six verses of Psalm 105 a rare and beautiful integration of four faith dimensions: memory, worship, seeking, and proclamation. In other words, the faithful are called, in the same breath, 1) to remember God's "wonderful works"; 2) to praise God for them; 3) to seek God because of them; and 4) to tell others of them.

The expression of these imperatives is so natural here that we are apt not to notice them as distinct features, but to see them, as the psalmist does, as one gathered expression of gratitude for God's faithfulness. It is perhaps only more recently that we have compartmentalized bible study, spirituality, worship, evangelism, and so on, understanding each as a separate pursuit or emphasis. In this delightful song, all of these are strands of single cloth.

Suggestion for prayer: **Pray or sing (in your own created melody) Psalm 105:1-6 as prayer. Then pray: God, may remembering your faithfulness emerge in my life as worship, seeking you, and sharing you with others. Amen.**

Wednesday, July 24 Read Psalm 105:7-11, 45*b*.

These five verses begin to do what will occupy the remaining 39 verses of this psalm: recounting certain central episodes in the historical faithfulness of God. The "call to worship" of verses 1-6 in the psalm charges the hearer to "remember the wonderful works God has done." In these verses we are given all the help we should need in order to do so.

The narrative of God's faithful action moves right away from the general to the specific, from the universal to the concrete: God's judgments span the earth; God remembers a covenant that has been made—even to a thousand generations; specifically, this covenant, *our* covenant, was made with Abraham and ratified with Isaac and Jacob. The content of that covenant? To give God's homeless chosen people a home in the land of Canaan.

Notice the collective tone of the psalm so far. The plural form of address is speaking to all, not just to one; the episodes recited are the community's stories, not those of one individual. The goodness of God can only be fully comprehended by all of the people together. It makes sense to speak of God's goodness to *me* only in the context of considering God's goodness to *us*, and to *all*. After all, as someone has said, some things are true even when I am asleep.

Suggestion for prayer: **Reflect on God's mercies toward you, your faith community, and all creation. Then pray: God, in singing the songs of your faithfulness, teach me the importance of sharing the singing with others and of finding my place in the songs that others sing. Amen.**

Thursday, July 25   Read Romans 8:26-27.

If some things are true even while we sleep, then, according to Paul, it is at least partly due to the Spirit's matrix of care and intercession in our lives. Whereas in the psalter the gathered community is the sign of memory deeper than my own, faith greater than my own, in Paul's letter to the Christians in Rome, the Spirit becomes such a sign.

My prayers falter; the Spirit completes them. My soul yearns for things too deep to put in words—to have a profound hope realized, to see creation whole, to be with God (vv. 18-25). I cannot even begin to speak these yearnings, "but that very Spirit intercedes for us with sighs too deep for words."

In the charismatic movement of the 1970s, this verse was cited as a warrant for praying in tongues. With all respect to that particular form of prayer, Paul's intent here goes deeper and ranges wider, so as to say: prayer need not be verbal to be expressed or heard. From such an understanding we can begin to see the value of many nonverbal prayer forms, such as gesture (movement, dance, exercise, kneeling, lifted palms), silence (meditation, deep contemplation), and vocalization (chants, humming, deep breathing, praying in tongues) as vehicles for prayer.

In this discussion, you and I are considering things we do not claim to understand, things literally "too deep for words." The assurance of Paul is that in the midst of such depths, the Spirit will help us; all we need is given.

Suggestion for prayer: **Introduce into your prayers today a nonverbal prayer form such as one of those mentioned above.**

Friday, July 26   Read Romans 8:28-39.

Coming from just anyone, we would suspect the words that
open this passage to be Pollyannish and simplistic: "We know
that all things work together for good. . . ." But they are not
spoken by an ivory-tower academic or an armchair positive-
thinker, but by an apostle who has experienced firsthand the
gamut of crises listed in verse 35: hardship, distress, persecution,
famine, nakedness, peril, sword. When one who has emerged
from such wreckage speaks about hope and providence, every
word is gospel.

This closing segment of chapter 8 is a consummate elaboration
of the truth pronounced in its opening verse: "There is therefore
now no condemnation for those who are in Christ Jesus." In these
verses Paul names all the demons, all the threats to our sense
of well-being, to our very lives. He lines them up in daunting
fashion, *twice* (v. 35 and vv. 38-39). Then he says, in effect, "What
matters finally is more profound than these or any imaginable
circumstance: we are held in God's care, God's freedom, God's
love, eternally, because of God's saving work in Jesus Christ." In
one of the most triumphant passages in scripture, we are given the
bold assurance that nothing "in all creation will be able to separate
us from the love of God in Christ Jesus our Lord."

I have heard that a particular Roman Catholic religious order
lists "hilarity" as one of the life-long virtues. What is meant by
this, I think, is a sense of holy perspective on the ultimate outcome
of things. By all appearances, things may be desperate, or even
deadly. In universal scope, however, even death has lost its sting
(1 Cor. 15:55), and that particular truth, like Paul's closing verses
of Chapter 8, is suitable for dancing.

Suggestion for meditation: **Read thoughtfully and prayerfully
Romans 8:37-39. Read these verses again. Is there a special word
for you or your congregation in them?**

220

Saturday, July 27   Read Matthew 13:31-32.

We have in today's parable a nest in the shade during a long, hot season. But to whom is the shade due? Presumably, the mustard seed was planted for the purpose of reaping its harvest later on, mustard being a cash stop with various medicinal and dietary uses. But Jesus' parable does not lead us to that end; the sower is removed from the story early on and never returns.

Instead, we are led to the conclusion that birds of the air become the beneficiaries of the full-grown mustard shrub. Right away we realize that any birds nesting in such a tree are freeloaders, never having lifted a feather to earn their place in its branches. Did they purchase the land? Did they prepare the soil? Did they plant the seed? Did they cultivate the young shrub to full growth? At best, they were a mere irritation of droppings and chatter along the way. But to them belongs the mustard shrub!

Ezekiel 17 offers a beautiful apocalyptic vision of the nation of Israel becoming a towering tree—great, strong, and noble. But in Matthew we get a dowdy, frumpy mustard shrub. And it is given over entirely to birds, who are only in it for the shelter and the shade. Unmeriting, undeserving, uncredentialed—just there to receive. In this parable, the kingdom of heaven is such a reality, a mustard shrub enjoyed by those who can never earn it, never pay for it, never create if themselves—who can only delight in it.

Prayer: **Loving God, open my heart to receive from you what I cannot earn from you—your gracious rule in my life. And open my heart to accept others I may have thought unworthy, who benefit from that very same grace. Amen.**

Sunday, July 28   Read Matthew 13:33, 44-52.

This parable of the yeast instantly appears more conventional than the one about the mustard seed. Even as we read we can begin to smell the fresh dough, the dust of flour, the warm air from an oven heating up for baking. But within this one verse is hidden what would be for the original hearers—and even for us—a bushelful of disturbing features!

For them "leaven" would have been a code word for evil and its spread. Jesus inverts the image to suggest that it is goodness, not evil, that spreads inexorably and eventually permeates all.

Secondly, a woman raised to the public level (such as being featured in a parable) would have been problematic at the time. And the image of a woman representing God or the Kingdom, a bakerwoman God, still challenges stereotypes.

Finally, the Greek word used here for "hid" or "mixed in with" is *krypto*, which normally has negative connotations of secrecy and deceit. Besides, why would anyone knowingly hide the work of the Kingdom, keeping it behind the scenes?

In one small verse, one innocent-looking parable, leavenness, femininity, and secrecy are all inverted to present God's realm in radically new ways. If these features make us nervous, we should consider the whole picture again—a warm, cozy kitchen, and the promise of bread enough for many to share. (Three measures of flour, about fifty pounds, enough to make over a hundred loaves of bread!)* From the abundance of God's kitchen, we are all fed.

Suggestion for meditation: **Seek to identify workings of the Kingdom of God around you and within you that are "cryptic," that is, those that normally go unnoticed.**

---

*Text note to verse 33, from *The HarperCollins Study Bible,* New Revised Standard Version, copyright © 1993 HarperCollins, Publishers, Inc.

CONTENDING WITH GOD

July 29—August 4, 1996   **Stefanie Weisgram, O.S.B.✤**
Monday, July 29   Read Genesis 32:22-26.

We each contend with God at some point in our lives. Some of us even do it continuously—or nearly so. But whenever we do, we never come out on the short end. Instead, we come face to face with God's compassion, which marks us, changes us, makes us new in some way. Jacob had such an experience.

Having cheated his brother Esau in years past, Jacob had reason to fear his first reunion with his twin. Jacob also had reason to send his precious family and possessions to safety while he stayed behind to "wrestle" with his worries. But his wrestling is with a man, a struggle that lasts the night. More surprising, the mysterious man does not overcome Jacob and finally has to strike and dislocate Jacob's hip joint. Even then Jacob will not give up, instead asking for a blessing.

Jacob does not push for victory; he knows when to stop. He seems to understand that his involvement is more important than victory, and he wants it to be acknowledged by a blessing.

So it is with us when we contend with God. What we come to realize is that we cannot remain passive in our relationship with God. We must personally strive within the relationship. Contending with God will never harm us, though it will leave us marked.

Suggestion for meditation: **Think of a time when you struggled with God. What blessing did you think you wanted? What blessing did you receive?**

✤Member of the Roman Catholic monastic community Sisters of Saint Benedict, St. Joseph, Minnesota; librarian, College of Saint Benedict/ St. John's University.

Tuesday, July 30   Read Genesis 32:27-31.

Jacob was willing to acknowledge his identity without hesitation, but he never learned the identity of his adversary nor gained power over him. We have to respect Jacob. Even with his worries over Esau and this strange episode of wrestling, Jacob listened to what this mysterious person said when he gave Jacob a new name and a new identity: *Israel*, one who has contended with God and with humans and has prevailed.

By hearing his own identity, Jacob learned the identity of the mysterious wrestler and acknowledged it. Jacob knew he had met God face to face and had survived. How often do we recognize God in our struggles, in our victories?

Often in hard times we forget God except to ask God to solve our problems. At other times we see God as the cause of our hard times and are ready to place blame.

But do we really struggle with God? Or are we afraid of the struggle because of what God might ask of us? Maybe, in spite of the pain of our hardships, we know our situation, our reactions, our feelings; and as long as we close our eyes to God's presence, we feel somewhat in control. But if we actually struggle with God "face to face," we know we will be changed. That possibility of change is frightening. We cannot predict the form or path it will take, nor can we predict what God might ask of us. However, we know from Jacob's example that we will come out with a blessing—perhaps with a new identity—and always with a knowledge of God's compassion.

Prayer: **God of Jacob, give me the courage to face your presence in my life. Empower me to be as open to your blessing as Jacob was, even when it might change how I know myself. Amen.**

Wednesday, July 31   Read Psalm 17:1-7, 15.

Psalm 17 seems an apt description of how Jacob must have felt and of how he might have prayed before and after his wrestling match. Of course, he had reason to fear Esau. He seems to recognize that, but we wonder if he is too quick to see his brother as his enemy from whom he needs protection, regardless of the cause of enmity. In this psalm the psalmist claims that his cause is just, his lips are free from deceit, no wickedness is in him. What arrogance! What total denial of reality! And what amazing faith and trust in God!

So often in the figures of the Hebrew scriptures we see real wrongdoing, real injustice. We also see acknowledgment of wrongdoing couched in the hypothetical, "If I have . . ." The Hebrew scriptures offer us extravagant claims of virtuousness. Perhaps here, more than in anything, is the recognition of the complexity of life. We do not always know why we do what we do, and we often mean well but make bad choices.

For both the psalmist and Jacob, God is their Savior whom they fully expect to see, whose wondrously steadfast love they expect to experience. Faith that recognizes and accepts faults and weaknesses and knows forgiveness exhibits a remarkable arrogance. Perhaps we cringe when we hear the psalmist's amazing claims of freedom from wickedness, of avoidance of violence, of holding fast to God's ways when we know our own sinfulness. But God is our Savior too. Maybe our arrogance lies in thinking we are too wicked to know God's steadfast and forgiving love.

Prayer: **God, show me your steadfast love. Take away my arrogance and let me know your mercy. Amen.**

Thursday, August 1   Read Romans 9:1-5.

Paul believes that nothing can separate us from the love of God in Christ Jesus our Lord (Rom. 8:38-39). And so Paul has special concern for his own people, the Israelites. They are the people of the promise from whom, according to the flesh, the Messiah comes. For Paul the problem is that not all the Israelites (Jews) have accepted Christ. They have chosen separation from him. This separation causes Paul such anguish and sorrow that he would rather see himself cut off from Christ than that his people be separated from Christ.

This attitude is a far cry from the "me first" attitude we commonly encounter today. In fact, its uncommonness makes it difficult for us to understand Paul's concern. After all, his people had their chance to know Christ and refused it. They are free to choose or not to choose. But Paul knows that we do not operate so simply or choose so easily. Furthermore, God has touched Paul's life, and he cannot simply stand by.

For Paul, God's touching his life gave it a new dimension. Paul loves with God's love; he loves as Christ loved, willing the good of others, even preferring their good over his own.

What about us? Are we up to this challenge? Can we be like Paul? Imitating Paul does not mean destroying ourselves or being a carpet under the feet of others. Living as though God has touched us takes discipline, love, and an openness that allows God to work in and through us. It means being like Paul; but even more, it means being like Christ.

Suggestion for meditation: **When has God touched my life? How can I enable God's love to touch others today through me?**

Friday, August 2   Read Matthew 14:13-14.

When Jesus heard about the beheading of John the Baptist, his response was the same as ours might have been. He needed to draw apart to be by himself. John was his cousin, probably his friend, and John's death hit two ways: Jesus lost someone he loved to a wasteful and unjust death. John's death served as a reminder that Jesus was following the same path as John with a great probability of its leading to death for him as well. No wonder Jesus went apart by himself—perhaps to "contend" with the Father. At this point Jesus needed affirmation, courage, and consolation.

But the people followed him on foot, bringing their sick. Jesus seemed to draw people. They sensed his goodness and wanted to be in his presence. And Jesus, even in his loss and need, responded with compassion. Jesus knew their distress, their desire for good, their need for love and healing.

Jesus had an uncanny way of knowing what people needed. He showed that he knew when to test their faith and when to respond in compassion. He knew when to challenge and when to console. He also knew himself and his own needs, and he knew when he could set aside his own needs to care for others. If Jesus had heard of John's beheading, had the people not heard as well? Did they not realize what Jesus was up against? Did they not have compassion for him? Was their love stirred?

And what about the disciples? They must have put two and two together and realized that Jesus could be in danger. Perhaps the great crowd of people gathered around made them edgy. Or perhaps they knew Jesus well enough now to share his compassion.

Suggestion for meditation: **Recall an occasion when you experienced Jesus' compassion. Savor the memory and express your gratitude.**

Saturday, August 3 Read Matthew 14:15-21.

Evening came, and after a day of healing and teaching, everyone was tired and hungry. The disciples wanted the people to go away so they could settle back and eat their scanty fare of bread and fish. But once again Jesus had another agenda. Once again, he saw the people through eyes of compassion, and he told the disciples to feed them. Just as Jesus had compassion on the individual who needed his help, so did he have compassion on the crowds. Jesus was a true son of the Father (God), who through the ages has treated people with compassion.

So what little food the disciples had, Jesus offered freely. But Jesus went even further: he made the disciples extensions of himself when he gave the blessed and broken bread to them to distribute. Those who wanted the people to go away to feed themselves find that they are serving the people instead, and there is food enough for all with leftovers besides!

We cannot help but wonder about the disciples and about ourselves. If we had been among the disciples, how would we have felt as the evening drew near? Like Jesus, the disciples, too, must have known that the Baptist's death did not bode well for them. A sense of insecurity may have caused them to distance themselves from possible trouble. Perhaps the people's faith did not impress them.

It is a challenge for us also to see others with Jesus' eyes, to see them with compassion. It is a challenge to let ourselves be open and vulnerable in the face of others' suffering, to serve them in their need.

Prayer: **Lord, let me be courageous and compassionate. Help me to see others through your eyes and to love them. Amen.**

Sunday, August 4   Read Matthew 14:13-21.

Jacob contended with God and received a new name, identity, and mission. Paul met the Lord and learned a compassion that made him willing to give up all if only others might accept Christ. We are like Jacob and Paul. Neither was perfect, although each was well-intentioned. Both accepted responsibility for the consequences of past actions. Both knew they had encountered God and allowed that event to change their lives and how they saw others.

Jesus shows us how God is rich in all things, especially in compassion. Jesus' own compassion allowed him to rise above his own loss and fear to care for others. He healed the sick. He showed the disciples how to care for others, enabling them to be extensions of himself.

Jesus teaches us to see with compassion and to serve with love. He shows us that he can satisfy all our hungers. Just as he healed the sick, fed the hungry, and empowered his disciples, he does the same today. Jesus is still with us, healing, feeding, loving, and working through new disciples. He works in and through us when we are open to him. And there is the rub. We need to be open to Jesus' presence in our lives and to see more nearly with his eyes.

We can feed the hungry, console the sorrowing, uplift the downhearted. We can do all of this, yet remain untouched ourselves. Opening our hearts to Jesus' presence can change us. Then we will be open to the pain and need of those we serve. We will be present in a new way as extensions of Jesus' loving hands.

Prayer: **Compassionate Jesus, be present among us. Use our hands and hearts to serve and heal each other in your name. Feed us with your love. Amen.**

229

THE PERSON WHO BELIEVES IN GOD

August 5–11, 1996   **Thomas R. Albin**✤
Monday, August 5   Read Romans 10:5-10.

The Epistle to the Romans has been recognized by many as the jewel of the New Testament epistles. One of the central themes in this important book is faith in Jesus Christ alone for salvation. In the opening chapter Paul proclaims, "I am not ashamed of the gospel; it is the power of God for salvation to everyone who has faith, to the Jew first and also to the Greek" (Rom. 1:16).

The word for "salvation" in the New Testament is the same word used to describe physical healing or the restoration to wholeness. Just as Jesus healed people's bodies, resulting in physical wellness, faith in Jesus Christ resulted in salvation and the healing of the spirit.

At the center of the Christian faith is the sure confidence in God and God's word that John Wesley expressed in the preface to his *Notes on the New Testament*: "The Scripture . . . is a most solid and most precious system of divine truth. Every part thereof is worthy of God: and all together are one intire Body, wherein is no defect, no excess. It is the fountain of heavenly wisdom."

The way to spiritual health and wholeness is to "confess with your lips that Jesus is Lord and believe in your heart that God raised him from the dead."

Psalm 1 says that the person who meditates on the word of God will be like a tree planted by streams of water. I would invite you to find spiritual health and wholeness this week as you read and meditate on the scriptures and give yourself to prayer.

Suggestion for meditation: **Meditate on the words of Romans 10:11: "No one who believes in him will be put to shame."**

✤Director of Contextual Education and Instructor in Christian Spiritual Formation, University of Dubuque Theological Seminary, Dubuque, Iowa.

Tuesday, August 6   Read Romans 10:11-15.

It is abundantly clear that Paul's purpose and passion is to see the salvation and healing of all people—men and women, young and old, Jew and Gentile, slave and free. "Brothers and sisters, my heart's desire and prayer to God . . . is that they may be saved" (Rom. 10:1). What is my heart's desire? What is it that I long for and desire at the deepest level of my being?

As a parent, my greatest desire when my children are ill is for them to be well. I think about it, I pray for it, I desire it with all of my heart.

Why? Because I love my children.

As a Christian parent, my greatest desire for my children is for their salvation, their spiritual health. I think about it, I pray for it, I desire it with all of my heart.

Why? Because I love my children.

The challenge in this passage comes to me at the point of my Christian discipleship. Do I love my neighbors as much as I love my children? Is my chief desire that they come to enjoy spiritual health and salvation? Do I think about this, pray for it, desire it with all of my heart?

Paul was motivated by the love of God and the confidence that "everyone who calls on the name of the Lord shall be saved." Because Paul cared, he traveled, preached, and prayed. Do I care? Do I love my neighbor enough to proclaim by word and deed the health and wholeness that comes through faith in Christ alone?

Prayer: **Lord, make me an instrument of your peace. Help me to proclaim your salvation to those who may not hear unless I speak. Amen.**

Wednesday, August 7   Read Matthew 14:22-27.

Jesus sent the disciples to the other side of the sea, while he dismissed the multitude fed through the miracle of the loaves and fishes. Then he went up the mountain by himself to pray.

Think about it carefully. If this was important for Jesus, could it be that this is recorded for our benefit as well? Do we, like Jesus, need time alone with God in prayer?

For those who question the importance and power of prayer today, we need only to look at the example of persons we know whose lives have been touched and changed by prayer. For me, the example of Korean Christians testifies to the power of prayer. The vast majority of their churches are alive and growing because of their emphasis on prayer. This past fall, during our seminary spiritual life retreat, exchange students from Korea inspired and challenged those present to make prayer our top priority.

The importance that John and Charles Wesley placed on personal prayer is well documented in their journals. It was from this solid foundation of time spent alone with God that the Wesleys and their early followers found the courage and compassion necessary for evangelical witness and social action.

Just as Jesus left the security of the prayer mountain to rescue the struggling disciples who were caught in the storm, so we are to follow his example. Surely the winds and the waves of life still seek to destroy his disciples today. Yet, Jesus comes to us where we are, even while we are buffeted by the wind and waves of life's storms.

Suggestion for meditation: **List some of the things that threaten to sink your "ship" or that of others you love. What are those things that threaten the congregation where you worship? Be honest and name real issues. Now take this list with you into your time alone with God in prayer.**

Prayer: **God, help me to follow Jesus' example in prayer. Amen.**

Thursday, August 8   Read Genesis 37:1-4, 12-28.

The text today makes it clear that Joseph was loved by his father and hated by his brothers. Because the story is familiar to many of us, it is difficult to read it without anticipating the "happy ending" that will come in subsequent chapters. This reading reminds us that God's faithfulness to Joseph comes only after some of the most terrible, emotionally destructive and spiritually challenging events that one can imagine.

Try to put yourself into the text. At the age of seventeen you are sent to visit your brothers as they tend the family flock in another region. When you arrive at that place, your brothers take away the coat your father gave you and throw you into a dark pit. While you cry for mercy, they debate how to kill you. Their decision to let you die of thirst in the dry hole is only modified when foreign slave traders happen by, giving your brothers an opportunity to make money from your demise. Although you are not betrayed by a kiss, you are betrayed by your own family.

Can you imagine the emotional and spiritual pain Joseph endured? Wouldn't you be deeply hurt, angry, enraged? What would your emotions be when you were lifted out of the pit, bound like a criminal and sold for twenty pieces of silver? How would you feel? What would you say to God? For what would you pray and how would you react when there was no deliverance from your captivity for many years? Would you be tempted to curse and hate your brothers? Would you be tempted to curse and hate God?

Prayer: **Almighty God, give me the ability to trust you even when everything in my life seems to be falling apart. Amen.**

Friday, August 9   Read Psalm 105:1-6.

One of the recurring themes in the Hebrew scriptures in general, and in the Psalms in particular, has to do with the importance of telling and retelling the stories of faith. The psalmist exhorts the people to sing as well as say what God has done in the past. There is something in the act of remembering that strengthens faith.

Today, seminary education places a great emphasis on telling and retelling stories as well. Students preparing for pastoral ministry learn how to preach narrative sermons, and they study the basic principles of narrative theology.

The psalmist tells the people to "*give thanks* to the LORD, *call on* his name, *make known* his deeds. . . . *Sing* to him, *sing praises* to him; *tell* of all his wonderful works. *Glory* in his holy name; *rejoice*. . . . *Seek* the LORD. . . . *Remember* the wonderful works . . . miracles . . . judgments" (*italics mine*).

I believe that we, who are today God's people, are instructed to do these things because the psalmist knows that living faith is active and dynamic. If faith is not growing it is dying. Left alone, our faith will naturally decline. Faith can be easy for us to forget, to question, to doubt.

Living faith is nurtured as we tell ourselves and others the truth about God and the nature of God.

Suggestion for meditation: **Reflect on one or more of the italicized words above. In your mind, picture yourself doing this action. Then commit yourself to do it as you close in prayer. Then act on your commitment.**

Saturday, August 10   Read Psalm 105:16-22, 45*b*.

The pastor to students at the seminary where I teach, Dr. Henry Fawcett, is a Native American from Alaska. At an early age he was adopted. Later he was sent to a missionary school away from his family. It was not an easy life. Yet, Henry has allowed God to use even the painful parts of his past to make him a gracious and understanding counselor. In his pastoral relationships he embodies what some call "a non-anxious presence."

In today's reading the psalmist reminds us of the physical and emotional pain Joseph endured as a prisoner bound with fetters on his feet and an iron collar around his neck. The story of Joseph's life is one of the foundational stories of the Hebrew people. It is important to tell and retell it today so that the people of God will realize that even through terrible suffering and times when our faith is severely tested, God is with us, working good from ill, blessings from seemingly accursed circumstances.

Spiritual growth often comes in the valley of the shadow, rather than the sunshine of the hillside. We are told that "the word of the LORD kept testing him" until the king of Egypt set Joseph free. After many years of testing, God was ready to use Joseph to free others—from starvation, from oppression, and, in the case of his brothers, from terrible guilt and then the fear of revenge. When this happens, everyone can acknowledge the hand of God at work and conclude with the final words of the psalm, "Praise the LORD!"

Suggestion for meditation: **Have you been hurt deeply? What are those circumstances that challenge your faith? How has adversity been a part of your faith maturity?**

Sunday, August 11   Read Matthew 14:25-33.

In Matthew's Gospel, the disciples are often presented as persons of little faith. When Jesus came to them walking on the water, their first response was fear, not faith. And when Peter asked for a sign that it indeed was Jesus, he was encouraged to act out his faith, to get out of the boat and walk on the water too.

There is comfort for each of us in this story. Are you frightened by the storms in your life? So were the first disciples. Have you failed to recognize Jesus Christ when he comes to you in troubled times? So did the disciples. Have you had the courage to step out in faith, only to lose your focus and begin to sink? So did those who later became apostles.

In Jesus Christ we see how God deals with the wind and the waves. We see how God cares for fearful disciples. And we see how God responds to those who have enough faith to get out of the boat and take a few steps on the water, even though they later begin to sink.

I encourage you to meditate on the nature of God as revealed in this passage. God always comes to us. (No one who believes in God will be put to shame.) God always reaches out to rescue those who are sinking and cry out with Peter, "Lord, save me!" (No one who believes in God will be put to shame.) God will save and heal! "You of little faith, why did you doubt?"

Let Jesus come and speak peace to the wind and the waves in your life, then you, like the disciples, can worship him, saying, "Truly you are the Son of God."

Suggestion for meditation: **As you worship today, do so in the knowledge that no one who believes in God will be put to shame.**

GOD OF MERCY

August 12–18, 1996
Monday, August 12

George P. Lanier✛
Read Romans 11:13-16.

In chapters nine and ten of Romans, Paul has made his case concerning the Jews' rejection of the gospel of Jesus Christ. In Romans 11:11, Paul asserts that because of the Jews' rejection of the gospel, the Gentiles became the recipients of salvation. Paul now wishes to use the Gentiles' salvation to entice the Jews into responding to the words of the gospel, in the hope that some of them would be saved.

Paul understands that the universal message of salvation does not come from Jews or from Gentile Christians but from the word of God. Paul understands that the glory was God's and could not be credited to a chosen or given group of people.

Receiving salvation through God's grace does not entitle us to place ourselves on some kind of pedestal. Rather, we have a responsibility to share this grace for the freeing of all people to worship God. I am overly amazed when persons rise above themselves and begin to look down upon other groups and even upon others within their own group.

We are heirs of the great Judeo-Christian heritage; we are branches grafted on by the Great Vinedresser. "If part of the dough offered as first fruits is holy, the whole batch is holy."

Prayer: **Have mercy, Lord. As your obedient church, we want to love our other brothers and sisters whose faith also centers in you. Make us one in you and with one another. Amen.**

✛Team leader and social worker, United Methodist Children's Home, Decatur, Georgia.

Tuesday, August 13   Read Psalm 78:17-20.

Why do we fight against God? We say that there is nothing God cannot do. I have found that we become rebellious when we demand from God according to our will as if it is God's will. The psalmist records the stories of how God provided everything the Israelites cried out in need for. "They tested God in their heart by demanding the food they craved. They spoke against God, saying, 'Can God spread a table in the wilderness?'"

Do we have attitudes similar to those of our siblings of old? This is why the writer reminds God's people of the present of the glorious deeds of the past. God fulfills promises made. "Can [God] also give bread or provide meat for his people?" The record will show that the Creator's will is to care for the needs of humankind.

Now that we know the answer, we must respond in faith. Can God feed the hungry in the inner cities? Can God also give aid to the homeless or provide for the needs of persons in the developing countries? Yes. If the church performs the will of God, as I know it can, God's record will prove it.

Prayer: **Have mercy, Lord God. Forgive us our negligence in obeying you and our failures in living in accordance with your will. Help us to be ever mindful of your promises and seek your guidance and strength to do our part in the fulfillment of your promises for all people. Amen.**

Wednesday, August 14   Read Psalm 78:1-3, 10-16;
                                                          Psalm 113.

The Israelites became ungrateful and unfaithful. The psalmist of Psalm 78 wants the generations to come to know about the disobedient side of their ancestors' past and for them to learn from former actions. What caused their ancestors to stumble? Psalm 78:11 reveals it to be a lapse of memory. Forgotten were those mighty acts that God had done for them as promised.

The Ephraimites did not keep God's covenant and refused to walk according to God's Law. Because of their action God took Ephraim's position and gave it to Judah (vv. 67-68). It is clear that when they forgot how God had been with them in the past, the future became uncertain. Those who forget can be neither truly faithful to nor thankful for the promises of old.

The theme of forgetfulness and the biblical reminder of God's care and intervention among the needy and powerless is repeated often in the Psalms. The Lord "raises the poor from the dust, and lifts the needy from the ash heap," says the writer of Psalm 113. Remembering and telling the Lord's acts of compassion, the Lord's *involvement* in the lives of people, is a vital part of our Judeo-Christian faith. This remembering and telling forms the foundation of our day-to-day relationship with the Lord.

Prayer: **Thank you, Lord. I honor you with praise for the mighty works you have done. You, Lord, delivered your people from Egypt. You, Lord, made the waters of the sea stand at attention to make a passage for escape. You, Lord, led your people day and night. You, Lord, gave water from the rocks for the thirsty and manna with the morning dew for the hungry. Lord, help me not to forget you or rebel against your will. Amen.**

Thursday, August 15   Read Exodus 16:2-15.

For the third time since the Israelites left Egypt, they had once again found something to murmur about concerning their trek to freedom: no food. Then the brunt of the Israelites' anger was directed at Moses and Aaron instead of God. Moses said, "What are we, that you murmur against us?" After all, God had heard their complaint, and God would see whether they would respond to the divine outpouring of love and thus walk in God's Law or not.

God's people can find themselves rebelling when they seek their sustenance through faith in human productivity alone. So we can choose to be comfortable slaves in bondage to the materialistic creation of human hands or co-creators to the eternal fulfillment of God's will. The former relies on the abilities of the self and the latter on a faithful life with God.

People who find new freedoms from old bondages develop their faith in new choices cautiously. We are free to make choices, but we are bound by the choices we make. God was saying to Moses, "I will see if they will choose me or not, as I respond to their needs" (AP). I am glad that God gives us choices, even the choice to rebel against divine love. But in the end, wisdom lies in our choosing to love and worship God.

Prayer: **Have mercy, Lord, upon those who would reject your love. Help us to see your response to us as good parental caring. We are your children and we thank you for your love. Amen.**

Friday, August 16   Read Matthew 15:21-28.

Jesus shows us how to love our neighbor. He, a Jew, was one day confronted by a Syrophoenician woman who asked for help. Jews and Canaanites were long-standing enemies. The woman persistently pleaded for help. Jesus' response was born from his struggle within: "I was sent only to the lost sheep of the house of Israel."

Jesus knew that all Jews were neighbors. He also knew that faith extended beyond geographic boundaries and all forms of separation. As Jews and Christians, our common call to faithfulness binds us together as brothers and sisters, children of God. Whoever believes and does the will of God is of God.

Jesus made another response to the woman. He said, "It is not fair to take the children's bread and throw it to the dogs." The Jews were the children, the Gentiles were the dogs (housepets). The woman then said, in so many words, "True, I am not a Jew, a child of your faith, but I do believe in your message." Because of such faith, Jesus helped this non-Jew, an enemy of his people and a person not on his present agenda.

Prayer: **Have mercy, Lord, when we are too busy, selfish, and non-caring to help a neighbor in need. Amen.**

Saturday, August 17   Read Matthew 15:21-23.

The predicament of people in need just will not go away. We saw how Jesus responded to the Canaanite woman in yesterday's meditation. Today we examine the disciples' response.

They said, "Send her away, for she is crying after us." But because of her love for her daughter and faith in a young Jewish rabbi, the woman was motivated to cry out. Jesus acknowledged her strong faith and answered her prayerful cry for the healing of her daughter.

If we are to be like Jesus, then we must not be quick to be judgmental disciples. We can ignore many human needs if we rationalize them out of existence: the poor do not want to work, the hungry want a free handout, the homeless are irresponsible.

To respond in the Christlike way to people in need, we must go to their place of living. We must stop, look, and listen to their life story. Even the unchurched person expects to be heard and cared for by the church if he or she is to believe in what the church stands for.

Prayer: **"Merciful God, we confess that often we have failed to be an obedient church. We have not done your will, we have broken your law, we have rebelled against your love, we have not loved our neighbors, and we have not heard the cry of the needy. Forgive us, we pray. Free us for joyful obedience, through Jesus Christ our Lord. Amen."***

---

*Prayer of Confession, *The Book of Services* (Nashville: The United Methodist Publishing House, 1985), p. 21.

Sunday, August 18   Read Romans 11:29-32.

Trading places is not what God had in mind. Paul evidently agrees. No one, no people have any better place or position with God than any other. Romans 11:32 says, "For God has made all people prisoners of disobedience, so that he might show mercy to them all" (TEV).

God's purpose in the plan of salvation is to redeem the total order of creation. Our freedom and obedience as believers do not center on our status or self-image. They center on the image of God as we, both Jew and Gentile, reflect God's will in our lives. And, as Paul says, "The gifts and call of God are irrevocable."

Paul's dream was that Jews and Gentiles will take their rightful place, together, as God's instruments of change for the people of the world. That the first shall be last and the last shall be first is like a revolving door. When pride convinces us we deserve to be at the head of the line, God makes the end the head. When all learn to walk together, side by side, God is pleased and we find freedom and equality.

Then, as Dr. Martin Luther King, Jr., proclaimed, "We will be able to speed up that day when all of God's children will be able to join hands and to sing in the words of the old Negro spiritual, 'Free at last! Free at last! Thank God Almighty, we are free at last!' " *

Prayer: **Have mercy, Lord. Guide us on your way that leads to righteousness. As vessels of peace, we want to be filled to overflowing, that all may receive that peace. Amen.**

---

*"I Have A Dream," Dr. Martin Luther King, Jr., Washington, D.C., 1963.

GOD'S EXTRA-ORDINARY PEOPLE

August 19–25, 1996   **Richard H. Summy✤**
Monday, August 19   Read Exodus 1:8-22.

Pharaoh had a plan. The powerful often do. He would "deal shrewdly" with the perceived threat of the Israelites. Shrewdly in this case meant forced labor, hard service, and ruthless administration of every menial task.

Surprisingly, although he seemed to hold all the cards, the dealer dealt himself a lousy hand. The more the Israelites "were oppressed, the more they multiplied."

And so Pharaoh dealt another hand.

But two Hebrew midwives, Shiphrah and Puah, played the unanticipated trump card of faith and outwitted the powerful, and supposedly wise, ruler. You see, they feared and respected God more than they feared Pharaoh.

Increasingly alarmed, Pharaoh shuffled the deck and dealt the cards once again. This time he thought he had dealt himself a winning hand. He ordered his people to throw into the Nile River every Hebrew boy newly born.

Yet, even while Pharaoh was enjoying his perceived victory, a male Hebrew child was born who would escape the water. His name was Moses.

The wild card in this game belonged to God.

The powerful still scheme and plot. The high and mighty deal shrewdly. They plan to stay on top by keeping others at their feet.

But schemes and plots, shrewd dealings, and arrogant devices add up to a house of cards that will, in the end, fall in the face of faith and the steadfast love of God.

Prayer: **Gracious Lord, grant us a simple and strong faith upheld by your steadfast love. Amen.**

✤Pastor, St. Michael's Evangelical Lutheran Church, Sellersville, Pennsylvania.

Tuesday, August 20   Read Psalm 124.

If it had not been for my next-door neighbor, I probably would be dead.

As a child, I had been sent to retrieve something from the metal china closet in the kitchen and decided that it would be fun to stand on the lip at the bottom of the cabinet while I held on to the doors—an indoor swing! That is the last thing I remember. The force of my weight brought the closet crashing down on top of me, slicing a large swath through my forehead that bled profusely.

Had my neighbor not been an ambulance attendant who knew how to slow the bleeding, I might have bled to death by the time the small town ambulance arrived. I have counted that blessing many times in my life.

In this psalm, Israel is being asked to count a blessing that spared its life. With enemies described in primal, powerful images providing the threat, Israel is poignantly and pointedly reminded of a time when, had God not been by its side, it surely would have been as good as dead—mere prey in the jaws of a ravaging monster.

The recollection has two results: thanksgiving ("Blessed be the LORD") and trust ("Our help is in the name of the LORD").

Remember that if not for the death and resurrection of our Lord, we, too, would be swallowed up by death. May we, like the Israelites, respond with thanksgiving and trust in the One whose blessings can be counted on.

Prayer: **Dear Lord, help us to count our blessings, to trust your saving presence in our lives, and to give you thanks. Amen.**

Wednesday, August 21   Read Exodus 2:1-10.

A fragile basket of papyrus plastered with pitch floats in the shallows of a reedy river. There is a child inside. The child, who was supposed to be dead, is the one God has chosen to deliver God's people from the oppression of slavery.

An unusual approach, I would say.

Fast forward a few millennia. Sheltered by a backyard animal stall in an obscure town, a manger matted with hay holds another child. This one is to be the Savior of the world.

Unlikely, to say the least.

God's actions—both great and small—often come wrapped in unusual packages.

And if Moses and Jesus are not sufficient examples, think of Abraham the liar, Jacob the cheat, Jonah the weasel. In other words, God often acts through people and in places in which we are least likely to look for anything good—let alone expect to find God at work.

Think of the Cross.

Now, look around your own life at the places you do not want to go. Look toward the people you would rather not see. Ask yourself if God might be working there too.

And while you're at it, take a good look at yourself. God just might have something in mind for you as well, don't you think?

The child in the fragile basket floating in an unusual place was rescued by a most unlikely person. He did not die but became a man and, by God, he set his people free.

The manger child did die, short of middle age. But by his death he set all people free.

God often acts in unusual places through unlikely people. Look around!

Prayer: **Surprising God, help us to look for you in unexpected places and unlikely people, even ourselves, and see you active there. Amen.**

Thursday, August 22   Read Romans 12:1-2.

It's tempting, isn't it, to want to escape from a world in which fourteen-year-olds sell drugs on street corners. It's tempting to wish to see the major problems of the world as residing in other places—in the city, say, or other countries. It's tempting, isn't it, to become unaffected by so much that is disheartening in this world.

To do so, though, is to begin to make of others something less than human. It is to begin to become a little less human yourself. Besides, God made the world to be very good.

The Apostle Paul did not intend for Christians to escape from the nitty-gritty of daily life and human interaction. To be sure, neither did he wish for them to be captive to the standards and siren calls of the day.

Paul's call to be transformed was a call to bear witness to another world—the world in which the Resurrection and the inbreaking of God's future kingdom is an already present reality—while very much living in this world.

Our call is to discern God's presence in the midst of daily life and to name it, that we all might become more aware of the grace that holds life together by a thread that is often all but invisible.

Elsewhere in scripture, Jesus told his disciples to be in but not of the world. *In* the world—no flights of fancy or fantasy, no artificial escape, no ducking the everyday. But *not of* the world. Just beneath the surface is a deeper reality, the real world, if you will, where God's good and acceptable and perfect will is seen.

This is the place where the gospel lives.

Prayer: **Dear God, grant that we may boldly witness in this world where we live to your otherworldly love. Amen.**

Friday, August 23 Read Romans 12:3-8.

"For as in one body we have many members, and not all the members have the same function, so we, who are many, are one body in Christ, and individually we are members one of another."

Paul exhorts his readers to maintain sober judgment and not to think more highly of themselves than they ought. He bridges the gap by placing all the gifts given by God on par with one another, neither exalting nor diminishing any gift. Thus, because all gifts have an equal value, no one will seek to have a better or more highly regarded gift. Each person is encouraged to exercise his or her particular gift to its fullest. The measure of whether the gift is from God is not how publicly impressive it is but whether it serves to benefit the good of the whole community.

These days the gap is not so much between ecstatic and administrative gifts as between lay and ordained ministries. Paul's words to the Romans are a reminder to all of us that certain gifts are not more valuable than others. All gifts that serve Christ are both necessary and good.

Prayer: **God, enable us to value the good gifts of others and to discover and use for the sake of Christ the gifts you have given us. Amen.**

Saturday, August 24   Read Matthew 16:13-20.

It is a wonder that Peter had the gumption to open his mouth at all. Of all the disciples, Peter, it seems, had the worst case of foot-in-mouth disease.

This time, though, he got it right. Thank God! Jesus *was* the Messiah, the Son of the living God.

Often, however, Peter was chief among the band of disciples who followed but often misunderstood Jesus. Peter was the one who tried to walk on water like the Lord, only to sink like a rock. Which disciple wanted to make dwellings on the momentary Mount of Transfiguration? Peter, of course. It was Peter who, seemingly just moments after his confession of faith, rebuked the Lord and who, in turn, was sternly put in his place. When Jesus was in custody, Peter three times denied that he even knew his Teacher.

It is a wonder that Jesus singled Peter out to be the "rock" upon which his church would be built. But the beauty of Jesus' choice of a special place for Peter is not that he was far and above the other disciples, but rather that he was, in many ways, typical of all disciples.

Peter, the rock of faith, was also sometimes thick and stubborn as a stone. Here is encouragement for us when we sink in doubt or misunderstand the Lord's purpose. Here is balm for our own woeful denials, betrayals, and shortcomings.

After the resurrection Jesus undid Peter's denial by eliciting from him a threefold expression of love. May we who are sometimes thick and stubborn as stones also be blessed by God to love the Lord Jesus as did Peter.

Prayer: **Lord, forgive us our denials and betrayals. Strengthen us in our faith. Help us to love you as Peter loved you. Amen.**

Sunday, August 25   Read Matthew 16:13-20.

For some people of his time he was Elijah or Jeremiah or some other prophet returned from the past.

He is, for some people today, the ultimate nice guy. "Do to others." "Turn the other [cheek]." "Father, forgive them."

He is, for some, a historical figure. Someone you read about in an old book with maddeningly thin pages. Someone who definitely belongs to the past.

He is, for some, the teacher of strict morals. "You have heard that it was said to those of ancient times . . . But I say to you. . . ."

He is, for some, a friend. "Come to me, all you that are weary and are carrying heavy burdens."

He is, for some, an itinerant storyteller who used simple beginnings and surprise endings. "There was a man who had two sons . . ." "Two men went up to the temple to pray . . ." "In a certain city there was a judge . . ." "Which of these three . . . was a neighbor to the man who fell into the hands of the robbers?"

He is many things to many people.

But, for Christians, Jesus is "the Messiah, the Son of the living God." This is an appellation which includes all of the above in some sense but also much more. It is a title that answers some questions but opens others. It is a confession that cuts to the heart of every matter and claims even the corners of our souls.

He came in flesh and blood, eternity wrapped in rags. He proclaimed and inaugurated God's kingdom. He died for us and was raised that we might live.

He is the One who made room in our lives for faith and the One in whom our faith is best placed.

Prayer: **Saving Lord, grant us the courage to make Peter's confession every day of our lives. Help us to place our trust in you and our hope in the Kingdom you proclaimed. Amen.**

THEOPHANY

August 26—September 1, 1996 **David W. Kerr✤**
Monday, August 26 Read Exodus 3:1-6.

"God took notice of them" (Exod. 2:25*b*). This announcement reveals God's compassion toward a helpless people. The words set the stage for today's reading as we see God's plan of intervention for the sons and daughters of Sarah and Abraham.

Traditionally the emphasis in today's reading underscores Moses' experience of theophany—the self-manifestation of God as God speaks to Moses out of "the flame of fire." We hear God calling him by name: "Moses, Moses!"

This unveils an important trait of God's nature: God seeks a relationship with people. To pursue this relationship with Moses, God invited him onto sacred turf. What are the implications for *our* faith? If God chose to speak to Moses out of a burning bush, where might a theophany be manifested for us today on our spiritual journey?

Let us be expectant! The good news reveals that God is continually initiating, always attempting to establish a relationship with us. "God took notice of them" is a theological statement as well as a historic reference. Amid our contemporary living as we, too, experience bondage, let us be assured that it is God's intention to call us each by name.

Prayer: **For your coming to us, for your knowing and calling us by name, O God, we thank you. In Jesus' name. Amen.**

✤Senior Pastor, Salem-in-Ladue United Methodist Church, St. Louis, Missouri. Previously, Director of Preaching Evangelism, General Board of Discipleship, The United Methodist Church.

Tuesday, August 27   Read Exodus 3:7-15.

We frequently hear the phrase *What's in it for me?* Somehow the human-divine dialogue in Exodus 3 seems to be an ideal spot to hear Moses uttering such a question; after all, God was asking Moses to sacrifice his life in the announcing of the divine plan before Pharaoh (v. 10).

While there are many implications in this fascinating reading, two in particular can be underscored. First, God's manifestation to Moses was not for Moses' personal glory. Moses was to tell others of the theophany in such a way that they could see the "why" behind this divine appearance. God established the human-divine encounter in order to exercise a purposeful call and mission for the remainder of Moses' life. The second important implication is that if we look carefully, we will discover a particularly striking picture of God. The biblical portrait depicts God as One who not only knows of human suffering, but even more significantly as One who is willing to become involved, to act as saving, redeeming Liberator for a helpless people. As my youngest son would say, "Awesome."

Through the movement of this second learning, may we be ever mindful of the implications. As Moses later struggles with his own response to God's call, it is important for us to realize God's assurance: "I will be with you." Throughout the pages of the biblical witness, from Genesis to Revelation, this promise of God's presence and help is continually repeated. We are to know that the theophany revealed in Exodus 3 is symbolic of God's ongoing intention. God seeks a relationship with us. This will be a purposeful relationship that will sustain us in purposeful living.

Prayer: **Amid the loneliness and brokenness of so many relationships, thank you, God, for your sustaining presence and love. In Jesus' name. Amen.**

Wednesday, August 28   Read Psalm 105:1-6, 23-26, 45c.

The call and mission of Moses is remembered throughout the Bible. Psalm 105 is an example of this.

This psalm is a community psalm of thanksgiving. Through the worship act of this psalm, the people carried forth the telling of the theophanies enjoyed by their ancestors. Their act of remembering was much more than a sterile remembering, more than a rote recitation. They believed God was continually reenacting the Exodus. Thus, through their language they were giving their contemporary community definition. By recalling the theophanies of old—"Remember the wonderful works he has done"—they sought reassurance of God's *ongoing* presence and love.

What implication does all of this have for our worship today? The Psalms were written in conformance with the Torah, the Law found in the first five books of the Hebrew scriptures. Similarly, doesn't our Christian worship conform to the church's earliest written witness in the Gospels and the Epistles? In using the language that helps us remember the New Testament theophany—of God manifest in Christ Jesus—do we have faith to believe that God is still coming, still calling, still empowering?

Paul wrote to the Corinthians these words: "I handed on to you as of first importance what I in turn had received" (1 Cor. 15:3a). God's manifestation in the death and resurrection of Jesus Christ was ongoing! Paul goes on to detail an account of the risen Lord's appearances to many, concluding, "Last of all, as to one untimely born, he appeared also to me" (15:8). Theophany!

Sacred space certainly can be anywhere. Wherever it is, let us know that in sacred space, and, yes, in the sacred space that is worship, we can *anticipate* theophany. For every theophany, for every anticipation of theophany, let us sing, "Praise the Lord!"

Prayer: As we remember your deeds, O God, may we anticipate their replication in our worship and service. In Jesus' name. Amen.

Thursday, August 29   Read Romans 12:9-13.

Whenever you see a "therefore" in Paul's writings, take notice. Such is the case in Romans 12:1. Paul's "therefore" references his arguments up to this point. He is stating that because of such theophany, we should eagerly live a life acceptable to God. It is our response to God's grace and mercy revealed in Jesus Christ. Verses 9-13 provide the detail of such a life.

In examining this unique life, let us magnify the particular type of love to which Paul refers. In Plato *eros,* another Greek word for love, symbolizes self-fulfillment, ecstasy. But, here in verse 9 Paul uses the Greek *agape*. This expression of love is not self-seeking but self-emptying. And so, hospitality will be more than mere wording in a mission statement. It will be the very emblem of the follower of the One who said, "Just as you did it to one of the least of these who are members of my family, you did it to me" (Matt. 25:40*b*).

Finally, what does Paul mean by "genuine"? The Greek word *anypokritos* denotes one who is "without hypocrisy." Paul is suggesting that this genuineness ("without hypocrisy") is a natural outgrowth of Jesus Christ's *agape*. Jesus did not put on a show for self-aggrandizement but instead "emptied himself, taking the form of a slave" (Phil. 2:7). The absence of hypocrisy rests on the transforming, justifying work of Jesus Christ. (See Romans 12:2, 3:26.) Genuineness is a gift that emerges by faith.

Prayer: O God, as your love surrounds us completely, we pray that others may come to experience your love as we reflect the theophany of your grace, given to us through Jesus Christ. Amen.

Friday, August 30   Read Romans 12:14-21.

Today's lesson from Romans bears similarity to the words found in the teachings of Jesus generally called the Sermon on the Mount (Matt. 5:1–7:27). Romans 12 begins with an image of persecution. It is followed with the petition to bless those who mastermind such cruelty. We can note how Paul has become a source through which the early apostolic memory of the Lord's teachings is being passed on: "But I say to you, Love your enemies and pray for those who persecute you" (Matt. 5:44). Paul did not cloak the theophany he had experienced, nor did he construct it to a private "blessing." He *openly* bore witness to his experience of the Risen One!

Whenever we see photos or newsreels or hear about persons killed or maimed by terrorist acts or by acts of war or by acts of racial hatred, we are confronted with the whole debate of retribution, that is, an "eye for an eye." (See Exodus 21:24; Leviticus 24:21*b*.) On the other side of the rushing desire to "get even" is the teaching that leaves no ambiguity: "Do not be overcome by evil, but overcome evil with good." We must become workers of God's good.

And so, let us yield to the biblical appeal that bids us take a higher road. In our respective lay and ordained ministries, may we be committed to actively promote the cause of justice and peace.

Prayer: **Bless, O God, those who because of their theophanies, their encounters of your divine peace, become peacemakers. In Jesus' name. Amen.**

Today's meditation was written following the tragic April 19, 1995 bombing of the Alfred P. Murrah Federal Building in Oklahoma City. It is presented in memory of those who died there and in honor of all persons who are actively passing on God's vision for justice and peace.

Saturday, August 31   Read Matthew 16:21-23.

"From that time on . . ." This reveals Jesus Christ's resolute focus. Principally, Christ's work was to show God's intimate identification with the suffering found in the human experience. God's words in our earlier Exodus reading were "I know their sufferings" (3:7). Jesus now embodies such language in his flesh. But beyond suffering and crucifixion is—yet to be revealed—resurrection! The human community is not left in desolation. Just as of old when God made possible the Exodus, so now, in Jesus Christ God continues to liberate and empower. Suffering and bondage will not have the last say!

Perhaps the most piercing words of the week's readings can be found in the Lord's statement to Peter: "You are a stumbling block to me"; yet, Jesus did not speak these words to Peter's ruination. You see, theophany is more than a onetime manifestation when we realize that Jesus is beckoning, "Follow me." God's Holy Spirit is continually revealing, reproving, and purifying as we are invited to take on the new clothing of Jesus Christ.

I recall the hour of conversation when a colleague, a diaconal minister, told me that her current church was not renewing her contract. In the difficult aftermath of this news, she revealed to me the example of what it means to live in harmony with God. Instead of bowing to a sense of defeat, she said, "God has never failed me, and I know God will sustain me through this trying time." Theophany! She knew God was alongside, identifying with her. This saint went on to claim the mystery of the Exodus and of Easter—freedom and resurrection! She believed she would not be left desolate. May our serving be accompanied by such strong faith in God's ongoing presence.

Prayer: **From this time on, O God, keep us focused on your divine call to enter the world's sufferings and to announce the Resurrection hope. In Jesus' name. Amen.**

Sunday, September 1   Read Matthew 16:24-28.

The scripture for today is one that is often quoted. Both Mark and Luke also write of these images. John uses such symbols as the towel and speaks of a servant ministry. All four Gospel writers offer a single strand of thought that is central to the church's theology. Authentic humanity does away with "me first" pursuits and discovers that ultimate meaning is connected to loving and serving God and neighbor. The church's peculiar symbol for this authentic living is the cross of Jesus Christ. Wherever I have traveled in the world, again and again I have seen the cross as the church's central sign.

Christ's message in the cross, his suffering and crucifixion, is to demonstrate how complete love can be. Jesus Christ loves us utterly. There is no boundary to the means he will undertake to express such solidarity with our circumstances. But it is because Christ is the "suffering servant"—who endured humiliation, degradation, and horrible pain and anguish—that we can hope and believe he is present to and with us in the agony of our pain and suffering.

Real trust is truly revealed in today's scripture. God is entrusting to us this divine message! God invites us to deny self and to receive the mantle of Christian ministry. If we say yes to God, we know not where such a calling will lead; but, we can be assured that God's Holy Spirit will surround us with the very power of the Exodus and of Easter. Praise the Lord!

Prayer: Theophany **is a good word, Lord, for it reveals your will to reveal yourself to us, to be here with us. Go with me as I seek to serve and bear witness to your appearing and to your pursuit of salvation for all people. In Jesus' name. Amen.**

SALVATION'S WAKE-UP CALL

September 2–8, 1996   **Carolyn E. Johnson✤**
Monday, September 2   Read Romans 13:11.

The watch alarm interrupted our laughter. It was time for our friend to leave. This was "family night" at home, and he had a lot to do in preparation. At least one night each week family together-ness had top priority amid many competing claims on the busy lives of our friend and his family. They treasured these special moments. As enjoyable as our group was, it was being replaced for moments far more significant.

Marking our spiritual journey are moments of good news; moments of relief and release; moments of insight, inspiration, and introspection; and moments of decision. Quantitatively a moment may seem insignificant relative to all moments that are ever to be—yet qualitatively each moment is precious; coming only once; never to be repeated, revisited, or changed. There are special spiritual moments so insightful in the profound truths revealed, so foundational in the depths to which faith becomes anchored, and so compelling in the courage and commitment they inspire. These are discerning, life-changing moments where meaning and direction are realized with new clarity.

Sometimes these moments awaken in us the call salvation demands on us. At these moments we are called to give renewed attention to our spiritual disciplines. These "salvation" moments, these "wake-up calls" embody both the instructive and sacrificial nature of salvation itself.

Prayer: **God, may this moment awaken us to your call on our lives. Amen.**

✤President, Women's Division, General Board of Global Ministries of The United Methodist Church; researcher at Purdue University; member, St. Andrew United Methodist Church, West Lafayette, Indiana.

Tuesday, September 3   Read Exodus 12:12-14.

The sacrificial moment: A call to remembrance

"Was that *really* me?" I asked myself while rummaging through a box of photos and mementos from my college days. A graduation tassel attached to some old letters caught my eye. I remembered wrapping the tassel around the letters as a reminder that graduation was made possible by the advice, support, and encouragement of my family. Rereading those letters brought a fresh appreciation of their love and care. I think about the sacrifices (although they would never have called them so) that my parents made to ensure a quality education. To them education was essential preparation for life. The tassel and letters became a reminder of the sacrificial moments undergirding the journey of maturation.

Forgetting can be a side effect of our busyness. Reminder notes, watch alarms, even the old string on the finger are symbols to refresh memory. As Christians, we have symbols that evoke memory and meaning . . . symbols which remind us of the sacrificial nature of the salvation moment. When we see the cross we remember who we are, where we have been, what has been given up for us, and the challenge of remaining faithful. Salvation is more than deliverance from bondage and sin. It is deliverance into a new life, an opportunity to be responsive to God's will for our lives; it is salvation *for* as well as salvation *from*. We must never forget in mind or heart what it has taken to become strong in the faith. From the precious lamb's blood on the Hebrew doorways to Jesus Christ, the Lamb of God dying for us, the sacrificial moment is a tangible expression of God's grace.

Suggestion for meditation: **Write a remembrance letter to yourself recalling sacrificial moments in your faith journey. What signs and symbols evoke these memories for you? Write these down or draw the symbols you picture.**

Wednesday, September 4   Read Romans 13:8-10.

The transforming moment: A call to love

What nothingness would we drift into if God's love were withdrawn? This is inconceivable. God is love . . . and it is this love and resulting grace on which our faith is anchored and our salvation based. God has promised continual love for us, and we are to love others. This is our debt.

Love is a unique debt, one we are not to try to pay off. Debt can sometimes be overwhelming and oppressive, creating a desire to be released from the burdens it brings. Even small debts, like owing someone dinner, a letter, or telephone call, can become a lingering weight. The willingness to be bound in love to others, because we are yoked in Christ, transforms the debt of love from burden to opportunity. We try to share with others that which God has so generously given to us—love, mercy, compassion, care, and respect. The yoke is not the burden but the means of managing and moving with life's ups and downs. In the same way that bills in the mail remind us of financial obligations, images of suffering awaken our senses as compassionate people.

Paul alerts us that fulfilling God's commandment to love is more than setting up complex laws. Laws can be followed without understanding their purpose or without a belief in their rightness, bringing about superficial changes but not a conversion of the heart. We Christians must be governed by the law of love, from which springs a concern for others which creates in us a constancy of loving behavior.

It is the law of love that calls us to understand that "neighbors" are those whose need places them in the residency of our hearts.

Suggestion for meditation: **Name some of the people who hold "residency in your heart." In your journal write a letter of love, expressing your compassion and concern about these people.**

Thursday, September 5   Read Matthew 18:15-20.

The redemptive moment: A call for respect

"Strike three, you're out!" yells the umpire. Like baseball, this passage might lead us to think there is a three-strikes-and-you're-out rule to repairing broken relationships. In salvation's call for reconciliation, the real issue is quality, not quantity, of effort.

Quality is measured by the *respect* we show for the dignity of the other; *tenacity* . . . we have to keep trying; and *sincerity* . . . we feel concern and communication about the issues at hand. Each try is a teaching/learning moment aimed at healing and renewal. We fail when we forget these standards.

Witness two women whose situations seem very different, yet are both relationship "strike-outs." The first woman had just received a public reprimand in front of colleagues and friends. Her tears were a mixture of anger, hurt, and embarrassment. The issue of what she had done took second place to the emotions of the moment. Afterwards, as people tried to provide comfort, she just kept saying, "Why wasn't I told in private before the meeting? Why?" The second woman was genuinely baffled, wondering what could have happened to cause cooling of the friendship. Whenever she asked her friend, the answer was, "Nothing's wrong," yet the distance became greater. Finally, the woman stopped trying to find out what had occurred. A friendship ended.

Correction and renewal are products of effort and communication. Our organizational and personal relationships are not well served if we retreat into silence instead of honestly and lovingly confronting those who have wronged us.

Salvation calls us to be reconciled with each other in Christ. There is no greater effort than this.

Suggestion for meditation: Think about your organizational and personal relationships. Are there strains? What additional effort or communications could take place? Prayer about this.

Friday, September 6   Read Exodus 12:1-11.

The preparatory moment: A call for discipline

Salvation calls us to a spiritually disciplined life. Preparation for living in the Kingdom requires both envisioning the big picture of God's plan for us and giving attention to the details of adhering to God's instructions for everyday living. At times, confident that we already know what to do, we resist following instructions, finding them cumbersome. Later, we wonder what went wrong when there are a handful of bolts left over and the assembled toy or furniture does not look like the picture on the box or work as it is supposed to.

Students were asked to take a "special" test requiring some rather unusual responses such as clapping their hands three times or standing up and walking around a chair. When starting the test, they were instructed to read through *all* the questions before responding to any of the items. Many failed to do that. If they had, they would have read the last item: "put down your pencil and do not take this test." Those who read and followed all the instructions had quite a chuckle watching their classmates do silly things. For those who disregarded the instructions, embarrassment was the expression of the moment.

Instructions are designed to ensure success for the task at hand. The reason for such detail may not be apparent until much later. Questions and creativity are still valued. Questions move our understanding to new depths, and creativity responds faithfully to God in these times. Jesus, the greatest teacher, instructed his followers in the life of discipleship. Moving from being controlled by the elements of the world to a self-control nurtured by the spiritual disciplines is one mark of discipleship. God's love has an instructive quality directing us in paths of the righteous life.

Prayer: **God, help me to become more disciplined, listening to your instructions and call. Amen.**

Saturday, September 7   Read Romans 13:11-14.

The urgent moment: A call for action

The alarm jolted us out of seats. Smoke pouring through the vents made us know this was not a drill; this was for real. Fire! Seemingly trapped in the top floor conference room of the high rise and in a country where another language was spoken only heightened the fear. Disbursing into the hallways, some rushed for the elevators, others for the stairwells. I went to the ladies room and thoroughly soaked the jacket to my "good suit." Covering my mouth with the jacket and staying low to the stairwell, I made it out just fine. From somewhere long ago lessons of fire safety were controlling my behavior. The "good" jacket was only as good as it could be surrendered and used for something more important. The priority was moving from a position of danger to one of safety.

If only it were easy to move from our current danger and crisis spots to positions of safety. Poverty, violence, children at risk, concerns for families, decaying morality and ethics, and many other issues capture our attention and demanding urgent action.

At times of urgency we may be sensitive to the necessity to act rapidly but not in panic. We sometimes are able to make rapid decisions utilizing all the spiritual lessons and disciplines at our disposal.

We enter into the "danger" spots with the full armor of Christ. We wear, in word, witness, and service, that which was Jesus . . . challenging injustice, bringing messages of hope to the downtrodden, teaching and sharing, feeding and nurturing, telling the good news. And we live lives where the excellence of our words is matched by the excellence of our example.

Prayer: Lord help us respond with urgency to the pressing cries of your people. Amen.

Sunday, September 8   Read Psalm 149.

The worship moment: A call for joy

"You got that for me, Daddy? Really?" the little girl exclaimed as they were walking into church. Looking up lovingly at her dad, she excitedly jumped up and down exclaiming, "You're the best daddy in the whole world—I love you this much!" stretching out her arms as wide as she could. He picked her up, and their mutual smiles reflected love and affection. We never found out what the gift was, but her joy was contagious, making us all smile.

Her joy came to mind later, as I sat in front as guest speaker. I watched the stern faces of the congregation. We had sung, prayed, and listened to scripture about the wondrous and redeeming nature of Jesus Christ; the enduring promises of God; the uplifting power of the Holy Spirit; and yet, the faces did not mirror the words. Remembering a friend's favorite saying, I reminded the congregation, "If you have the love of Jesus Christ in your heart, be sure to tell your face." It took a moment, but smiles started appearing, and chuckles and laughter began filtering through the group. What a difference it made looking at joyful faces! The seriousness of the message at hand was not diminished, nor was there any minimizing of the intensity about critical issues facing our lives.

God is worthy of praise and joy. This is not mere happiness caused by external factors but comes from the ability to have inner joy because we are a saved people. It is this joy that makes all the instructions and sacrifices understood in their fullest meaning— we are loved by God. This is our great joy and our salvation!

Prayer: God of our salvation and source of our joy, may the love in our hearts be expressed in all our being. "Praise the LORD, my soul! All my being, praise his holy name!" Amen. (Psalm 103:1, TEV)

1997

Now is the time to order your copy of
The Upper Room Disciplines 1997

Published for over 35 years, Disciplines is one of the most popular daily devotional books available. Year after year, Disciplines continues to appeal to more and more Christians who, like yourself, desire a more disciplined spiritual life. Be sure to order your copy today, while the 1997 edition is still available.

THE UPPER ROOM DISCIPLINES 1997
$7.95 each, 10 or more copies $6.76 each
Ask for product number UR747

To Order Your Copies,
Call: 1-800-972-0433
Tell the customer service representative your source code is 97D.

Or Write:
Customer Services
The Upper Room
P. O. Box 856
Nashville, TN 37202-0856

Shipping Charges:
On **prepaid orders,** we pay postage.
On **"bill me" later** orders, the shipping charges will be added to your invoice.

Please prepay, if your order is under $10.00.
All payment in U.S. funds, please.

THE UPPER ROOM DISCIPLINES 1997
is also available at most bookstores.

A COMMUNITY OF FAITH

September 9–15, 1996
Monday, September 9

Lonni Collins Pratt✤
Read Exodus 14:19-20;
John 1:5-9.

Two realities exist side by side in the world. Dark and Light. Evil and Good. This is not news to anyone who has lived long enough to encounter both realities. When injustice seems to reign, when night cuts dark and long, we easily forget the opposite reality.

"The cloud was there with the darkness, and it lit up the night; one did not come near the other all night." John put it another way, "The light shines in the darkness, and the darkness did not overcome it."

There is no getting around the reality. It gets dark sometimes. But that is not the end of the story. Against the darkness there always burns a pillar of fire.

You and I are sometimes called out to burn against the night. We are called to be, like John the Baptist, the one "sent from God, whose name is John," or Maria or Frank or whatever your name might be.

For the Hebrew people, a perilous probability stood behind the fiery pillar. No military campaign or human might could reach them through the night or across the great sea.

If there is a lesson to be learned on the shores of the Red Sea for the community of faith, it is that God alone will get us through the night. God is more than enough, more than we ever imagined. A surprise awaits those who expect impending doom. God is a saving God.

Prayer: **Cut into our darkness, Saving God, and give sight to our unseeing eyes. Amen.**

✤Freelance writer, speaker, and retreat leader; Lapeer, Michigan; associated with Saint Benedict Monastery in Oxford, Michigan.

Tuesday, September 10   Read Exodus 14:21-23.

Moses stretches forth his hand. It is human effort cooperating with God, and in the human ascent to God faith is birthed; faith against the threat. Moses, who is the leader of the community, is also the leader of faith. It is the example of the leaders Moses, Aaron, and Miriam that will build and encourage faith in the people.

For those who look to Moses in the face of crisis, it is crucial that they see the community leader walk to the edge of the raging waters, confront the danger, and lift his hand to cooperate with God in their deliverance. For all Christian leaders, this text calls us to consider whether or not we have shown this kind of courage and faith. Am I a woman who lifts my hand with God or against God? Do my actions resist God or support God's will? Will my response in the face of fear, injustice, and danger inspire those around me to confront the darkness?

What does my response say about what I expect God to be like? When I lift my hand in deliverance, in favor of justice and release, I witness to a faithful, saving God who delivers. This kind of leadership requires something from the one who leads. It means taking a position on the front lines, making the hard decision, maybe even looking foolish in the process.

It can feel like risky business when we follow God to the edge of the danger and look at its face with only God separating us from it. It reminds us of our helplessness. But the community of faith needs leaders and members who, if they are convinced of nothing else, are convinced of their helplessness and utter dependency on the God who saves.

Prayer: **Great God of the waters, move us with holy-inspired courage toward what we fear. Enable us to lift our hands to the tasks you set before us. Amen.**

Wednesday, September 11   Read Exodus 14:24-31.

We have all heard this story of the parting of the sea. We wonder how deep was the water, really? Is the story no more than part of a body of Hebrew legend? To a people of faith, these arguments miss the point.

The point is that we can trust God to care. God is involved with us. God does not abandon us. If we can count on anything, we can count on God to come through during the worst of times. God is a God of the impossible.

Here, in the middle of the sea on dry ground, is where the lessons of faith are learned. Here, trembling as we make our escape while the enemy shouts behind us, we discover the joyful reality of who God is and what God is like.

This knowledge pushes against much bad theology and legalistic notions about God as a punishing God. No! God delivers. God saves. God opens a way through the worst and rescues us. God is a saving presence for the pilgrim people.

If we focus on the logistics of the miracle of the parting of the sea (the facts and only the facts), we miss what is happening *in* the people of God. They are passing from death to life. They are being birthed by water and fire. The people of God are being called forth and named as God's own by the One who swirls winds and waters.

The building of community is inherent to these passages. While each person crossing over on dry ground is an individual, to God they are called together as one group, saved together, commissioned to be the *people* of God—a community. And here, in the passage often referred to in the New Testament as a type of baptism, they are baptized into God as a community.

Suggestion for meditation and prayer: **Ask yourself,** *How have I built community? Have there been times when I have dismantled genuine community?* **Ask God to show you the places and ways that you can be a loving, nurturing partner in community.**

Thursday, September 12   Read Exodus 15:1*b*;
                                                    Psalm 114.

These scripture passages are songs of rejoicing over God's saving power—how the worst of enemies is defeated by God's presence among God's people. But notice this: most of the celebration has the tone of those who are caught completely off guard.

There is an element of surprise in all this singing, as well as an inherent knowledge that singing and dancing, happiness and celebration, are rightful kinds of response in the presence of God. The people seem to have just discovered that God is a saving God.

What is the human response to this incredible revelation? Excitement! Enthusiasm! God can be counted on. God is a saving God. These women did not expect to be singing on the other side of the shore. Their image of God would never be the same. God is not some Tyrant in the Sky. God is not someone from whom we need to be saved. God is the One who saves us. "This is my God!"

Old images abandoned, the new birthed. A new possibility about God considered. The awesome idea that God—think about it!—*God* is on our side. With God we find not someone to appease, convince, or dread, but our Champion and Defender.

God is for us. And "if God is for us," as the Apostle Paul asserts, "who is against us?" (Rom. 8:31*b*) Compare the power resisting us to the One who resists evil. God will stop at nothing to save us; this is what the people of God have learned. So they are dancing and singing. Consider the incredible, too-good-to-be-true possibility: God will never settle for anything less than humanity rescued, humanity saved.

Suggestion for meditation: **What are my predominant images of God? Do my images of God give me reasons to celebrate? How would I be changed if I thought of and saw God differently?**

Friday, September 13   Read Romans 14:1-4.

A vital principle for any cooperating group is the respect of differences and distinctions among its members. The lections this week challenge us to honor and respect those who arrive at conclusions different from our own. This is not always an easy thing to do, especially when one's convictions go deep.

The key to genuine respect is a loving honor for others. When we love others, we are willing to admit that they, too, are loved by God.

We live our lives before God; we must live in honor of our calling, in gratitude for the gifts of God and God's salvation plan in our life. Because each of us lives with an awareness that it is ultimately God alone who marks our lives as valuable and significant, it is before God that we must let ourselves stand or fall. What seems legalistic, unnecessary, foolish, incomprehensible to one is crucial to another.

Christian love means loving the "other." The one who disagrees with you. The one who isn't like you. The one who doesn't live in your neighborhood, go to your church, dress like you dress, go to the same meetings, care about the same causes. It means listening to her, loving him, acknowledging that he or she is also responding to God.

If this is not how we love, then according to Jesus' teachings our loving is not any big deal. It is what everyone does, even those who are not following Jesus. If we are not continually learning to love more and more, we have missed the point.

Prayer: **Holy One, we have not loved as we ought to have loved. Our hearts and minds close easily against someone who is different from self. Infuse us with greater love—a love sent from above. Amen.**

Saturday, September 14   Read Romans 14:5-12.

We must allow others to need something we don't need. Part of accepting another person means letting that person be who he or she really is, including accepting his or her struggles to believe.

"Let all be fully convinced in their own minds." There is a peace of mind that comes with knowing what we know. But no one can do it for us. Conviction, when fully bloomed, makes human beings stand tall, act bravely, and resist oppression.

At the same time, we must remember that we are being saved *as a community* of faith. One friend told me how she cringes when she hears someone use the words *personal Savior*. She says the same Savior everyone else has is just fine for her.

The heart of community is honoring all persons as fully human and fully sacred, while living out and receiving the gifts and graces of individualism in the community. We neither deny our uniqueness nor insist on special rights. It is a balancing act, a gradual integration of the "we" and the "me." It is not easy, but it is the way God has chosen to save us.

We can survive on our own, but we will not move closer to the image God had in mind when God created humankind. That takes the challenges and joys of community.

Suggestion for meditation and prayer: **Think of a time you felt the need to convince someone of some point or conviction. Reflect on why it mattered so much to you. Ask God how you could have handled the situation differently. Ask God how you can demonstrate acceptance of those in your local community of faith.**

Sunday, September 15   Read Matthew 18:21-35.

Listen to Peter. He thinks he's being generous. "As many as seven times?" Not seven times, Peter. Think bigger, kinder, more lovingly and wildly, dear Peter.

This talk represents a new way of life that God is trying to establish, a new outpost. Those who live angry, get-even lives discover that the same is extracted from them. Anger breeds anger.

We are not the king in the story who gets to settle accounts. We are the slaves, our senses dulled from years of believing ourselves unworthy, unloved. We must be moved to compassion by the condition of our sisters and brothers. The king wants peace and a settling of accounts; the slave wants recompense.

The first person owes a debt to a great king, one who is mighty and powerful. The king can extract the worst kind of recompense but chooses not to do so. This is the choice of grace contrasted with the choice against grace.

All the passages we have read this week seem to be about community, life in community, and community values; about how we relate to one another and how we understand God. God has chosen to save us, to be gracious toward us, to love us. This seems to come as a surprise to those women and men who dance on the shores of the sea, alive rather than dead. We are called to give the gift we receive: grace.

Do we understand God as a God who will throw us to the torturers, or do we understand God as a saving God? Do we realize that we are being saved as a people? Community matters, this parable tells us. We are a saved community called to lift the burdens of those stooped under the weight of oppression, injustice, and sin. Grace is what the people of God are all about.

Prayer: **Gracious God, as we have been loved, let us love. As our arms open wide to receive your abundant grace, so let us show the same graciousness to a burden-laden world. Amen.**

GOD'S WONDERFUL GIFTS

September 16–22, 1996   **John F. Clifford✣**
Monday, September 16   Read Psalm 105:1-6.

It was a late August evening in West Texas. The hurricane was breaking up over the High Plains of the Texas Panhandle. Just before sundown, the clouds lifted from the horizon and the sun peeped through. Suddenly almost directly overhead was a full double rainbow, the brightest I have ever seen. Since the campsite was otherwise deserted, nobody heard my singing or saw the little jig I danced in the mist!

When was the last time you happened upon a breathtaking "wonderful work of God"? How did you respond to the realization that you were in the presence of the Lord?

We have become fairly well adjusted to technological marvels. Now, it seems, we reserve the term *acts of God* for whatever natural powers we cannot control. Storms, earthquakes, fires— these are the forces we identify with the Lord. Occasionally, even in storms, we can see signs of God's presence. Then we are called to sing praise!

For some, singing praise feels strange. So many people worship a judgmental, angry God, that to see God as good is very hard. Yet Christians declare it is so. We have "good news" to tell the world. We follow a gracious Savior!

The psalmist suggests that telling of God's wonderful works is the best way to praise our Lord. The two go together—the acts of God on behalf of a chosen people and the praise of the people in return. We look to the past to know the works God has done so we are attuned to discover the present works of God.

Prayer: **Lord, give us eyes to see your mighty works, voice to sing your praises, and the spirit to dance our joy! Amen.**

✣Pastor, First United Methodist Church, Mart, Texas.

Tuesday, September 17   Read Psalm 105:37-45.

It was my first pastorate. I was fresh out of seminary, in a new community, not at all confident in my ability, unsure even of the way to organize a worship service (I had taken history, not worship courses!) I settled in to see what would happen. The church had scheduled a dinner to welcome me that first Sunday night. Perhaps you know why, but I did not, and the "pounding" took me off guard. Each person brought a pound of some canned good or staple for the kitchen—a chancy thing to do for a young single man! But if these people wanted to stock the larder of the new preacher, I suspected they were on my side, and I took new confidence from that.

I suspect the Hebrews felt just as nervous about where Moses was leading them and just who this "Yahweh" he took orders from really was.

But the psalmist takes us directly to the "pounding." Look at the gifts of God's presence! Gold, silver, the guiding pillar of cloud and fire, and—most of all—food! and water! God isn't out to destroy but to sustain! The outcome is foregone—the people will come into the promise and the promised land. All that is in doubt is whether these people will keep the ways of the God who has been so bounteous to them.

Now do you understand the praise and joy of the people? Not only does God do wonderful and mighty works but God also cares for the people's most basic needs of food and water. God's grace and love truly never fail.

Prayer: **For the nurture of our souls and bodies, we give you thanks, O God. Amen.**

Wednesday, September 18   Read Exodus 16:2-8.

It's not unusual—it happened in our town this past fall. After building a tradition of winning football teams, a bad season came. As among the Israelites, there was murmuring among us. *We should have kept the previous coach* [who moved on his own initiative]; *this coach doesn't know what he is doing! Why did things have to change? We had it better in the "good old days"!*

Something is not right on this rescue mission God is orchestrating, and the people are nervous. They want to be reassured, to know that God really is up to the tasks they face, that they are not getting themselves into a worse situation than they experienced as slaves in Egypt.

And so they approach Moses, their leader—the one who has been speaking with God and arranging all the details of this trek. Moses speaks to God. And God responds with the most reassuring of gifts—food! They will find enough to last them each day, and it will be continually renewed. What more can they ask?

Even today we murmur against the Lord and against all the powers that be around us. We want reassurance. We want a sign. But when we complain, we need also to look for the ways God may be trying to answer us—the manna of those nurturing gifts that we too often overlook when we are busy complaining. God does not let us down—we merely forget how to see God's blessings.

Prayer: **Lord, help us take time out from our murmuring to look for the gifts you put in our world today. Amen.**

Thursday, September 19   Read Exodus 16:9-15.

My wife came to Texas from New York, and I continue to try to educate her in the delights of Mexican food. Often she will ask questions like, "What's in it? How do you eat it?" and, most important of all, "How spicy is it?" Dealing with the unknown is always a source of uneasiness and questions.

Or murmuring. When we stop to consider how unfamiliar to the Israelites is the wilderness in which they have found themselves, we may have a better feeling for the distrust they show. They do not know how to survive here—they have spent their lives in the Nile Valley, not wresting a living from the desert. They do not know whether Moses can do any better for them. And they really have not come to trust the Lord who has called them to come to this desolate place.

What they need to restore their confidence is a miracle. And so Moses and Aaron call them together and announce one. They will have food! Not entirely familiar, perhaps, but nourishing—quails flocking to be caught, and this strange new food they called "manna." "What is it?" they ask. Moses tells them—"This is the sign of God you asked for, the miracle that assures you of God's presence. It is the bread that the Lord has given."

Well, there you have it! God does not abandon this people, but rather shows mercy in yet another wonderful gift.

Prayer: **Almighty God, even when we are in new or strange places, help us remember your presence with us, your love to bless us and care for us. Amen.**

277

Friday, September 20   Read Matthew 20:1-16.

The computer age has taught us to think in binary terms—in an either one or zero, on or off, this or that, and either/or frame of mind. This is, of course, not the only way to see the world; many things are better seen as a spectrum of choices. But some things *are* either one or the opposite, with no middle ground.

When we think of Jesus' parable of the workers in the vineyard, hired by the master throughout the day, we are encouraged to think in spectrum terms. After all, we are told of the various hours of engagement, and the way the master went back repeatedly to see if more workers were available. Certainly this leads us to see this as a parable about levels of service, doesn't it?

And then the payoff comes, and each worker receives the same pay, the same denarius as every other. *What's going on?* we wonder. This is a parable we have trouble with, for it offends our sense of justice. We think of equal pay for equal work. We believe in moving up the employment ladder to "reach the top." What Jesus describes in the parable is truly a mystery, something we do not understand.

But what if the coin of the realm is God's grace? Can this be divided? Or is it something that either is or is not accepted? It does not matter *when* we receive God's gift, we will receive all of it, for it cannot come any other way. The first receive all of it, and the latecomers receive no less. Is our Lord suggesting that we either take the grace offered or we do not, and that *when* does not matter? God continues to amaze us with love and care!

Prayer: **O God, your grace continues to astound us; but help us rejoice in it today. Amen.**

Saturday, September 21   Read Matthew 20:1-16.

Our workaholic culture is busy with "production" all the time. Work itself becomes an idol. And so it is only cautiously that we look at the idea Jesus presents in this parable. While God rewards all the workers equally, only those who accept God's offer and "work in the vineyard" are paid. Certainly others were with them when they were offered the work; what of those who preferred not to take the offer?

It seems, you see, that receiving God's gifts, God's grace, demands both a response of faith and a response of service. To say "I'll work for you, Lord," but not head for the fields, hoe and pruning hook in hand, is a false acceptance, not to be graced. It is by leaving the sidelines for the action that we put ourselves in the presence of grace.

The people of Israel learned God's presence most when they left Egypt behind. Whoever stayed there lost the promise; those in the wilderness nurtured and shared it. The workers who went to the vineyard received the wages of a gracious God.

Prayer: **Lord, help us be in the places you visit and to respond with our whole hearts and minds and souls and strength. In Jesus' name. Amen.**

Sunday, September 22   Read Philippians 1:21-30.

The Christmas shopping frenzy is now three months away. There will be voices encouraging us to consider alternative gifts of various sorts. (After all, I have enough after-shave to last several years . . .) How should we respond to God's loving gift of a Savior, the most wonderful of all God's blessings? What is the best way to acknowledge the gracious care God has shown us?

Paul struggles here. He is anxious to be with Jesus, in the heavenly kingdom. But he realizes that the most fitting response to God's grace is to share the gift of love he has received.

This is why Paul puts up with the suffering and difficulties of his missionary trips, going from town to city to preach the gospel. He has Christ to share, to give away, and nothing else matters (as he told the Roman church). This is why he encourages others to live lives worthy of their Lord: those much blessed are called to be great givers—not so much of material things, for few early Christians seem to have had much, but of the love and mercy Jesus has given them.

What better way to recognize God's wonderful gifts to us than to share them as widely as possible? Truly God has blessed us in wonderful ways!

Prayer: **O God, may we have our senses alert to the many ways you have been with us wherever we have been. In Jesus' name. Amen.**

THE NECESSARY HUMILITY OF GOD'S PEOPLE

September 23–29, 1996   **Ruth Heaney✚**
Monday, September 23   Read Exodus 17:1-7.

This week's readings begin with a complaint. Unfortunately, it was not the first that the Israelites had lodged against Moses because they had no water, nor would it be the last (see Exodus 15:22-27 and Numbers 20:1-13).

Note that when God sweetened the water at Marah, he gave the people a statute and an ordinance. It was not a promise to see that the Israelites got whatever they wanted whenever they wanted. Yet the Israelites seemed to have interpreted it that way, for now it was as if God had failed them.

The people once again found fault with Moses' divinely appointed leadership. "Why did you bring us up out of Egypt, to kill us and our children and our cattle with thirst?" (RSV)

Worse yet, despite all the miraculous things God had done for them, they dared to ask, "Is the LORD among us or not?" (RSV) It was an outward eruption of an inner rebellion.

What ignorant, arrogant people these ancient Israelites were! we may think. If we do, we overlook frightening instances in our own lives when we have questioned God's love and purpose—even God's presence.

Prayer: **Lord, sometimes, I, too, need water—your living water. Remind me that the Source is always with me, leading me by day and by night. Strengthen my faith that I may follow you without doubt or fear. Amen.**

✚Christian writer; Wenonah, New Jersey.

Tuesday, September 24   Read Psalm 78:1-8.

Although Psalm 78 is not listed as one of the wisdom psalms, (such as Psalms 1, 3, and 112), in today's verses it has the tone of one. We see in verses 1-4 an intention to use Israel's history to teach a spiritual lesson.

Asaph, David's appointed choir leader (1 Chron. 16:4-7), quite possibly was the author of this psalm. In it he set history to song in an attempt to instruct. Clearly, he wanted his contemporaries to learn this lesson well enough to pass it down to their children.

People will remember more if details are presented in a catchy manner that encourages repetition. How many TV commercials can we recite without even wanting to? But the same is equally true of weightier matters. Consider Henry Wadsworth Longfellow's poem "Paul Revere's Ride":

> Listen, my children, and you shall hear
> Of the midnight ride of Paul Revere . . .

Psalm 78 is a *maskil* (*maschil*), meaning an artistically composed song with didactic (teaching) elements.* Because of its composition it required greater skill to perform. Because of its wide vocal range, most of us cannot comfortably sing "The Star Spangled Banner," yet we recall the history of which it tells.

Only part of Asaph's intentions are clear in these first verses of the psalm. As the psalm continues, God's people will be humbled as they are forced to recall their sinful disobedience.

Prayer: **Lord, teach me a song of the history of the people of faith to whom I belong. Help me to remember that my own past was not as glorious as I want to claim, that my accomplishments are but reeds shaken by the wind when compared to you. Amen.**

---

*See notes on Psalm 32:1-11, p. 827, *The HarperCollins Study Bible,* New Revised Standard Version, copyright © 1993 HarperCollins, Publishers, Inc.

Wednesday, September 25   Read Psalm 78:12-16.

Historical accuracy has apparently given way to poetic license in the verses prior to today's reading (vv. 9-11). The Ephraimites, already introduced to us in 1 Chronicles 12:30 as "mighty men of valor" (RSV), now come under attack by the psalmist. Perhaps Asaph had lumped together the northern tribes and called them Ephraimites as he recalled the events of Judges 1:27-36. Why should he target only Ephraim when Manasseh, Zebulun, Asher, and Naphtali also failed to drive out all the Canaanites?

A possible explanation given by some theologians is that the choir leader is using the term *Ephraim* to refer to the entire Jewish nation for failing to attack the land of Canaan (see Numbers 14:1-9). Verses 67-68 of the psalm, however, make that theory somewhat questionable.

Although the identity of Ephraim remains unclear, the results of Ephraim's actions do not. Today's reading begins the humbling recitation of all the miraculous events that Ephraim forgot. One cannot help but wonder if Asaph had lapsed into gross exaggeration at this point. How could any group possibly forget a sea divided, a guide formed from cloud and fire, a drink from a rock?

This prodding picks up again in verses 23-29 and verses 42-45 and is followed by God's resultant punishments (see verses 59-64). Yet Psalm 78 concludes on a tremendously reassuring note. Despite the fact that Ephraim forgot, God does not.

Suggestion for meditation: **The quality of my life is enhanced by a continuous thread of blessings that God weaves throughout my earthly days. Some of these blessings are miraculous, others minute. All are essential. I will spend time in the Lord's presence today specifically recalling with gratitude the abundant blessings I have been granted from the Lord.**

Thursday, September 26   Read Philippians 2:1-11.

The Philippian church was in danger of splitting because of two quarreling women. Both Euodia and Syntyche were important to Paul because they were former co-workers of his and obviously committed Christians. Unable to be there in person to mediate the quarrel, Paul begged a third church member, addressed only as "true yokefellow," to help these women reach an agreement (Phil. 4:2-3, RSV).

As an interesting parallel to today's reading, note that in his letter to Corinth, Paul was forced to attack the very same problem of self-exaltation as that which arose at Philippi. To the Corinthians he decided to handle it by pointing out how vitally necessary it was for the body of Christ to be diverse (1 Cor. 12:12-21). Here, in his letter addressed to the Philippians, Paul chose to stress the importance of single-mindedness.

A careful analysis of these letters reveals that the two views are not contradictory. There is, after all, nothing more solidly unified in function than the various parts of one human body. Conversely, there is nothing more richly diversified than a common mind-set when it is shared by many different personalities.

For the church of Christ to flourish, Paul obviously felt that its members need to differ in responsibilities, gifts, and talents while maintaining the same focus.

To refocus the church at Philippi, Paul pointed to the supreme example of Jesus' selfless humility. Humility was the cohesive force needed to bond diversity and single-mindedness.

Prayer: **Lord, the church at Philippi is so very far away in culture and in time. Yet I can look across that distance and see a church that is frighteningly like many in America now. Teach us in this country, in this year, how to wear the humility of Christ so that we can lead by serving. Amen.**

Friday, September 27   Read Philippians 2:12-13.

My copy of the Revised Standard Version Bible gives the heading that precedes today's verses as "Obligations of Christians." There is an assumption here on which these obligations rest, and it is simply this: We can only work out of ourselves what God has already worked into us.

The reason we know this to be true is the issue of salvation mentioned in verse 12. Personal salvation is not something for which we can take credit. "For by grace are ye saved through faith; and that not of yourselves: it is the gift of God: not of works, lest any man should boast" (Eph. 2:8-9, KJV).

In like manner, we can in no way boast about the Kingdom work we accomplish for the Lord. We are incapable of performing any service unless the Lord has worked into us both the will and the gifts to accomplish it.

Why, then, the "fear and trembling" that Paul recommends in working out one's salvation? It might be helpful to compare Paul's use of the same expression in 1 Corinthians 2:3 where he applied it to his feelings when he met the Corinthians for the first time. In 2 Corinthians 7:15 he used it to describe the emotions of the Corinthians when they initially welcomed Titus.

There is nothing more humbling—or more comforting—for Christians than the realization that God never intended for us to meet our obligations in the natural or the external. Our obligations are to be the fulfillment of a spiritual trust that has already been worked within us by God.

Prayer: **Lord, thank you for working salvation into each of us, for desiring life not death for every person. Help me to "work out my salvation" so that the things I say and do will convince those who need you of your love and desire for them. Amen.**

285

Saturday, September 28   Read Matthew 21:23-27.

Not immediately apparent but crucial to the question raised in verse 23 is the fact that Jesus had driven the money-changers from the Temple the previous day (vv. 12-13). Not a member of the Sanhedrin, not an "ordained" rabbi, not even an accredited teacher, Jesus had clearly overstepped his bounds this time.

He might have gotten away with such flagrant behavior if the authorities had been willing to concede that Jesus at least appeared to be a prophet of God. Instead, they tried to persuade those who flocked after Jesus that he was nothing more than a dangerous rebel. And now this rebel had dared to draw a line in the dirt.

A confrontation was unavoidable. "By what authority are you doing these things, and who gave you this authority?" (RSV) If Jesus claimed an earthly authority, he would be reported to Rome. If he claimed a heavenly authority, he would be accused of blasphemy.

Instead, employing a popular teaching tool used by the rabbis themselves, Jesus answered their question with a question. "The baptism of John, whence was it? From heaven or from men?" (RSV)

Given the opportunity to discover the truth for themselves, the chief scribes and elders decided to ignore it. They deliberately chose the path of evasiveness. "We cannot tell," they answered. (KJV) Torn between truth and prestige, they opted for the latter. By doing so, they lost both.

Prayer: **Lord, draw me to your word with such a hunger that I cannot possibly stay away from it. I need to see your truth more clearly and, having seen it, to step out in obedience. Amen.**

Sunday, September 29   Read Matthew 21:28-32.

Today's reading is a simple parable of two sons and two responses. Son number one replied to his father's request, "I will not." Son number two said, "I go, sir."

We are, however, left to draw inferences about both sons. The second son's response could have meant one of two things. He was either lying and had no intention of going to the vineyard or he was telling the truth. If the latter was the case, he somehow got waylaid. If the former, we can only conclude that this son was either uncommitted to his father or to the proposed assignment.

The first son seemed to exhibit a definite lack of commitment. "But afterward he repented" (KJV). In this parable, Jesus didn't mention the quality of the first son's work when he finally got to the vineyard or how long he remained at the task. Was this, perhaps, a deliberate omission?

The parable's application appears to be simply the fact that the first son *tried* to obey his father. Although a seemingly clear application, the danger lies in assuming that we are obeying our heavenly Father when, in reality, we are not.

The scribes and Pharisees, ever obedient to their Temple rituals, had gotten so mired down in formality that they began to ignore God's will. Jesus' disciples, on the other hand, were a worldly lot that included tax collectors and harlots. They, however, *obeyed* the Lord and went into his vineyard to work. To these "misfits" he gave the keys to the Kingdom of heaven (see Matthew 16:19).

Suggestion for meditation: **My noblest intentions are meaningless unless I carry them out. If I never progress beyond the planning stage, is this an indication that I don't trust God? that I think I know better than God does? Where does repentance fit in? Is this the necessary first step to laying down certain burdens and clearing my heart to follow God's will? When was the most recent time that I repented and received God's cleansing grace?**

KNOWING AND DOING GOD'S WILL

September 30—October 6, 1996   **William E. Smith**✤
Monday, September 30   Read Exodus 20:1-4.

By what standards do we live? What values do we hold most dear? Do they reflect the sensate culture and moral relativism of our time, or are they rooted in the will of God?

The giving of the Law to Moses reminds us that God is the transcendent One whose presence is made known in the crucible of history. God leads the children of Israel from slavery to freedom, provides for their care in the wilderness, and communicates the divine will to Moses.

God also shows a clear desire to live in a closer relationship with Israel, specially called to be the people of God. "You shall have no other gods . . ." was difficult for the people to accept, surrounded, as they were, by pagan deities. We, too, are lured by the gods of material success, power, and privilege.

The price of rebellion then and now is estrangement from God and from our better selves. When will we learn that obedience to God alone brings true freedom and lasting joy?

Prayer: **Help us to reject the false gods that claim our loyalty but lead to destruction. Restore us to singleminded devotion to you, O Lord, in whose will is our peace. Amen.**

✤United Methodist clergy, Pinehurst, North Carolina; retired professor, The Divinity School, Duke University, Durham, North Carolina.

Tuesday, October 1　　　　　　　　Read Exodus 20:7-9.

Israel was to be a community separated from the world and consecrated to the service of God. It was in this covenantal context that the Decalogue was given: "You shall be for me a priestly kingdom and a holy nation" (Exod. 19:6). The keeping of the Law, that is, the doing of God's will, defined the identity of the Israelites and demonstrated their relationship with God.

"You shall not make wrongful use of the name of the LORD your God." You shall not invoke God to perform magical tricks for your benefit or call down divine wrath upon your enemies. God does not wait for our beck and call. God's name, God's very being, is holy and must not be besmirched by association with the profane.

The sanctity of the Jewish Sabbath was made very clear to me during my recent visit to Jerusalem. On the Sabbath, room service was suspended in our hotel; only a cold buffet supper was served. Businesses were closed. No work was done. It was a holy day. Families with young children gathered in the hotel lobby. They were having a delightful time. I must confess I envied them when I returned to a secular culture in which keeping the Sabbath holy seems so very quaint.

Prayer: **We thank you, Lord, that every day is holy because it is a gift from you. Enable us also to boldly reserve special times for rest, for worship, and for loved ones—thus, may we remember who and whose we are. Through Christ our Lord. Amen.**

Wednesday, October 2   Read Exodus 20:12-20.

The rampant moral confusion of our times begs a question: How can we restore a sense of right and wrong, of moral accountability to God and humanity?

Fashioning a stable society begins at home. Who we are and how we function as adults are shaped by our relationships in childhood and youth. For parents there is no nobler task than rearing children.

The basics of moral accountability begin in the Ten Commandments.

No murder! Do no violence directly or indirectly to or against anyone. That is God's uncompromising word to all people in all times and places.

No adultery! This corrective is desperately needed in an era when sex, separated from love, responsibility, and commitment, is viewed as an end in itself. "Enjoy the moment with whomever" must give way to "those whom God has joined together . . ."

No stealing! No lies! Integrity before God and one another is absolutely essential. The people of God are to be trustworthy!

No coveting! Envy has been described as "sorrow at another person's good fortune." Covetousness corrodes the human spirit. Envy, jealousy, greed—by whatever name we call covetousness—spoils interpersonal relationships. The more I focus on my desires, the less I am concerned with what God wills. Do not covet, even in your fantasies, that which is another's.

In these commandments we find the moral foundation essential in every age for building a stable society.

Prayer: **Create in me, O Lord, the desire to obey your will in all things and so discover the joy of those who live in harmony with you and humankind. Through Christ our Lord. Amen.**

Thursday, October 3   Read Psalm 19.

Psalm 19 originally consisted of two distinct parts: the first extols God's glory in creation (vv. 1-6); the second celebrates the wonder of God's Law (vv. 7-14). At some point these two parts were brought together in praise of the Lord of creation and the Law.

The words in verses 1-4 recall the glorious anthem from Haydn's *Creation*: "The heavens are telling the glory of God." There is a language, unheard by human ears, that nature speaks in celebration of God's handiwork. There is a perpetual anthem sung night and day, extolling God the Creator. Poetic imagery? Indeed, and speaking a universal language: "The hand that made us is divine."

The next two verses make me want to ask, Have you seen the sun rise out of the mists like a big, orange ball? Have you traced its course across the heavens until it sets in the depths of the sea, while clouds reflect its rays long after it disappeared? We see God the Creator in the majesty and mystery of creation.

Verses 7-10 tell us that God is also revealed through the Law, which expresses the divine will. The psalmist heaps words of praise both for what the Law is (perfect, sure, simple, right) and for what the Law does (rejoicing the heart, enlightening the eyes, and so forth).

Yet for all his gratitude the psalmist knows that the Law also condemns: "Clear me from hidden faults." Hidden from God? Not likely, but perhaps from one's own memory. This acknowledgement of hidden faults leads to earnest petition: "Save me, Lord, from overweening self-confidence, like the insolent who flaunt their sins. Let them not run or ruin my life! Then hopefully I can live up to your commandments" (AP).

The psalm ends with a very personal prayer: "May these words that come from the depths of my being be as acceptable to you as a temple sacrifice, O Lord, my rock and my redeemer" (AP).

Prayer: **O Lord, be thou our Rock and our Redeemer. Amen.**

Friday, October 4   Read Philippians 3:4*b*-14.

Does being a Christian mean we can forget the Law given in the Hebrew scriptures? Not according to Paul. He himself was a Jew: of the tribe of Benjamin and a Pharisee. But "whatever gains I had in being a legalist," said Paul, "I count as *rubbish* that I may gain Christ and be found in him" (AP). Righteousness now comes not from the Law but through faith in Christ.

Here is the key to salvation and the heart of Christian morality. *Knowing Christ* and being found *in him* go beyond the Law. Now my goal as a Christian disciple is no longer to display my virtue by outward performance ("a righteousness of my own that comes from the law") but to be open to a deeply personal relationship with Christ (a "righteousness from God based on faith"). For Paul this is a mystical experience: "It is no longer I who live, but it is Christ who lives in me" (Gal. 2:20). Being *in Christ*, dying to sin and rising again with him to newness of life, results in fruits of righteousness, good works. Doing good deeds does not make one righteous. Because one is righteous, having been redeemed by Christ, one will do good deeds!

Does this mean, Paul, that you have reached perfection? Paul would answer, "By no means!" In language reminiscent of a race in which the prize is displayed very prominently at the point where the race will end, he declares:

> One thing I do . . . is to forget what is behind me and do my best to reach what is ahead. So I run straight toward the goal in order to win the prize, which is God's call through Christ Jesus to the life above. (TEV)

Prayer: **Grant, O Lord, that we may "run with perseverance the race that is set before us, looking to Jesus, the pioneer and perfecter of our faith."***

---

*Hebrews 12:1-2

Saturday, October 5   Read Matthew 21:33-40.

Jesus told this parable during the final days of his earthly ministry. Included in all three Synoptic Gospels, it anticipates Israel's rejection of Jesus as the Messiah and Jesus' acceptance as the Messiah by his disciples who became the church. By the time the Gospels were written, animosity between Jews and Christians, and especially between Jewish converts and those Jews who rejected Christ, had become intense; and this scripture passage may well reflect that tension (compare Acts 13:44-46).

Isaiah 5:7 spoke of Israel as "the vineyard of the LORD of hosts" from whom God expected justice, "but saw bloodshed; righteousness, but heard a cry!" Violence, then as now, was a way of life.

There is unrelieved pathos in this story, the ending of which is never in doubt. Although entrusted with the stewardship of the vineyard, the tenants looked to their own interests first. They rejected the owner's servants and even killed his son, hoping, somewhat incredulously, to inherit the property.

What will happen to the wicked sharecroppers? Judgment will be swift and sure (see tomorrow's meditation). What of our own stewardship? When the owner comes, will we be found faithful?

Christ has a way of forcing decisions: "Whoever is not with me is against me" (Matt. 12:30). "Everyone who hears these words of mine and acts on them will be like a wise man who built his house on a rock" (Matt. 7:24).

Prayer: **Gracious Lord, save us from rejecting him who was sent to be our Savior. Remind us that Christ's worst enemies are those who know better but habitually make wrong choices. Lord, have mercy. Amen.**

Sunday, October 6   Read Matthew 21:40-46.

The story of the wicked tenants ends with swift retribution. Remember, these are hard sayings; Jesus was keenly aware that he would be rejected by his own people, and he did not mince words.

"Have you never read the scripture?" he asked, as if to say, "Have you who pose as authorities ever exposed your beliefs and practices to the searching light of God's will?" If they had, they would have discovered that the prophets repeatedly foretold the destruction of the sinful nation (Isa. 5:1-7; Hos. 10:1-6; Jer. 2:20*ff*). Psalm 118, which foretells that the rejected stone will become the cornerstone (v. 22), is also the source of the Messianic welcome as Jesus entered Jerusalem: "Hosanna, blessed is the one who comes . . ." (v. 26).

The showdown is near and the stakes are high. At the moment Jesus has the upper hand. The Temple functionaries, realizing that Jesus was referring to them in his parables, stopped short of having him arrested because the crowds regarded him as a prophet. How quickly that would change!

There is judgment here for those who reject Jesus. While the scripture clearly refers to the Christian church replacing the old vineyard (Israel) and bearing "produce at the harvest time," we must beware of self-righteousness, the very attitude that rejected Jesus. Our righteousness must not be like that of the Pharisees! We must also take care not to use this passage to support anti-Semitism. Christ, himself a Jew, bids us love our neighbors as ourselves and thus love God, in whose image all are made.

Prayer: **Gracious Lord, we thank you for Jesus Christ, the chief cornerstone upon whom rests the whole structure of our faith. Help us to follow him with such conviction and courage that we may know and do his will always. Amen.**

STANDING IN THE GAP

October 7–13, 1996 **Steve Harper**✣
Monday, October 7 Read Psalm 106:1-6, 19-23.

"I don't know what I would have done without you." Words like these remind us of the indispensable role people play at critical moments to affect our lives. Every passage in this week's readings reveals a crisis that must be faced and God's provision of someone to address it. As we journey through our texts, we will see the grace of God using people to stand in the gap. We will hear a challenge to open ourselves to being used in this way for the sake of others.

The psalmist has given a lengthy account of Israel's sins, confessing that "both we and our ancestors have sinned." The history of God's people has been a roller coaster of highs and lows. There were moments of great deliverance (vv. 8-12) and periods of deep darkness (vv. 13-22). At the time when destruction was imminent, Moses stood in the gap, turning away God's wrath.

If we look closely at each of this week's texts, we see that "forgetfulness" is at work in one way or another. At such times in our own lives, we need someone who can remind us about what is right and who will pray that we will get the message. People who stand in the gap are not always appreciated or followed, but they are means of grace through whom God awakens us and sets us back on the true path. In the next three readings we will see some of the circumstances in which we need another's help. As we draw the week to a close, we will discover how we stand in the gap for others.

Suggestion for prayer: **Think of any persons who have stood in the gap for you, persons whom God has used to renew or redirect your life. Give thanks to God for each one by name. Thank God that you are not left to face life's difficulties alone.**

✣Executive Director, A Foundation for Theological Education; founder of Shepherd's Care ministry to ministers; Lexington, Kentucky.

Tuesday, October 8   Read Exodus 32:1-10.

The people of Israel were vulnerable when Moses delayed in returning from the mountain. They made an idol they could worship as a substitute for the Lord. People and priests alike found themselves offering worship at counterfeit altars.

Are we in danger of idolatry when God does not seem to come through on time or according to our expectations? Do we manufacture our own golden gods to make up for the real thing? Do we exert pressure on our religious leaders to provide god-substitutes when direct contact with the living God is eclipsed? These are serious questions raised as we read about the experience of our Israelite ancestors.

We have seen the rise of the gospel of prosperity. It makes materialism an almost-literal golden calf. We have experienced the "celebrity syndrome" in Christianity, which appears to leave little room for ordinary people with unspectacular testimonies. We have become enamored with mega churches that too easily mimic the "bigger is better" mindset of the fallen world. We support a multi-million dollar "Christian market" that keeps an endless line of products coming our way. We do not like to have to wait for God; we want something new and immediate. We prefer stimulation over obedience. We are not as far from the campfires of the Exodus revelry as we might think.

Like our spiritual ancestors we need someone to stand in the gap—to save us from our own idolatry. We need a Moses who can call us back to faith in the one, true God.

Prayer: **O God, open our eyes to the making of our golden calves today. Forgive us for our idolatries, which shout out a distrust of you. Cleanse us from our sin of chasing after God-substitutes. Send us priests and prophets and ordinary persons of faith who will bring us back to our senses. Amen.**

Wednesday, October 9   Read Philippians 4:1-9.

A major Protestant denomination surveyed its clergy, asking what they most needed help with. The number-one response: "We need help with conflict management." This same denomination reported that it spent more money on hospitalization of clergy for "stress-related illness" than on any other item. Disagreements in the church wear us down and exact a high price.

The Philippian church's problem is ever with us! Conflict between the Euodias and Syntyches continues to plague the church. We are not told what the nature of the conflict was, but it was significant enough for Paul to urge a reconciliation. His pastoral heart could not rest knowing there was unresolved division in one of his favorite congregations.

We must not miss the fact that both Euodia and Syntyche are clearly identified as Christian leaders. They were Paul's fellow strugglers, his co-workers in the ministry of the gospel "whose names are in the book of life." We must not make the mistake of defining all conflict as having its spiritual and un-spiritual parties. Even sincere Christians can vigorously disagree about things, as these two women appear to be doing.

Nevertheless, someone is needed to stand in the gap. Euodia and Syntyche have apparently lost the ability (and the will?) to achieve reconciliation by themselves. Paul calls on a loyal companion to be that person. His task is to help the women "be of the same mind in the Lord."

Verses 4-9 provide a prescription for conflict resolution. Rejoicing, gentleness, prayer, foregoing worry, seeking God's peace, and thinking of lofty things are appropriate courses of action for those caught in the downward spiral of disagreement.

Prayer: **Great Shepherd, when disagreement divides us, send us persons who can bring us back into the one fold that we may breathe again the air of your grace. Amen.**

Thursday, October 10   Read Matthew 22:1-14.

"That's no reason, that's just an excuse!" Words like these tell us that people are trying to weasel out of some responsibility. Each person in today's reading had been previously contacted. Sometime earlier each had said in effect, "Yes, I'd like to be at the banquet. Let me know when it's ready."

They did not mean it, for when the servants were sent out to say the banquet was ready, everyone backed out. Matthew shows what was really going on by saying, "They made light of it and went away." Their problem was not an unexpectedly crowded schedule; it was a failure to commit in the first place. A second invitation only intensified their rejection, including the murder of the messengers.

God takes seriously our stated intentions. In the end, a superficial commitment is worse than no commitment at all.

This story reveals another great irony. Whereas we have seen God's provision of someone to stand in the gap in our two previous lessons, today there is no one to do so. The story has a ghostly silence about it as God leaves the pretenders to themselves and to the consequences of their fate. Sometimes the only thing that stands between us and disaster is the integrity of our own words and actions. Sometimes no one comes to the rescue.

The invitees had violated their consciences for so long that they were double-minded, double-tongued, double-intentioned. They perished under the weight of their own superficiality, confirming the saying "A man's only as good as his word."

Prayer: **God, you are Word and you take words seriously. Work in me through your Spirit that my words and my deeds may work in harmony. Save me from debilitating superficiality and from believing that I can say one thing and do another without consequence. Amen.**

Friday, October 11   Read Matthew 22:1-14.

This reading is a difficult one. It does not have a happy ending. It flies in the face of cultural religion that says, "You can have your cake and eat it too." It shows how God works in the gaps, how God seeks us even when we are not interested.

We noticed yesterday that no person was there to stand in the gap, as there was in the golden-calf episode (Exod. 32) and in the church conflict involving Euodia and Syntyche (Phil. 4). But a deeper look reveals that another mediator was at work. The threefold invitation extended by the king—through his "slaves" (God's prophets)—produced genuine accountability from the people invited.

Military schools allow students three responses: "Yes, sir." "No, sir." and "No excuse, sir." In the military school environment no one is able to claim ignorance but, rather, only to assume responsibility. In a more gracious way, God comes to us, creating life in such a way that we are genuinely accountable; we are *response-able*.

The original invitation might be compared to our being made in the image of God, created with a built-in hunger for the divine. If we heed the original invitation, we find ourselves willing and able to respond to the subsequent overtures from God.

The second and third invitations might be compared to the "God moments" that come as we move through life—those wooing, drawing, inviting experiences. These fill us with confirmation that God is real and that we are meant to enjoy fellowship with God.

True accountability makes people's refusal in the Gospel lesson all the more unfortunate. No one had to miss the party. Neither do we!

Prayer: **God of invitation, I want to feast at your banquet. Let me so live that I may be aware of your original invitation expressed through my being made in your image. Let me so live that your subsequent invitations evoke my yes. Amen.**

Saturday, October 12   Read Exodus 32:11-14.

Sometimes life gets so out of control, by choice or circumstance, we must either have outside help, or perish. So it was for the Israelites as they handed in and melted down their gold to make a calf-god. Perhaps beginning in anxiety over their situation, their actions soon turned to self-destructive revelry.

Moses prayed. God had already said, "Let me alone." Divine wrath was going to burn hot against the Israelites and consume them. But Moses prayed. "And the LORD changed his mind about the disaster that he planned to bring on his people."

Prayer sometimes stands in the gap. Years ago, Maxie Dunnam challenged me when he wrote, "Suppose there were things which would not happen apart from prayer. How would that change your prayer life?" While not completely removing the mystery of intercession, his words made clearer what my role is to be. I am to pray.

If more things are wrought by prayer than this world dreams of, then surely we want to commit ourselves to being change-agents! We face a choice. We can spend our time viewing the hopelessness of circumstances, or debating the role prayer plays, or we can do what Moses did. We can pray.

One evening, nearly 25 years ago, I stood on a street corner in Lexington, Kentucky with Billy. I was a seminary intern. Billy was a homeless alcoholic. We had been meeting for several weeks. That night we were at a crossroads. I was at my wit's end. Billy was hanging on by a thread. Let him describe the thread for himself, "Every time I think about ending it all, I remember that somewhere my mother is praying for me!"

Prayer: **God, who delights in hearing our prayers, move in my life so that I may spend my time standing in the gap through intercession rather than standing on the sidelines analyzing prayer. Amen.**

Sunday, October 13   Read Psalm 106:1-6, 19-23.

If we look back over the scripture texts and the week's meditations, one overarching principle stands out: we are not alone. We live and thrive in community. Our problems are worked out in community. A look at the Philippian church shows how true this is, both with respect to the general benefits of living together in the church and with regard to the particular conflicts that emerge in our relations with others. We should often give thanks for Christian fellowship, which is truly the "tie that binds."

The psalter lesson roots our community life squarely in worship. We can only imagine how many times the people gathered for worship and recited these words. Even though the lectionary text only highlights selected verses, the whole psalm is a total recall of sin and of God's faithfulness. It ends with the exclamation, "Blessed be the LORD, the God of Israel, from everlasting to everlasting. And let all the people say, 'Amen.' Praise the LORD!" (v. 48)

Worship which restores contains a strong element of memory. The psalm is largely a recounting of Israel's infidelity and God's intervention. Time after time, the people crawled out as far as they could on the limb of life, only to find God present, willing, and able to forgive and restore them. Among other things, worship provides the opportunity for us to rehearse our defections and God's deliverances. It is an occasion for all of us to claim kinship with our Jewish ancestors, to confess that we, too, violate the highest and best we know over and over—yet, God is always there to offer hope and a way back. As we worship, we do not find it difficult to echo the words of our forebears, "Praise the LORD! O give thanks to the LORD, for he is good; for his steadfast love endures forever."

Prayer: **This day, O God, I claim my inheritance as your child. I renew my commitment to find my place in the community of faith, your church, which stands in the gap for me. Amen.**

October 14–20, 1996   **Richard L. Morgan**✤
Monday, October 14   Read Exodus 33:12-23.

"I don't always recognize God's presence in my life, but now that I am older, I can look back and see God's hand at work." This comment at a spiritual autobiography group reminded me of Moses asking God to "show me your glory."

Moses learned that seeing God's glory is more than a mortal can bear. However, when God passed by, Moses *could* see God's back, how God was present in Israel's journey.

Remembering need not be looking into the rearview mirror, yearning for the good old days. Many times Moses had to contend with the Israelites wanting to go back to Egypt. Neither is remembering a stubborn refusal to go forward into the unknown. Remembering is realizing God's presence in our spiritual journey, discerning how God was at work in the twists and turns of our salvation history. We call these times "grace moments."

One member of the group suggested we each write the events of our lives in black ink, and in red how God was present! How many moments Moses must have recalled of God at work in the lives of the people. What about God's hand at work in our own story?

Suggestion for meditation:* Recall some turning points or crises in your life. Ask yourself, *How was God present in that moment?

✤Older Adult Enabler for the Presbytery of Western North Carolina; editor, AGEnda, Presbyterian (USA) publication on aging; parish associate for older adult ministries, First Presbyterian Church, Morganton, North Carolina, and Grace Ridge Retirement Center.

Tuesday, October 15   Read Psalm 99:8-9.

They sat in a circle and remembered their stories. Ten people in a nursing home, trying to recall their past so they could live in the present. One man ruefully said, "By the time you are my age, there is no eraser left on your pencil's end. You're condemned to the choices already made. All you can do is pay for the trip you have taken."

The unbearable silence was broken by a woman in a wheelchair, who was diagnosed with Alzheimer's disease. Softly she said, "All I know is that God is still my eraser. God has rubbed out all my blunders and sins." That is all she said. But it was enough, a gentle touch of grace for us all.

Her words echoed the psalmist who reminded Israel that the Lord enthroned was a forgiving God. "O LORD our God, you answered them; you were to them a forgiving God." It is important to recognize God's transcendence. Someone once reminded a group who claimed that "God is other people," that "God is Other, people." But we need the reassurance of God's forgiveness that erases all our sins.

It was appropriate that we ended our group meeting by singing the familiar words, "What a friend we have in Jesus, all our sins and griefs to bear!" Even in that place where sickness was all too present, and death lurked around the corner, one woman reminded us of God's forgiving love.

Suggestion for meditation: **Visualize some moment from your life when you made a mess of things . . . some stupid blunder, a moment of weakness, unkind words that broke relationships. Imagine that God is saying to you, "I forgive you. Go in peace."**

303

Wednesday, October 16   Read Psalm 99.

"The Lord is great in Zion . . . exalted over all the peoples." This psalm of the Lord's enthronement rather remarkably reminds us of God's presence in our history. The psalmist recalls how "Samuel also was among those who called on his name." Not only did God call Samuel as a young boy when he ministered under Eli, but throughout his life Samuel called on God for himself and for others.

I remember such a woman. She had always been a tower of strength in her church, the faithful teacher and counselor to many. Then, with the swiftness of a sudden summer storm, she was stricken with cancer. Painful surgery, the endless ordeal of treatment, days and nights facing the unknown ensued. Yet, through it all she remained a person who "called on God's name."

Her invincible faith and indomitable courage brought her through to a measure of health. Through it all she prayed for herself and others. She even wrote her memoirs and told me, "One way or another, we are always remembering. For me, life's difficulties have become means of grace."

Remembering our past can be disquieting, especially if it conjures up memories of broken dreams, painful ordeals, and unresolved conflicts. But even these memories can be reconceptualized in light of God's grace. Moments when life seemed to offer *nothing* become occasions of discovering God's *everything*.

Prayer: O God, whom we seem to know best in life's darkest hours, help us not to despair when we face threats to our very being. Rather, help us to see you in those difficult moments. Amen.

Thursday, October 17 Read 1 Thessalonians 1:1-10.

Paul remembered how God had worked through people in the church at Thessalonica. He wrote, "We continually remember before our God and Father your work produced by faith, your labor prompted by love, and your endurance inspired by hope in our Lord Jesus Christ" (NIV).

In other letters Paul mentions faithful members by name, but here they are nameless. Perhaps this is symbolic, reminding us that God is a God of the nameless people, those we are likely to forget, yet whose work of faith and labor of love leaves an eternal memory.

These are the people who do not care who gets the credit, as long as God gets the glory. Like the two-talent man in Jesus' parable, their faithfulness and dependability get the job done without having to be in the limelight. Such as Gene and Shirley, Ray and Hattie, J.E. and Ruby, Buddy and Linda, and countless others.

Paul reminded the Corinthians, "We are ambassadors for Christ, since God is making his appeal through us" (2 Cor. 5:20). On the tombstone of an English missionary, whose life had been dedicated to serving others, were engraved these words, *This man had the kind of life only Jesus Christ could explain.*

We remember that God came finally and fully in the life of Jesus Christ, but God still comes to us through people who imitate Christ's spirit.

Suggestion for meditation and prayer: **Imagine that you are sitting inside a circle of light, where the source of each beam of light is a significant person who has touched your life. Identify them by name. Then, in a moment of quiet, thank them for their love and presence. Close with a prayer of thanksgiving for their presence in your life.**

Friday, October 18   Read Matthew 22:15-22.

It looked like Jesus' enemies had hit the jackpot in their clever question about paying taxes to Caesar. If Jesus says *no* then he appears subversive of the Roman state; if he says *yes* then he seems to collaborate with a foreign occupying force. No way he could wriggle out of this one.

His timeless answer resounds through the centuries. "Give to Caesar what is Caesar's, and to God what is God's" (NIV). While acknowledging the authority of the state, final authority remains with God. The state can require our money and services but never our souls. Jesus had already practiced what he preached. He had paid the temple tax (Matthew 17:27) in spite of his condemnation of much that went on there.

Judge Sam is a classic example of someone who gives to Caesar and to God. Son of Senator Sam Ervin of Watergate fame, Judge Sam has continued that legacy of justice for all, reminding us that a public office is a public trust, and where laws end, tyranny begins.

However, I think of him as a loyal churchman, faithfully present at worship, offering his counsel as a ruling elder and teaching classes in the church school. His commitment extends beyond the "second mile," and he has served as a mentor to many young people who have entered the legal profession.

Jesus' reply to his accusers is an open-ended answer. He leaves it to every person to decide what is rightfully Caesar's and what can be claimed by God alone.

Suggestion for meditation: **Ponder these words of Micah 6:8: "And what does the LORD require of you? To act justly and to love mercy and to walk humbly with your God" (NIV). Can you remember someone who epitomized those words? If so, give thanks to them.**

Saturday, October 19 Read 1 Thessalonians 1:4-10

George was not the typical role model for Christians. He called himself a "pagan" because he refused to worship the prevailing gods. He had spent most of his seventy-nine years as a small-town lawyer in a rural area of southern Maine. Quite a character he was, riding down Main Street on his bicycle, stopping to argue about politics or modern physics. He was often seen handing out candy to little children, or attacking oncoming cars with his walking stick.

He lived out his life in the same small town, surrounded by family and friends. He married his childhood sweetheart, reared two children, and stayed a lawyer. He seemed to be a "tower of stability" in a shaky world, where everything that was not nailed down was coming loose.

But it was his spirit that made him such a memorable person. My brother, John, called him "a high priest of the ordinary," a person who took delight in others, in trees and the sea, the sun going down on a lonely lake, good books, quiet conversation. George's life calls us to ourselves, while the sirens of our times call us elsewhere. More than that, he calls us to nature and to the Holy Presence.

I only knew George through what my brother told me. I wish I had known him in person. For me, at least, he was a classic example of what Paul wrote to the Thessalonians, "You became a model to all believers. . . . Your faith in God has become known everywhere" (NIV).

Suggestion for meditation: **Think for a moment of some person you remember who was "a high priest of the ordinary," someone whose quiet dignity of life made you feel the presence of God.**

Sunday, October 20 Read Exodus 33:14-23.

In times of distress it is all too easy to lose sight of God, even to believe God is nowhere to be found. There were two such moments I remember from my spiritual journey. A painful divorce wrenched me from my former life and thrust me like a newborn babe into an existence far more uncharted than any I had known before. This was a time of serious doubt—doubt that God was at all present or even cared.

A few years ago a serious illness hurled me into an agonizing time of seeking contact with God but finding only empty isolation. The religious beliefs that had sustained me when I was healthy were no longer working. I truly felt that God had abandoned me.

Now, with the healing perspective of time, I can discern God's presence in both events of my life. The word that came to Moses became a word to me. "My Presence will go with you, and I will give you rest" (NIV).

God was at work in my painful divorce, not as a "fix-it person" to suddenly turn my despair into a success story, but as a steady, faithful presence. God, who seemed so absent, so aloof to my needs, was nonetheless there. Now I realize, too, that the key to life sometimes is not found in health but in what we experience during illness. I began to experience a strange new Presence in my life. Faith had found a gentle beginning that still continues.

Remember when God . . . ? How can we forget?

Prayer: **In your presence, O God, I remember those difficult moments in my life journey when I thought you had forgotten me, when I prayed and the heavens were brass, when I cried and no one answered. Now, I thank you that you were there with me, gently nudging me to newness of life. Amen.**

TRUST IN GOD'S LOVING PROVIDENCE

October 21–27, 1996 **Susan Muto✣**

Monday, October 21 Read Deuteronomy 34:1-12.

When we do not see the final outcome of our plans, we may say that we are like Moses. Under God's direction, Moses did all the hard work. By performing great signs and wonders, he persuaded Pharaoh to let Israel go. He led Israel through the wilderness for forty years, years full of the people's complaining, arguing, and disobeying the God who had liberated them.

All of the struggle would pay off, however, when Moses got to enter the promised land with the people he had led so faithfully—except that God allowed Moses only a view of that long-promised land before he died; for Moses, too, had been *unfaithful* to God (see Exodus 17:1-7). So even though "his sight was unimpaired and his vigor had not abated," Moses died after a mere glimpse of the promised land from atop Mount Nebo.

Yet even at this moment of understandable disappointment, God's promise to Moses held true. Moses died in the assurance that his trust in God's loving providence was not unfounded.

Although we may not see the outcome of God's plan in our lifetime, we can be sure God's mission for us will come to fulfillment. If we open ourselves to God's leading, we, like Moses, can glimpse the land promised to us—God's kingdom here among us.

Prayer: **Ever loving God, at the close of my life as at its inception, may I experience something of the intimacy Moses knew with you. Grant that I may be a servant of and witness to the coming of your kingdom. Amen.**

✣Executive Director of the Epiphany Association, Pittsburgh, Pennsylvania; professor of literature and spirituality; speaker and consultant in the field of Christian formation.

Tuesday, October 22   Read Psalm 90:1-6.

This psalm, called "A Prayer of Moses," is a meditation on human mortality. It is at once a hymn (vv. 1-2) and a lament (vv. 3-6). It juxtaposes a number of experiences in which we, God's chosen, share. The verses recall how over the ages divinely initiated acts brought Israel into existence with a nurturing love.

God's power enabled the conquest of many an enemy. God raised up leaders and men of vision like Abraham, Isaac, and Jacob. God enabled Moses to lead the people through the desert to the threshold of the promised land.

The opening verses capture the awesome initial moments of Creation as well as the consequences of the fall. It is as if Moses wants to review for God how the almighty power and the everlasting trustworthiness of the divine promise have been so important to the people of Israel.

The contrast between our finitude, we who are but dust, and God's infinite power is striking. The contrast evokes in us humility. Not false displays of power but docility drew the heart of Moses into the heart of God.

This prayer attributed to Moses does not mince words. The human is the human. The divine is the divine. God is eternal; we are mortal. In God's sight a thousand years might as well be no more than a day or a night.

Moses' prayer helps us sense the reality of life's brevity. Our yesterdays, our todays, and our tomorrows all fade like grass that flourishes in the morning and withers by evening. Of what then have we to boast? Perhaps the transience of our lives calls us to transcendence in faith.

Prayer: **Infinite God, help me see each day of my temporal existence against the horizon of eternity. Give me the grace to make every moment count, to take no gift of yours for granted.**

Wednesday, October 23   Read Psalm 90:13-17.

Not only are we humans conscious of our mortality but we also bear the weight of being miserable sinners, deserving of God's wrath. No wonder the depth of divine mercy astonishes us!

In this psalm, called "A Prayer of Moses," Moses knew how angry God could be. The disobedient group who dared to call themselves God's chosen made God fume with anger. The people saw that they were like flies God could swat, but God wanted to teach them another lesson instead.

A wise heart is of more worth than an angry or a fearful one. Thus, Moses could appeal to the Lord, as he did throughout his sojourn in the desert, to have compassion on God's servants and not to make them cringe under the power of divine wrath.

The kindness God shows—the steadfastness of God's love—saves us from being worthless as grass to an indifferent mower. God is a God of love. The Giver of all good things wants our songs of joy. For this reason, Moses, a normally meek, God-molded man, has the audacity to ask at the end of his prayer that the days and years of our gladness at least equal those of our affliction. For all the years we have seen evil, Moses prays that we will behold the ultimate triumph of good. Moses asks that the greatness of God's saving work be seen in us, God's servants.

Such showing forth of divinity is enough to convince our children's children of the truth Moses knew: that God's favor rests upon us. The work of our hands will bear fruit because both the grace to begin it and the stamina to bring it to conclusion come from God.

Suggestion for meditation: **Recall an event in your life when lamentation turned to joy because of the compassion showed to you by God. What made this event an epiphany (a showing of God's power, favor, and glory)? How has God allowed the work of your hands to bear fruit most recently?**

Thursday, October 24   Read 1 Thessalonians 2:1-8.

Paul's letter is a moving testimony to trust in God's guidance and the truth of the gospel. Suffering and shameful mistreatment at Philippi could not dampen his spirit. The appeal of his mission has nothing to do with the deceits of impure motives that make people play to the crowd and judge truth by virtue of popularity.

From whence, then, does the appeal of Paul's message spring? He knows, as Moses did, that he is no self-declared prophet. There was a time when he did not trust God at all, when he blatantly opposed all that was Christian. He did not choose God; God chose him.

God's trust humbles Paul and makes him a trustworthy teacher. In line with the prophets of old, his aim is not to please mortals but to please God in all that he is and does. He has no interest in flattering people or in using preaching as a pretext for greed. Paul neither cares for notoriety nor asks for special compensation, such as room and board, for his services.

Paul sets high ethical standards. He addresses people from the viewpoint of personal experience. He perseveres in the face of persecution and urges his brothers and sisters in the faith to do likewise.

In the end, God will test our hearts. Will we pass the test of humility, or will vanity obscure our delivery of the divine message? Paul's heart remained humble before God. Can we say the same about ours?

Prayer: **Source of strength, let your purifying grace cleanse my heart. Help me rise above ungodly influences and strive to teach your gospel wherever I go, in all that I am and do. Keep me from discouragement when facing opposition. Make me a living witness to your everlasting love. Amen.**

Friday, October 25   Read 1 Thessalonians 2:1-8.

This passage gives us a picture of a true apostle, the kind of person Paul was, the imitator of Christ and a role model for his followers (see 1 Cor. 11:1). Theirs will not be a trouble-free existence. On occasion they may have to defend their ministry. Paul wants them to develop the inner dispositions they will need to be Christian leaders. Then such accusations as being avaricious and a charlatan will not apply. Paul and his companions in the faith must be determined teachers as well as gentle nurses, "tenderly caring for [their] own children" (v. 7).

The key to discipleship is self-donation—giving of oneself as well as sharing the gospel of Christ. Paul preaches what he practices. Thus, his message of love is doubly convincing. He proclaims the gospel free of charge not to an elite few but to all who care to listen.

Paul's aim is not to become a financial burden on the community (v. 9). After meeting his basic needs, he keeps nothing for himself. He shares what he has with others. In doing so, Paul proves the old adage that actions speak louder than words. His love is so overflowing that he tells the Thessalonians how dear they are to him. Wouldn't it be wonderful to feel such warmth toward others as a rule rather than as an exception?

Inspired by Paul and his companions, we perhaps need to reconsider the centrality of firm and gentle caregiving love in our churches today.

Suggestion for meditation: **Before being entrusted with the mission of proclaiming the gospel, what "harsh edges" in you would need to be gentled? When do you find yourself seeking to please people more than God? Which method of evangelization do you prefer: an aggressive activity or a gentle appeal? What is the reason for your preference?**

Saturday, October 26   Read Matthew 22:34-40.

The Pharisees were always trying to put Jesus on the defensive. They wanted to trick him so they could accuse him of false teaching or blasphemy. With the question in this passage, they thought they had found the ultimate test. They asked him a question the answer to which, in effect, had to be a summary of Israel's law. What would Jesus say? Would he point to one of the many minor laws of his day? Would he focus on the essentials?

Jesus unhesitatingly replies that the first and greatest of the commandments is to love God with all one's heart and soul and mind. Such love is not mainly a feeling; it is a *willingness* to remain faithful in all things to the covenant of love between God and us.

The second part of the commandment is, therefore, that we love our neighbors as we love ourselves. As the Golden Rule indicates, we are to do for others what we would have them do for us (Matt. 7:12).

On these two commandments, says Jesus, "hang all the law and the prophets." From the love of God, neighbor, and self, all other laws derive and find support. This point is so crucial that Matthew makes the Law itself depend upon the deeds of love.

Jesus probably stunned the Pharisees with his answer. Imagine proving his fidelity to the Jewish tradition and his commitment to a way of life that emphasizes the essentials in two short sentences!

Love is the real test of a Christ-centered life. It is an indisputable point.

What teacher but Jesus could cut through the tangle of observances to the principles on which all were based?

Prayer: **God of holy love, help me give myself to you heart and soul and mind—holding nothing in reserve, loving you with my whole being. Give me the strength I need to share your love in me with all those entrusted to my care.**

314

Sunday, October 27   Read Matthew 22:41-46.

If the Pharisees could ask Jesus questions, then in all fairness he could turn his interpretive skills on them. What was their opinion of the Messiah? Whose son was he?

Jesus knew, of course, that messianic speculation abounded and was a divisive factor in Judaism. The Pharisees quickly replied that the Messiah was the son of David. Jesus then pushed the matter a step further by raising another question: If David calls him Lord, how can he be his son?

By citing scripture (compare Psalm 110:1), Jesus deliberately places past traditions in conflict with the new work God is accomplishing through him. The old has value, but so does the new. These doctrinal experts cannot give Jesus an answer. Jesus knows that his significance is not confined to Israel, for he has a higher calling in fidelity to God's plan of salvation. His transcendent dignity makes him David's Lord also. Rather than probe these issues with minds open to new truths, the Pharisees, much like those who blindly defend the status quo in any age, are stymied. Such bankruptcy on the part of these religious leaders—who do not even dare to ask Jesus any more questions—leads into his attack on their teaching. (See Matthew 23.)

Through his passion, death, and resurrection, Jesus will reveal that he alone is the Messiah, the Son of the living God, the One who alone sits at the right hand of the Father and makes his enemies a footstool.

Suggestion for meditation: **How do you view Jesus in your life today? Do you see him as Savior, Friend, the Word Made Flesh, Son of God, Emmanuel (God-with-us)? How do these descriptions of the Lord enhance your knowledge and personal experience of his saving power?**

LIVES THAT BECOME THE GOSPEL

October 28—November 3, 1996   **Thomas R. Hawkins✤**
Monday, October 28   Read 1 Thessalonians 2:9-13.

When we say something is an *imitation*, we usually mean that it is second rate, not quite as good as the original. Paul, on the other hand, uses this word very differently. It lies at the heart of his understanding of evangelism.

Paul reminds the Corinthians to "be imitators of me, as I am of Christ" (1 Cor. 11:1). He similarly asks the Thessalonians to imitate him (see 1 Thessalonians 1:6). Paul describes how he modeled Christ's life among them—working to support himself, conducting himself with holiness and righteousness, and acting as gently as a nurse yet as firmly as a parent (2:7, 11). Others will then look to the Thessalonians as a model to imitate (2:14). The gospel spreads through this ever-expanding imitation of Christ.

When Paul draws attention to his own behavior, it has nothing to do with arrogant bragging. He believes Christian growth is best accomplished through imitation of an example. Educators today call this social learning, that is to say, learning by observing someone else. The model can later be brought to mind through memory as a guide for action and decision.

The gospel still spreads by imitation, by modeling. It is not just a cliché to say, "Your life may be the only Bible someone reads." Does my life so model Christ that others can look at me and know what it means to be Christian?

Prayer: **Gracious God, may your word be so at work in us that we model Christ's life before others. Amen.**

✤Dean of Doctoral Programs and Associate Professor of Ministry, McCormick Theological Seminary, Chicago, Illinois; a United Methodist.

Tuesday, October 29   Read Matthew 23:1-12.

Jesus does not question the values of the scribes and Pharisees. In fact, he expresses appreciation for their teachings. Jesus condemns not their words but their example: They do not practice what they exhort the people to do.

By contrast, Jesus commands his own disciples to let the pattern of their lives be a living performance of the good news. Our Christian witness is most powerful and most authentic when the lives we lead point to the Word we follow.

When our two sons were baptized, my wife and I were asked whether we would lead lives that become the gospel to Robert and Jonathan. It took time for me to understand the importance of this vow. I now realize that little children are great imitators. Children love to mimic what they see adults doing. We learn to be human by imitating the examples we see around us. Children, and even adults, learn what it means to be Christian by seeing how other Christians perform the gospel with their lives.

When my wife and I were asked if we would live lives that become the gospel to our sons, we responded, "We will, by God's grace." The power to become a living performance of the gospel comes not from our own resources. It is a gift of the Spirit. Our witness depends not on us but on God. It comes as gift and not achievement. The scribes and Pharisees, in their proud arrogance, forgot this truth.

Prayer: **Loving God, grant us the gift of your Spirit so that we may lead lives that become the gospel to a watching world. Amen.**

Wednesday, October 30   Read Joshua 3:7-17.

Features of Joshua 3 suggest a solemn reenactment of Israel's crossing from Shittim to Gilgal: a period of ritual sanctification (3:5), a carefully orchestrated procession with the Ark of the Covenant (3:4), the presence of memorial stones (4:2, 19-23). Israel gathered annually at Gilgal to rehearse how God led them across the Jordan River into a land flowing with milk and honey. Israel did not just retell how they crossed the Jordan River. They ritually reenacted this crossing so that future generations could see it and experience it for themselves.

Similarly, Christian worship is sometimes described as a time mystery. The reality of past events is made present through our reenacting them in worship. In baptism we imitate Jesus' baptism and experience the heavens parting and a voice proclaiming, "You are my beloved." As we repeat Jesus' actions in breaking the bread and pouring the cup, we are given a model for how we are to break open our lives and share ourselves with others. We stand for the reading of the Gospel, thereby modeling for one another how to stand up for God's truth in a world tempted to cut ethical corners.

Our individual performance of the gospel is crucial to Christian witness in the world. Equally important is how the Christian community, gathered for worship, models what it means to be alive in Christ—reenacting as well as retelling its old, old story so that others may see it, experience it, and make it their own.

Prayer: **We pray today, O God, for Christian communities and their leaders. May our Christian worship and common life reenact the gospel, opening again for us new life in Christ. Amen.**

Thursday, October 31   Read Matthew 5:1-12.

Perhaps children enjoy Halloween because they crave the treats of bubble gum, candy bars, and suckers. I prefer to believe Halloween is fun because children love to imitate adults. Ballerinas, firefighters, and doctors roam our streets on this night. Children sometimes choose to imitate the darker side of human nature, dressing up as menacing characters, monsters, goblins.

To counter this, some churches sponsor Halloween parties. Children dress up as one of the church's saints: Saint George wearing armor or Saint Teresa of Ávila in her nun's habit. Saints, however, are not just for children. They are examples worth imitating in our own adult lives.

On All Saints Day we remember the multitude of saints from every nation, tribe, and people who now surround the Lamb, endlessly singing their hymns of praise and waving their palm branches (Rev. 7:9-10). The lives of the earliest saints became the gospel for the early Christians. The lives of the saints through the ages, as well as those of quiet everyday Christians we have known, remain examples that inspire us, enabling us to see more clearly how we should live if we are to be faithful disciples of Jesus Christ.

On All Saints Day I give thanks for the cloud of witnesses[*] who surround me: My grandfather, a social worker who cared passionately about justice for the marginalized. My aunt who taught me quiet confidence in God as she faced a painful death. A pastor who modeled God's compassion when I was a child. Their lives became the gospel for me and remain guideposts for my spiritual journey.

Prayer: We thank you, God, for that great cloud of witnesses who have helped us to discern more clearly the life to which you call us in Jesus Christ. Amen.

---

[*]See Hebrews 11–12:2.

All Saints Day

Friday, November 1   Read Matthew 5:1-12.

Saints are people whose lives are patterned on Christ's life. They see and do things differently from most people. They model service rather than domination, forgiveness rather than animosity. They are people who work for peace, comfort the grieving, turn the other cheek, go the second mile. They feed the hungry and speak out against injustice. They risk their lives for the sake of life and the Light.

While Jesus may bless these qualities, the dominant culture often rejects them. Those around the world whose lives become the gospel are often marginalized, sometimes persecuted precisely because their behavior seems strange to the convention of the society around them. Jesus reserves his final blessing for these saints precisely because he knows they will be persecuted for righteousness' sake.

When we are tempted to conform to the values of a society often at odds with God's justice and shalom, these models of holiness and wholeness encourage us. Their lives witness to the transforming power of God's grace, which allows ordinary people to point beyond themselves to God's promised blessings for all people.

All Saints Day provides an opportunity to remember with gratitude those individuals whose lives reflect the blessings of God revealed in Jesus Christ. When our commitment weakens, we have their example to imitate, knowing that our witness comes as gift and not achievement.

Prayer: **God of the living and the dead, we praise you for those who rest in you. Encouraged by their example and strengthened by their fellowship, may our lives reflect the blessings you make known in Christ. Amen.**

Saturday, November 2   Read Psalm 107:1-7.

Many Jewish exiles returned to Jerusalem after Cyrus defeated the Babylonian Empire in the mid-sixth century B.C.E. These exiles had wept by the waters of Babylon. Now they were returning home, gathered in from east and west, north and south.

Although this was a journey to which God called them, it was a difficult and dangerous one. A vast, hostile desert stretched between Babylon and Jerusalem. Some returning exiles lost their way, wandering hungry and thirsty in the desert. In their distress they cried to God, who brought them by a straight way to Jerusalem. The psalmist reminds these men and women to give thanks to God for their deliverance.

Leading lives that witness to God's reign can be as risky and uncertain as the exiles' journey across the desert. A small, urban congregation experienced its glory days twenty years ago, before open housing led to white flight. The congregation's journey since then has included desert wastelands and mountaintop visions.

Modeling Jesus' solidarity with the marginalized has cost them members and brought them to the brink of extinction. Yet that same faithfulness has given them new life through a neighborhood health center and an AIDS clinic.

Leading lives that become the gospel is risky and ambiguous. The outcomes are never certain, at least not in this world. Yet amid this ambiguity and uncertainty, we can trust that God's steadfast love endures forever. For that reason, we, too, always give thanks for God's grace and goodness.

Prayer: **Your steadfast love endures forever, O Lord. Strengthen us for the risks of being faithful witnesses to your love and justice. Amen.**

Sunday, November 3   Read Psalm 107:1, 33-37.

After giving thanks for God's mighty acts in history—delivering Israel from desert wastelands, breaking the iron bars of imprisonment, assuring safe passage through stormy seas—the psalmist turns to God's wonders in nature. God is the great Transformer of nature. God turns fruitful land into a desert and fills the parched land with springs of water. This upheaval happens for a purpose: The hungry are given a place to plant, harvest, and multiply.

Both human history and nature are expressions of God's self-giving love that acts to deliver, redeem, and renew. The appropriate response is praise and thanksgiving. God's grace inspires our gratitude just as a voice evokes an echo. Grace and gratitude belong together. Thanksgiving does not look at the gift and express appreciation. It looks at the Giver and expresses trust. Above all else, sin is ingratitude, a failure to acknowledge with thanksgiving God's steadfast love toward us.

The central prayer of Christian worship is the Great Thanksgiving. It thanks God for creating the natural world, making covenant with a people, and sending Jesus to live, die, and rise for us. More importantly, the Great Thanksgiving offers a pattern for our lives that we are to imitate. We receive our lives as they are given to us, we bless and praise God for these lives, we break them open in self-giving love, and we share ourselves with the hungry and marginalized. Our lives become the gospel when this pattern of receiving, blessing, breaking, and sharing becomes the pattern of our lives.

Prayer: **Help us, O God, to give thanks to you, the Giver of all good things. Empower us to receive, bless, break open, and share our lives with others. Amen.**

PRESERVING THE COVENANT TODAY

November 4–10, 1996   **Tommy Cresswell**✤

Monday, November 4   Read Joshua 24:1-3a; 14-25.

The form of covenant

Bible scholars inform us that the form of the covenant that Joshua uses, like that found in Exodus and Deuteronomy, is based upon a common ancient treaty formula: 1) a preamble ("Thus says the LORD . . ."); 2) historical prologue (of God's work in prior generations); 3) covenantal stipulations and warnings; 4) witnesses; and 5) drawing and depositing a document of the agreement. Reread today's scripture and spend some time reflecting on these elements of covenant as they affect your life.

We know the Lordship of Jesus. We know his commandments and promises. So much for preamble and stipulations. But, can you list your own historical prologue—what God through Christ has done in *your* life, in your parents' lives, and the generations before? Would you profess it in front of witnesses and put it in writing? Take time today to write down the evidence of God in your life. Then sometime this week share this with a friend or family member.

Prayer: **O Lord, too often I come before you with petitions for my present and future needs. Too seldom do I proclaim your mighty acts and the joy of my salvation. Heavenly Father, keep me ever in remembrance of your awesome power, your immeasurable love, your unfathomable grace, and your unequaled peace. Help me, Father, to make known all the good and miraculous things you have worked in my life and in the lives of those I love. Amen.**

✤Professional actor and attorney; certified lay speaker in The United Methodist Church; Nashville, Tennessee

Tuesday, November 5   Read Psalm 78:1-7.

Covenantal reaffirmation

The psalmist reminds us that God commanded that we retell his glorious deeds and wonders. The purpose is not just that the next generation might know them, but so that they will not forget God's works and they will trust him and keep his commandments.

You know that God had made the covenant with God's people generations before. Yet, recall how Joshua called the people forth for them to *reaffirm* the covenant. Ages had passed since Moses proclaimed God's promise on Sinai, and still more since Abraham built his first altar to God in Canaan at Shechem. (See Exodus 19:5-7 and Genesis 12:7.) Wasn't God's covenant still good? So, why reaffirm it?

Perhaps you belong to a club, a civic group, a business association, or other organization. When new members join, they are asked to sign or affirm that they will obey the rules and regulations already in place. New church members are asked to profess openly their faith in the Lordship of Jesus as Savior and their commitment to the church. Why?

Without our affirmation to the covenant to which God calls us, the agreement is unilateral, with no commitment on our part. God is ready, willing, and able to keep the divine promise to us, but we must *accept* it for ourselves. And our willingness to accept it often depends on how the covenant and God are explained and proclaimed to us by the prior generation.

Is your historical prologue from yesterday complete? Is it accurate and convincing? Would others who hear it want to "set their hope in God, and . . . keep his commandments"?

Prayer: Dear God, keep the wonders of your love in my heart and on my lips so that by your power through my witness, people will accept your covenant for the generations to come and declare Jesus as Lord and Savior. Amen.

Wednesday, November 6   Read Matthew 25:1-13.

Covenantal preparation

This parable of the ten bridesmaids has been explained sufficiently that we know Jesus was telling us to be ready for his second coming. The first word of this parable in most versions is *then*. The NIV translation begins "At that time . . ." Consequently, the story also represents what will take place at the time of his return.

We do not like to think about the fact that some people will not be received by Jesus on his return, but that is clearly what Jesus is saying. Five of the bridesmaids tried too late to obtain oil, and when they sought entrance to the wedding feast they were refused. In fact, "the door was shut." Some are saved, some are not. Whew! Hard words for people who try to be "inclusive" and "accepting"—two guiding words of our day.

For a moment, look at the end of Matthew, the last verse of which begins "teaching them to obey everything that I have commanded you" (28:20). We have become strong on God's grace and love, but do we remember that Jesus admonished his followers to obey what he commanded? Our obedience is both a response to his love and a responsibility he demanded.

When you witness to others, do you tell of the difficult words of Christ as well? Are we guilty of letting bridesmaids get all dressed up but forgetting to remind them of the requirements of oil for their lamps? All were bridesmaids; all were asleep; all had lamps—but some did not have oil.

Prayer: **Heavenly Father, free me from witnessing to "cheap grace," good news with no response or responsibility. Lord, let my witness to your covenant transform the lives I touch. In Jesus' name. Amen.**

Thursday, November 7   Read Matthew 25:1-13.

The individuality of covenant

Since difficult words are best reviewed, let's look deeper at this parable. In Jesus' time, there were two phases to Jewish weddings. The first involved the groom coming to the bride's home to obtain her and observe certain ceremonies. Then the groom took his bride to his home, resuming the festivities. The oil carried in the bride's lamp was only enough for the wedding procession.

We are taught to share when we are young. Jesus taught us about sharing in a deeper sense, and he set an example for us concerning providing for others out of our resources. In this parable, the "wise" bridesmaids do not share with the "foolish" ones, yet they are not chastised for this action.

The oil of the lamp represents our own individual spiritual preparedness. This cannot be shared. Each of us, on our own and by God's help, must develop our spiritual communion with the Lord. The bridesmaids might well have asked, "Give me your faith." But, we each must develop our own faith. It is through divine grace, the witness of the Holy Spirit to our spirit, and the testimony of our forebears that leads us to the point where we can affirm for ourselves our assent and consent to God's covenant.

We may joyously proclaim our faith corporately in worship as believers, but we meet the Christ of the cross one-on-one. He died not for all of us, but for each of us, and we, as individuals, must join his covenantal body.

Prayer: **Lord God, I declare that you are Lord of all. I regret that there are those who do not yet know Christ as their personal Savior. Your grace is sufficient, Lord. Make my witness sufficient that all whose lives I touch will know of your glorious deeds and their lamps will be full of oil and ready when your time comes. I pray in the name of your Son. Amen.**

Friday, November 8   Read 1 Thessalonians 4:13-18.

The endurance of the covenant

This passage is frequently referred to as "The Rapture," which comes from the Latin translation of the phrase that "we . . . will be *caught up*" with Jesus and those who died before. Paul sought to allay the concerns of the church at Thessalonica about what would happen to those Christians who died before Jesus' return in glory.

Where do you place your greater concern: on those Christians who have already joined that great crowd of witnesses who go before us, or your un-saved friends, family members, and business colleagues and acquaintances who have yet to hear and learn the truth of Jesus' gospel? And, note the emphasis on *Christians* who have passed on.

In the New King James translation, Paul is quoted as referring to the dead ancestors as "those who sleep *in Jesus*." Similarly, the New International Version reads, "those who have fallen asleep *in him*." Indeed, the New Revised Standard Version must be read this way, otherwise those dead whom Jesus brings with him would not be distinguished from dead relatives of "others . . . who have no hope." Also, verse 16 refers to the "dead *in Christ*" who will rise first. (Author's emphases added.)

Yesterday, we reflected on the personal nature of our assent to God's covenant. Each bridesmaid must have her own oil, or preparedness. But, before Christ's return what is our responsibility for showing others where to find the oil?

Prayer: **Loving and merciful Father, I do not trust in my own strivings to do good, but I rely wholly on the righteousness of the Lamb who was sacrificed for me. Lord, you say to be anxious for nothing. Teach me not to worry about those whose earthly lives have passed on. Guide me in your will that I will declare your mighty works that others may believe. I ask in the name of your holy Son. Amen.**

Saturday, November 9

Read Psalm 78:2-4;
1 Thessalonians 4:18.

Invitation to the covenant

If I had a nickel for every time my parents or teachers (school and Sunday school) said that a half-truth is as bad as a lie, I would be a rich man. Remember that gnawing feeling in your stomach when you have given someone an explanation but conveniently left out some pertinent facts?

God's love for us is paralleled in the Bible to the love of a parent for a child. In this generation, there is a risk of losing the significance of this imagery. We live in a time when so many children are growing up without a sense of security within the family circle; "latch-key" children are becoming too common-place; and unspeakable atrocities committed by fathers and mothers make headline news too often.

Does hiding the glorious wonders and ardent love of Almighty God seem so bad in comparison? Okay, so we forget to read the Bible at home; they'll hear it at church, won't they? So our prayer time isn't regular, and we omit "grace" at the table; God still loves us, doesn't He? Skipping church from time to time is not such a big deal; most of the people where I work don't even go to church. So what?

Are we a lost and dying generation not because we have hidden the truth but because we have forgotten our tradition of declaring the wonders of our God and King? We have not hidden anything. We have just forgotten. Nothing intentional, just an omission. We'll make it up—tomorrow.

What? Jesus is returning today? Sorry. That isn't convenient.

Prayer: Lord, you who are ever faithful, help me to be faithful to the calling on my life that you prepared for me before the foundation of the world. Let me not hide your truth, even by just forgetting to tell the story. Amen.

Sunday, November 10   Read Joshua 24:14-15.

Preservation of the covenant

Choices. We love 'em, and we hate 'em. Food at the buffet: great choices. Miss your deadline on your report, or miss your child's activity: bad choices. Ah, but those are the simple ones. What about the rich young ruler who was told to sell all that he had? What about giving up your fishing business with your father to follow a carpenter turned itinerant evangelist?

Joshua was clear that the people must *choose this day* whether to follow the Lord. And, if they chose the Lord, they must put away the other gods. Of course, the Ten Commandments addressed that, too, didn't they?

All right, half the world or more goes to bed hungry; millions are starving. Wars are raging. Disease is pandemic, and crime in America has the country living in fear. But, say! How about that new house? And have you seen my 32-valve sports coupe? The kids? Super videogames, never miss a night of television, and catch all the latest movies . . . into soccer, ballet, horseback riding, violin, art, and whatever the neighbor's kid thinks of.

The church at times seems uncertain about its stance on many perplexing contemporary issues, lifestyles, and problems. But society says that, . . . uh, I mean the contemporary view in psychology and sociology is, . . . well, the economics and politics of the situation require . . .

Are we prepared to choose God and choose now? Are we desperately trying to hold on to gods of our own creation? Do we know when Jesus will return?

And, say, uh, could you spare a little oil?

Prayer: Dear God, I have made you too small; I have trusted the words of people, and I have failed to tell the generations of your marvelous works. Have mercy on me, merciful Father. Jesus Christ alone is my hope of salvation. Let me say and do, "As for me and my house, we will serve the Lord." Amen.

November 11–17, 1996   **Joe Dunagan**✤
Monday, November 11   Read 1 Thessalonians 5:8-11.

It is funny how things work out. I never would have dreamed that I would find myself at this time in my life living in Texas and working with hospice patients. My ministry with the hospice allows me to work with some terrific people who as a team help terminally ill patients and their families cope physically, emotionally, and spiritually. As part of our program, I facilitate a grief support group for survivors. We gather each week. They are widows and widowers, young adults whose parents have died, and parents whose children have died. The sorrow shared by the members of my group would not surprise you. The laughter might.

Sometimes we laugh about stories of happy times with their loved ones. Sometimes we laugh because of the absurdity of a group member's feelings. It is not uncommon, for example, for a member of the group to be angry with his or her loved one for dying. I tell the group that the goal of healthy grief is to learn to live.

The support group provides a strong means of encouraging one another—to feel, to breathe again, to learn to live past the experience of a loved one's dying and death. This, along with the whole of the hospice ministry, meets people where they are and builds them up in the love of Christ.

Suggestion for meditation: **Reflect on your destiny of hope and joy in Christ and the way you share Christ with others.**

✤Clergy, South Georgia Conference of The United Methodist Church; Clinical Chaplain, Vitas Healthcare Corporation, Houston, Texas.

Tuesday, November 12   Read Matthew 25:14-30.

We use the word *talent* to refer to a natural ability such as that of an athlete or musician. Originally a *talent* referred to a measure of weight. By the time of the parable the word *talent* had come to refer to the value of a coin that weighed that much.

A talent was a considerable amount of money, representing a worker's wages for more than a decade. Thus, even the person who received just one talent received a huge sum of money. That helps explain the master's anger when he returned to find that the slave had not invested the talent.

Investing money can be scary. Putting our talents to work can be scary too. Sometimes we fail. Sometimes we lack confidence simply because we have not tested ourselves. I suspect the greatest concert pianist or the record-breaking Olympic medalist is nervous before a performance or event. Yet, the applause at the completion of their task is overwhelming. Those ovations would not have come had the pianist (no matter how great) or the runner (no matter how fast) never risked investing his or her talents.

In the parable, when the owner returned, the servants who had invested their trusts received their ovation. The owner said, "Well done," and invited them to share his joy. That joy made all their work worthwhile.

Helping people who are near death through the hospice has taught me that people live life as a talent. Some bury their talent; they are bitter and filled with remorse. Others invest their time in such a way as to get the fullest return. When they come to the end of life as we know it, these persons have few regrets. They are ready to enter into God's joy.

Suggestion for meditation: **Consider how you are investing the greatest talent God entrusts to you, life.**

331

Wednesday, November 13   Read 1 Thessalonians 5:1-11.

When I received a commission in the Navy Chaplain Corps, I knew nothing about being in the military. I reported for duty at a U.S. Marines infantry battalion at Camp Lejeune in North Carolina. The chaplain I was to replace was a graduate of West Point and a veteran of service in Vietnam. I tried hard not to let anyone know how nervous I was.

When I met the Colonel, he instilled in me tremendous respect and some fear. He welcomed me to the command, gave me some advice, and generally sized me up. I can only imagine what he must have thought about losing an experienced officer for a South Georgia preacher with a brand-new commission.

My battalion was scheduled for cold weather training that winter. Early one Sunday morning we were bivouacked high in the mountain. The snow crunched beneath our feet, and the morning haze seemed to crystallize in the sun. The Colonel found me already up and serving breakfast to Marines. Later, he referred to that incident often. When the Colonel saw me out there with the troops that cold Sunday morning, he figured that what I lacked in experience I made up for in dedication. When it came time for my evaluation, the Colonel told me that he had been surprised. He said, "I wasn't expecting much out of you, but you've done pretty good."

When we Christians put on our uniforms with the breastplate of faith and love and the helmet of hope, we don't have all the answers. Sometimes we are torn about what is right; sometimes we are not eloquent. That is not the measure. When we are found faithful, we know the joy of hearing, "Well done!"

Suggestion for meditation: **Consider the Christian's uniform of faith, hope, and love. How are these qualities woven into your life?**

Thursday, November 14   Read Psalm 123.

An interesting thing about this psalm is the manner in which its language begins in the singular and continues in the plural. Perhaps verse 1 served as a call to worship. The leader of the people says that he lifts his eyes to the one enthroned in the heavens. The congregation then responds with the prayer. The prayer describes looking to the Lord as servants look to the hands of masters or mistresses. The servants look to the hands anticipating instruction not wrath. They watch until God shows the way in mercy. The people call for mercy in the face of contempt and scorn from those who are comfortable or easy.

I believe society's problems are systemic. Everyone is connected. If we are to successfully address the great challenges of violence or disease in society, we must learn to deal with them individually. As the psalm moves from individual prayer to corporate, from *I* to *we*, so must the faithful of our time recognize our connectedness and act upon that understanding. How often, for example, when we pray the prayer of Jesus do we consider what it means to say, "*Our* Father"? Do our prayers connect us with those who know scorn, or do we relate better to those who are contemptuously comfortable?

Someone has quipped that the mission of the church is to comfort the afflicted and afflict the comfortable. Today's psalm addresses the scorn of those who are at ease. It reminds us that contempt is possible only with a sense of superiority. Therefore, the petition in the psalm is for mercy, not revenge. When we lament the contemptible behavior or attitudes of the comfortable, we must call for God's mercy rather than wrath!

Suggestion for meditation: **Consider first that you are part of a community at prayer. Then consider how comfortable you are with that understanding. What does that understanding mean in your life?**

Friday, November 15   Read Judges 4:1-7.

"He was a man *of* his times." I heard this statement recently when a famous statesman died. The commentator had spoken at length of the tremendous work this man had done in his political career. When he had to mention the record of the statesman's opposition to Civil Rights legislation, the speaker attempted to excuse or at least explain it by saying that he had just been a man of his times, and that we should not be too hard on this otherwise progressive politician. His congressional record simply reflected the "accepted standard" of his generation. The commentary concluded with a quote from the late politician himself explaining that his election depended on his representing the sentiments of the majority. A man *of* his times.

We might describe a prophet as a person *for* his or her times. Yet prophets are not content with the status quo. Such was the case with Deborah. She could have been a woman of her times and simply accepted Canaanite rule. It was, after all, the Israelites' just reward for having done evil in the sight of God. But the people had prayed for mercy, and God had heard them. God used Deborah to mobilize the armies of Naphtali and Zebulun by moving Barak to action.

Our destiny as disciples of Christ is to be men and women *for* our times, not just *of* our times. We can see the needs of the world and simply respond with a shrug of the shoulders or a sigh. But our mission is to envision how things could be, then to roll up our sleeves and get to work. The attitude of the prophet and of the believer is why not, with God's help and grace, make the world better?

Suggestion for meditation: **Consider whether you are more often a person *of* your generation or *for* it.**

Saturday, November 16   Read 1 Thessalonians 5:1-11.

My street in Houston reminds me of the small town where I grew up. Most of the neighbors have lived in their homes for decades. I asked the ninety-year-old woman who lives across the street from me how she got a rose bush in her yard to grow so big. She responded that you just plant it and then wait thirty-five or forty years!

Most of my neighbors are widows. They have raised their children on this street. Now they are alone in their homes—and frightened. They have seen the neighborhood go from a quiet street on the edge of town to a busy, noisy oasis surrounded by urban pollution and, unfortunately, crime. They have addressed their fear by supplementing the street lights with security lights in their yards. The block is almost as bright during the night as it is during the day!

Today's lesson speaks of the day of the Lord coming as "a thief in the night." That is a very frightening thought if one does not have spiritual security lights. Indeed, the writer speaks of the fact that believers belong to the day. We are to be awake and in the light. The Day of the Lord will come unexpectedly but it will also be welcomed. Those who are awake and alert will live with Christ.

Suggestion for meditation: **What are your sources of spiritual light?**

Sunday, November 17   Read Matthew 25:19-21;
1 Thessalonians 5:2-10.

I have been with a lot of people as they faced their destinies. I have learned that people die as they have lived. Some people have great peace and express no regrets. Others can only be described as desperate. I worked with a man in his nineties who was very upset and angry because he was not going to live to be one hundred. One's attitude toward death does not seem to have a lot to do with age. It has more to do with the way people face life.

I knew two young men, each suffering from a terminal illness. One was angry that this was happening to him; he perceived himself as a victim. He wanted to die and asked each of us who tried to help him to assist him in killing himself. One day he managed to accomplish this on his own. The other young man fought his illness even as he continued to embrace life and to look to the future. The last time I visited him, he was painting a room in his house and planning how he would use the room when it was completed.

A day of reckoning will come. The nation, in the story of Deborah, found itself under foreign rule (see Judges 4:1-2a). The trustees of great sums of money in the Matthean parable finally had to report back to the owner and account for their investment returns. The Epistle reading reminds the church of the coming of the Day of the Lord. Each instance involves judgment but also offers hope. Once Deborah's generation turned to God in prayer, Deborah was moved to call for action to restore the government. In the Gospel, for those who had invested their talents, it was a day of great joy. And the writer of the Epistle sends word to all generations that "God has destined us not for wrath but for obtaining salvation through our Lord Jesus Christ."

Suggestion for meditation: **Seek God's guidance in how best to invest your talents.**

AND WE, LIKE SHEEP

November 18–24, 1996   **Eradio Valverde, Jr.**✤
Monday, November 18   Read Ezekiel 34:11-16, 20-24.

The image of a shepherd at work had been a part of the identity of the people of Israel. In that image was everything good and positive about their life and economy. Also in that memory was the commitment of a "good shepherd." A good shepherd was one who loved the sheep and who would lay down life and limb for the protection of the flock. If left to themselves the sheep would wander off, often into harm's way. So the good shepherd was alert, always watching.

In the reading for today, Ezekiel quotes God as saying that God is the good shepherd. God will search, seek, bring, and feed God's flock. What better strength and protection could the people of God possibly want? God promises to be shepherd for God's flock. What better hope could people want, especially when they find themselves far from God?

God calls to the near and to the far, to the gathered and to the scattered, with a promise that a great day is coming when they all will be together.

Prayer: **God of our flock, cover us with your protection, care, and nurture. Help us to follow your example of caring for others. Amen.**

✤Pastor, Iglesia Metodista Unida El Mesías, Mission, Texas (Conferencia Río Grande).

Tuesday, November 19   Read Ezekiel 34:11-16, 20-24.

To the scattered flock of Israel the True Shepherd has spoken. The True Shepherd has shared a word of hope and promise. God has called them home with the promise that all would be welcome, regardless of condition. The promise of God was to mend and heal those who had been injured and sick. Where else but one's home can better healing and restoration happen?

God also has spoken a word of judgment that is coming to those who have exploited others. God knew the sufferings of those who had been exiles in other lands. God heard the cries of pain of those being shoved and pushed aside as if they were nothing. Those whose lives had been as prey of others would be so no longer. The promise was the establishment of one true shepherd, who would feed and protect them. This was the promise of salvation.

Prayer: **God of justice and God of our flock, let us be open to the cries of those in our midst who are exiles from their homelands. Let us share home and hope with them, who have left their homes and who seek new lives in and among us. Let us not judge them with anger and suspicion, but let us welcome them with love and joy. We pray in the name of the Good Shepherd, Jesus. Amen.**

Wednesday, November 20   Read Psalm 100.

This is the psalm many pastors invoke when presenting a new hymn to the congregation, one that hardly anyone knows. But it is an invitational psalm used by the psalmist to speak of the great joy and gladness that comes when being truly in the presence of the Lord, which is true worship. To enter into worship we must enter with the proper attitude toward God. We remember that it was God who made us, that we are God's people, and that we are sheep of God's flock.

Here is that image again, that the people of God are the sheep of God. Have you not heard a flock of contented sheep? If sheep could reason and be thankful, they would be thankful for things that we humans take for granted. How often do we take life for granted? Food? And how often have we stopped to just say, "Thank you, God, for all that we have"? Unfortunately, the attitude in this country often is to leave the official giving of thanks until Thanksgiving Day.

Not so, says the psalmist. "Enter his gates with thanksgiving, and his courts with praise. Give thanks to him, bless his name."

If we are to worship God, we are to do so with the right spirit and attitude.

Prayer: **Dear Provider God, forgive us for neglecting the most precious of your blessings. Open our lips and spirits to always say thank you. In Jesus' name. Amen.**

Thursday, November 21   Read Ephesians 1:15-23.

Scripturally, this is known as Paul's prayer for the Christians in Ephesus. Here he gives thanks for the great faith and love they have in the Lord Jesus Christ. Their fame was widespread in that their actions reflected faith and love. In this prayer Paul also is petitioning God to give these believers a spirit of wisdom and revelation of the hope that he himself has received. And the hope of that petition is for the church to have the marks of a true church: stronger loyalty to Christ and stronger love for one another. The writer of this Epistle knew these two things went hand in hand. One cannot profess to love Christ if she or he does not love one another. True expressions of Christ are found in expressions of love and charity for our fellow human beings.

Many have been the churches of our past and present that have measured their successes with stained glass and cushioned pew. Sadly, what has happened in the hearts of the people who make up these churches is that their vision is stained and their hearts are cushioned to the hurts and needs of a world in pain. The call from God is to go beyond the material to the spiritual and physical needs of everyone.

Prayer: **O God of all people, open our hearts to the needs of your world. Let us receive more knowledge of Christ as we serve you more, through our compassion toward each other. In Christ's name. Amen.**

Friday, November 22   Read Ephesians 1:15-23.

This day marks an anniversary that we wish had never happened. It is an event forever marked in the minds and hearts of those who remember it. Thirty-three years ago our nation lost its president to an assassin's bullets.

For the writer of Ephesians the event that would forever mark its place in his heart and soul was the resurrection of Jesus. And he calls us as Christians to make that event the central event of our lives, for the power used in the Resurrection is the power at work in, through, and among us.

The Christian church of today is a powerful agent of God. It cannot live its life or fulfill its calling with anything less than the power of the Resurrection. God's power cannot be surpassed. If a church is of God, seeking God's power through prayer, worship, and faithful service, then the power of that church cannot be surpassed either. In Paul's terms that church would be rich spiritually just as God intended. Yet, how many of our churches refuse to cash that check promised us in terms of power, content instead to live as if bankrupt. Many are those who come to the church with arms crossed expecting entertainment rather than enlightenment, or a handout rather than a handle on how to better live one's life.

Prayer: **God of grace and God of power, grant us all we need to be powerful in our service, our faithfulness, and our love. In the name of Jesus we pray. Amen.**

Saturday, November 23   Read Matthew 25:31-46.

It seems almost humorous. When the disciples became like proud tourists visiting their spiritual capital in Matthew 24, Jesus lets loose with a long sermon on the end days. And part of the teaching centers on the immediate needs of one another rather than in sky gazing and the looking for signs of same.

Jesus speaks of the final judgment when the people of the world will be judged according to their faithfulness. Those who would receive eternal life will be those who had seen, heard, and responded to those who were in need. The way that Jesus presents it, those who were blessed with eternal life could not believe how simple it had been. Jesus says that the believers should respond to the most basic of human needs: thirst, hunger, loneliness of the stranger, clothing, and visitation of those who are sick or in prison. To further stress the importance of such acts, Jesus says that when we do it for the least of these "who are members of my family, you [do] it to me."

The accursed will cry out with the same question, and they will receive the reply, "Just as you did not do it to one of the least of these, you did not do it to me." The accursed will respond that for reasons of safety and caution they could not help everyone. The accursed will also respond that for the sake of national boundaries they could not help everyone. When we deny someone these things, we deny Jesus himself.

Prayer: **God of one global family, let us see, hear, and respond to the needs of everyone. Let us see beyond boundaries and personal safety to the cries of your people in need. In the name of Christ, whom we will be helping. Amen.**

Sunday, November 24   Read Matthew 25:31-46.

The children of the church loved the idea. The parents could be heard to gasp as I asked the children during the children's sermon to line up in two lines, those who were sheep and those who were goats. It was two little boys, barely two years old, who lined up as goats. The others, either through personal knowledge of the scripture or through imitation of others, knew to line up as sheep. It did set the stage for me to preach on this passage, and the parents seemed more attentive. I also knew the moms of those two little boys had a lot they wanted to tell their sons after church.

The message of this Matthean passage remains so powerful. In our acts of kindness, those acts that we do almost without thinking, we are conveying to others the love and compassion of God. These are acts of kindness that do not involve large contributions of money; rather, they are the simple sharing with those in need of things we already have.

My wife in her childhood lived near the border between Mexico and the U.S.A. Many persons stopped at her home asking for water and food, and all received these things from her father and mother. Many of us can remember days that our parents and grandparents did the same in sharing food and water with those who braved asking. The same can be said of neighbors who shared their clothing with those with lesser means. Many of us also remember parents, grandparents, aunts, or uncles going to visit the sick, going to visit those in prison. Our family members' examples of compassionate action have *shown* us Christ's words, "Just as you did it to one of the least of these who are members of my family, you did it to me."

Prayer: God of one flock and family, let us with loving kindness this day and all days share with those in need the basics of human life. Amen.

WAITING FOR GOD'S PROMISES

November 25—December 1, 1996   **Harry Y. Pak✤**
Monday, November 25   Read Isaiah 64:1-5*b*;
Mark 13:32-37.

"Life is difficult." * With these words M. Scott Peck succinctly sums up the human condition. There is a yearning in the human heart to transform the difficult present into a brighter future. The same yearning is reflected in our Isaiah passage.

In our activist culture we assume that such transformation would come through human efforts. The prophet, however, was convinced that God would have to bring it about because human efforts had proven futile. So he pleaded and waited for God to come down.

Waiting provides a relevant theme for the Advent season, which we are about to usher in. While waiting, Isaiah's people looked for spectacular signs of God's appearing, such as mountains quaking and fire kindling brushwood, causing water to boil. At the first Christmas, too, people waited for the Messiah's coming in splendor and might. Thus, except for a few shepherds, they missed the cry of a baby coming from a Bethlehem stable. In search for the spectacular, it is easy to overlook the ordinary events through which God appears.

Prayer: **O God, may this Advent season be for us a time of expectant waiting for your coming, especially through common, ordinary events of life. Amen.**

✤Pastor, LaVerne United Methodist Church, LaVerne, California.

*M. Scott Peck, *The Road Less Traveled* (New York: Simon & Schuster, 1978), p. 15.

Tuesday, November 26   Read Isaiah 64:5c-7;
                                                          Luke 3:1-18.

While waiting for God to come down, Isaiah becomes intro-
spective. He becomes aware that "we have sinned," causing him
to repent. Repentance is an appropriate theme for Advent, the
season of waiting, which begins this Sunday. While waiting we,
too, need to repent.

But what does it mean to repent? At First United Methodist
Church in Honolulu, where I used to pastor, there is an annual
lectureship of some importance. In conjunction with the lectures a
reception is held at the parsonage to honor the lecturers. My wife
and I would spend some time cleaning the house. Invariably, we
were left with excess clutter. In desperation we would designate
a bedroom where we would dump all the unsightly things. But
during the reception we could never completely relax, knowing
that the house was not altogether in order. In our minds was, *What
if the guests want a tour of the house?* This is an analogy of how
not to repent.

By contrast, Isaiah completely bares his outer and inner life
before God. This is true repentance. True repentance is what John
the Baptist urges for us in preparation for the coming of the
Messiah. The preparation John insists we make is the cleansing of
the whole life by repenting.

It may be that precisely this call to repentance can prompt us to
clean up the inner clutter of our lives, especially as we prepare for
Advent and Christmas. There is joy born of true repentance. This
feeling of joy is not unlike the joy of a patient, who, after major
cancer surgery, is told that all the malignancy has been removed.

Prayer: **O God, may Advent be for us a time of repentance, that
we may find the true joy of Christmas. Amen.**

Wednesday, November 27   Read Psalm 80:1-7, 17-19.

The season of waiting, Advent, inevitably leads to the season of fulfillment, Christmastide. In actual life, what happens if the season of waiting seems interminable? This is the psalmist's predicament expressed in today's reading.

The psalmist prays, but God is silent and indifferent. Even worse, God seems to be cruel and heartless. So to the prayer for bread, tears are offered. In the people's thirst, they are given more tears. They are humiliated before their enemies, who deride them and taunt them. Still the psalmist does not lose hope. Still he pleads for God to come to save: "Restore us, O God of hosts, / let your face shine, that we may be saved!"

Reginald Fuller gives this passage a Christological interpretation, since, he says, passages referring to the earthly king of Israel may be transferred to the messianic King. Interpreted in this way, the phrases "man of thy right hand" and "son of man" become references to Christ and the passage becomes a petition for God to intervene by sending the Messiah.*

Let us take this psalm to heart. Then our waiting will be expectant, even if the fulfillment does not neatly follow the liturgical calendar. Terry Anderson, a U.S. journalist and former hostage in Iran, is an example of expectant waiting. Often in solitary confinement, he waited six years for his release. He was tortured physically and mentally. But he never gave up. His faith and stubbornness kept him going.

Prayer: **O God, may our waiting be faith-filled and expectant, no matter how dark the present circumstances may be. Amen.**

---

*Reginald H. Fuller, *Preaching the Lectionary* (Collegeville, MN: Liturgical Press, 1984), p. 202.

Thursday, November 28   Read 1 Corinthians 1:3-9.

What is the meaning of Advent, the season of waiting, for us Christians for whom Christmas has happened already? Are we simply to play-act as we wait for another Christmas? Today's Epistle reading answers this question.

Paul wrote after Jesus was born, lived, taught, faced the cross, resurrected, and ascended. Paul explained the meaning of waiting in this post-Resurrection era as he deals with a problem he faced in the Corinthian church. Leaders of the church boasted of their advanced knowledge of the gospel, their eloquence, and the variety of their spiritual gifts. While offering thanksgiving for these gifts, Paul immediately sets them in the context of the future, of the things yet to come. He reminds the Corinthians that in spite of all their present knowledge, God still has more truths to disclose. God sent God's son into the world that first Christmas. But Christ will come again to complete what the first coming started.

Paul reminds us, too, that even as we give thanks for the gifts we already possess, we wait for Christ's coming again to complete our Christian life. But the second coming need not be only the distant end-time event. Christ's coming can be any time when our lives are touched and renewed by the Holy Spirit. Thus, Advent is the season of thanksgiving that Christ has already come *and* the season of anticipating Christ's coming again to complete what he has begun.

Prayer: **O God, may we come more and more to a spirit of thanksgiving for Christ's coming and a sense of anticipation for Christ's coming again. Amen.**

Friday, November 29   Read Matthew 13:24-30.

The three parables of Jesus, which constitute the texts for the next three meditations, all deal with future fulfillment of what is now only an unpromising beginning. They are appropriate texts for Advent, the time of waiting and preparing.

One day, as I was pulling into the church parking lot, I caught a glimpse of a familiar figure going into the church office. He had already come three times that week asking for help. I immediately concluded that he had come again to ask for more help. When I entered the office, our church secretary was beaming. She explained that this man, who, I thought, had come to ask for more help, had come to give a donation to the church. This experience taught me not to hastily judge another person.

The parable of the wheat and tares addresses this issue. Among other things it deals with the difficulty of distinguishing the good from the bad. God allows the bad to live side by side with the good until the harvest time. This is a message of promise as well as warning. Here, the analogy of seeds to human life breaks down. Weeds cannot possibly grow up to produce a crop of wheat. But human beings can be changed! Even if everyone else may consider us weeds, God, who knows us inside and outside, sees the potential in us for bearing good fruit. That is the promise. But we must conscientiously seek to cultivate our lives to produce good fruit. That is the warning. The season of Advent is a time to cultivate our lives.

Prayer: **O God, may our lives measure up to the promise, and in due season produce good fruit. Amen.**

Saturday, November 30 Read Matthew 13:31-32;
Mark 13:28-31.

The parable of the mustard seed has reminded me of the days when I was a seminary intern serving as one of the campus ministers at the University of California, Berkeley. I was leading a Bible study of just four participants, including me. In the meantime, our mandate was to serve some thirty thousand students with the saving word of the gospel.

A similar experience must have faced the first followers of Jesus. As they tried to quantitatively assess their ministry as Jesus' disciples, the result seemed meager. This parable was an answer to this discouraged band of disciples.

It is also an answer to us in our times of discouragement in discipleship. The mustard seed was one of the smallest of all seeds. But when it was fully grown, it often reached a height of eight to ten feet, and the birds could perch on its branches to find shade. So we ought not to be discouraged by small beginnings. What is important is all the potential stored in that small beginning.

But the growth is not ours to dictate. God, in God's own time, will bring about growth and harvest. In the meantime, we need to wait—a relevant thought for Advent.

Our waiting, however, is not passive waiting. Before the seed can be planted the ground needs to be prepared. The planter must make sure the seed is provided with the most fertile place to germinate and grow. Then, and only then, do we wait—expectantly.

Prayer: **O God, having done our best to prepare the soil and plant the seed of the gospel, help us to wait patiently and expectantly, trusting in your power to bring forth growth. Amen.**

Sunday, December 1   Read Matthew 13:33-35.

In today's scripture, Jesus draws a very familiar picture of Palestinian home life. It is the picture of a housekeeper mixing a tiny amount of yeast into the dough before baking, and then waiting until the whole dough is leavened.

A small amount of yeast can leaven the whole dough and change its quality. Just so, what really counts in Christian influence in the world is the indwelling dynamic force of the Spirit.

There is a further lesson. Once the yeast is put into the dough, the yeast does its work silently, almost imperceptibly. Like yeast, the kingdom of God expands silently and almost imperceptibly. The growth of the kingdom is dynamic, yet silent. This contrasts with our cult of noise in which we think the desired results will come if we can only shout long enough and loudly enough.

Faithful Christians are few. We know all too well what it means to find few others at our work or in our class in school who seek to witness to Christian concern for moral values, honesty at work, or peace with one another and among nations. Christ's followers are but a small minority—but we are the yeast in the world! As we quietly witness to our faith, there is in us a hidden dynamic to revitalize others.

The kingdom of God works like the yeast. There is a silent yet steady indwelling of the present by God's future. So even as we wait in this Advent season, the future which God has in store for us is already permeating this present world.

Prayer: **O God, trusting in the promise of a silent but dynamic force hidden in the yeast, help us to recommit ourselves to witness for our faith. Amen.**

HASTEN THE COMING OF CHRIST

December 2–8, 1996   **Roy I. Sano✤**
Monday, December 2   Read 2 Peter 3:8-15a.

We can make a difference

"Hastening the coming of the day of God."

During Advent we recall God's coming to us in Jesus of Nazareth. We also look forward to Christ's fulfilling God's reign. Finally, during Advent we celebrate Christ's coming to us in the interim, time and again, and transforming us and this world.

We read an amazing point in verse 12: We are not only "waiting for" but also "hastening the coming of the day of God" by bringing people to repentance. Regardless of human dependence upon God's grace, we can never trivialize human contributions. God works through us humans to further the kingdom of God on earth.

In eighteenth-century England, Christians from Moravia reminded John Wesley that he would be "by grace . . . saved through faith . . . not the result of works" (Eph. 2:8-9). On May 24, 1738, while attending a meeting in Aldersgate-street, he felt his heart "strangely warmed" and experienced assurance that he did indeed trust in Christ for his salvation.

An excessive occupation with faith, however, led some Moravians to become passive. They were called "quietists." These distortions of faith eventually led Wesley to balance faith with works. He turned to the Apostle Paul's call for "faith working through love" (Gal. 5:6).

This week we will focus on specific works that can help bring God's kingdom, works that our piety and dogma often manage to overlook when we read and study the Bible.

Prayer: Embolden us, dear God, to do your work to pave the way for Christ's coming in fullness. Amen.

✤Bishop, Los Angeles Area, The United Methodist Church; California.

Tuesday, December 3   Read Isaiah 40:1-2.

Costly comfort

When the children of Israel returned to Jerusalem from their Babylonian captivity, the site of the devastation was a crushing blow to them. Isaiah 40, therefore, begins with a call to speak tenderly to them a word of comfort.

The word is clear. Israel is forgiven because she has paid for her sin. People *pay* for the forgiveness of their sin? Some will cry, "Heresy!" "Blasphemy!" at that assertion.

Misguided zeal in our piety and excesses in our dogma, even though based on valid points, prevent us from seeing in the Bible the contributions we are called to make. Without this recognition, forgiveness degenerates into cheap grace. We are let off the hook too easily.

Wholesome forgiveness comes from remorse, repentance, and trust in God's grace. Forgiveness (justification) cannot, however, be separated from restoration of health in us and those we have violated (sanctification). Restitution offers a token or sign of the restoration which faith nurtures in us. Restitution for individuals or nations can feel like a term served, penalty paid, and demands which are double for our sins.

Most of us are not ready for this costly task. If we only trust God's grace we encourage a cozy comfort. Faith brings a task and gives us strength to work with love (see Galatians 5:6). Beyond trust, therefore, healing calls for painful choices in the long process of salvaging the damage we have created. We can only take comfort in integrity when through caring, if costly, acts we try honestly and humbly to rectify wrongs.

Prayer: Comfort us, dear God, to know we bear witness to your forgiveness and healing when we seek to make restitution to those whom we have wronged. Amen.

Wednesday, December 4   Read 2 Peter 3:8-15a.

Speed up a slow God

Early Christians had expected Christ would return more quickly to end their suffering and clear up the mess in the world. They grew impatient because Christ seemed so slow in coming.

This passage reminds believers that a loving God works on a different schedule because of another agenda: "not wanting any to perish." God's supposed delay was creating more space for "all to come to repentance."

Creating more space where people can turn from their old ways and give themselves to new possibilities in Christ is one way we can help to hasten the coming of Christ. We create space in all kinds of ways. John Wesley started a movement which gathered people into "classes" of eight to twelve persons. There they shared what was happening to them and opened the Bible to hear God's word. They prayed for each other and collected offerings to extend their care. Classes gathered in chapels for worship. Along with other classes, they formed a United Society as a leaven in the larger society.

Collectively, they promoted self-care and personal development. They changed the face of England, which was suffering the human degradation and disruption caused by industrial development and urban congestion.

Today we see an adaptation of the classes in a host of Christian churches, in other religious traditions, and in groups with no explicit religious affiliation. When Christians create spaces for human interaction, they speed up the coming of Christ into the lives of individuals and spread hope-filled changes in neighborhoods.

Prayer: **Come, Lord Jesus, as we create spaces for you to move through human interaction to transform lives. Amen.**

Thursday, December 5   Read Isaiah 40:3-11.

"If . . . , then . . ."

> Every valley shall be lifted up,
>   and every mountain and hill be made low,
> Then the glory of the LORD shall be revealed.

The future tenses in Isaiah 40:4 seem to be imperatives: if these conditions are met, then the glorious and blessing filled consequences promised in verse 5 will happen. We can prepare the way for "the glory of the LORD" to come.

Lifting valleys and lowering high places symbolize the acts of the Sovereign Savior promised in Mary's *Magnificat* (Luke 1:46-55). So sure is Mary of God's promises that she states them as accomplished facts. The Lord who will come into the world through her "has brought down the powerful from their thrones, and lifted up the lowly" (Luke 1:52).

What appears in the *Magnificat* as promises of God's action appear in Isaiah as human responsibilities. The lowly people in captivity are to be lifted up; the mighty on their thrones are to be brought low. If they do that, then the glory, or the awesome and rich presence, of the Lord will come in conspicuous ways.

Preparing a way for the Lord's coming also includes straightening out the circuitous routes we impose on people to achieve the same gains we have obtained and leveling the playing field where we live out our lives. If we promote equity in these weightier matters of justice (see Matthew 23:23; Micah 6:8), then all people shall see the glory of the Lord together.

Prayer: **Gracious God who works for justice, renew our resolve to bring down the obstructions, straighten out the crooked paths, and level the rough roads people must travel to obtain dignity and the necessities of life, so that your glorious presence will become conspicuous for all. Amen.**

Friday, December 6   Read Isaiah 40:1-11.

Impossible starts

Those who are forgiven break with the past. They are free then to launch a fresh start.

There is a sure sign of our capacity to make changes. In the face of devastations, when the landscape is desolate and without promising possibilities, we "prepare the way" for the Lord's coming. Oh, the seeming cruelty of God's demanding grace! No indulgences in cheap grace here!

Persons who have been through a Twelve Step program, such as Alcoholics Anonymous, know that they start in the depth of a life in ruins, a life they have let slip from their best self. But, praise God, they also radiate the courage to make a new start. They prepare ways for healing and strength to come coursing through them despite the devastations they face. In their wilderness, they are preparing a way for the God as they know God to come to them. Hallelujah!

We now face all around us the long haul of recovery from the wreckage left in the wake of the Cold War. As a nation we pushed for common defense and neglected domestic tranquility. Our versions of the havoc left by the Cold War in Eastern Europe haunts us as well.

Thanks be to God, therefore, for those who bear witness to the advent—the coming—of the Sovereign Savior into our abandoned cities, into hovels hidden deep in the hollows of the hill country, and into lonely hamlets far removed from the resources of urban centers.

Prayer: **Wreckage abounds, dear God, and yet you call us to make a fresh start in unpromising circumstances. Because you create community out of chaos, we join you in rebuilding our lives, our neighborhoods, our nations, and our churches. Amen.**

Saturday, December 7 Read Mark 1:1-8;
2 Peter 3:10-13.

Break from sin and evil

While we undertake works, "faith working through love" (Gal. 5:6) is, after all, faith at work. We generally think of faith as an act of entrusting our lives to Christ, who loved us, gave himself for us, and was raised from the dead. We focus, therefore, on the central events of the past.

By contrast, Second Peter 3:10 and 12 directs our attention to the climactic actions of God in the future. Faith in this framework is our response to the promised coming of Christ. Two dimensions in the climactic coming of Christ appear in Second Peter 3. First, God will bring an end to the heavens, the elements, and the earth, which are now familiar to us; and second, God will usher in "new heavens and a new earth" (v. 13).

Tomorrow we look at the new heavens and a new earth. Today, we consider faith as an act of joining this God who is bringing an end to the old world. We enter into God's activity through faith when we accept and yield ourselves to the course of action which this God pursues in order to end the power of sin and evil.

With this faith we turn away—repent—from our sin and from evil, and move toward a repentance John the Baptist first called us to: "a baptism of repentance for the forgiveness of sins." In the last half of the twentieth century, we have seen the erosion and eventual fall of the principalities and powers of European colonialism and of Communism that occurred when people denounced and renounced sin and evil. We bear witness, even if in modest measures, to the melting away, dissolving, and ending (2 Peter 3:10, 12) of the powers of sin and evil that will occur climactically in the coming of Christ.

Prayer: **Dear God, we do not at present fully embody the end of sin and evil. We wait for Christ's coming and cry out, "Come, Lord Jesus!" Amen.**

Sunday, December 8   Read Psalm 85:1-2, 8-13.

New heavens and a new earth are coming

Through faith active in works of repentance, we join God when we choose to leave behind what God is bringing to an end. The God who will end sin and evil in this world also promises to bring "new heavens and a new earth" (2 Peter 3:13).

In Psalm 85 we read that "surely [God's] salvation is at hand for those who fear him." We find here several features of this salvation in the new heavens and a new earth. First, earthly changes will occur. The psalmist was not speaking symbolically, but speaking literally of ecological transformation on this earth (vv. 1a, 12). The material world will be pervaded with a spiritual dimension because glory will dwell in the land. Heaven and earth become compatible, no longer separated because of human sin!

Second, this glory, or awesome presence, of God will "speak peace" to what we experience as divisive distinctions. While tenderness of love often clashes with zealous faithfulness, "steadfast love and faithfulness will meet" in God's realm. Crusading for righteousness can cause turmoil just as those pursuing peace can overlook evil. But the glory of the Lord will cause these two to "kiss and make up," as it were, in God's reign.

Third, "faithfulness will spring up from the ground, and righteousness will look down from the sky" (see also 2 Peter 3:13). Heaven and earth will be joined; the Creator and creation will be united. The vision of the psalm joins Revelation 21:3 in proclaiming, "The home of God is among mortals. He will dwell with them as their God."

This week we have named contributions we can make through works of faith, contributions that will bring our world closer to the new heaven and new earth that God desires. May God grant us the courage and faith to persevere in that work.

Prayer: Dear God, speak peace to your creation. Amen.

EMPOWERED BY THE SPIRIT

December 9–15, 1996
Monday, December 9

Loretta Girzaitis✤
Read Isaiah 61:1-4.

The opening verses of Isaiah 61, like the Servant Songs in Isaiah 42 and 49, emphasize the role of the servant who is to bring justice to the nations. The servant is one who is chosen (Isa. 42:1) and God delights in him. The affirmation of being chosen and beloved is later given to Jesus at both his baptism and transfiguration (see Luke 3:22 and Matthew 17:5).

In Isaiah 49 the prophet feels he has failed in his work. Despite his discouragement, he recognizes that he is important in the sight of God and that his reward and strength are from God (v. 4).

This theme is repeated in Isaiah 61 when the prophet underscores this dependence upon God through the Spirit who has given him a task. Explicitly, this task focuses on justice issues: "to bring good news to the oppressed, to bind up the brokenhearted, to proclaim liberty to the captives," and freedom for those languishing in prison; to comfort all who grieve.

The prophet also emphasized the need to announce the year of the Lord's favor when all will be forgiven. The people recognized this year of the Lord God's favor to be the "sabbatical year" when all debts were to be cancelled and all slaves freed.* Their brokenheartedness would be healed as they began life anew.

Prayer: **Lord God, through the centuries you call us as your favored ones to become servants to those in need. Help me in this ministry. Amen.**

✤Spiritual director based in St. Odilla's parish, Shoreview, Minnesota; Roman Catholic layperson; St. Paul, Minnesota.

*See Leviticus 25 (esp. vv. 1-17); Deuteronomy 15:1-11; Jeremiah 34:8-22.

Tuesday, December 10   Read Isaiah 61:8-11.

Isaiah 61 continues with the emphasis of God's yearning for justice. God's words are both eloquent and threatening as Isaiah emphasizes God's love of justice and hatred of oppression and robbery. He assures us that God will make a covenant with those who are just and promises that everyone will recognize that God has blessed those who work for justice. The promise of God is also that justice will prevail just as certainly as the earth produces growth and the seed yields its fruit.

The Lord God's yearning for justice has stirred many hearts and changed lives. However, it seems that those who choose to become prophets pleading for justice are not blessed but suffer rejection, loss of reputation, and condemnation. This happened to Jeremiah, Elijah, Micah, and other prophets of old.

It is a risky business becoming a servant of the Lord in seeking justice today for the homeless, the refugee, people who are HIV positive or have AIDS, the poor, those in prison, the lonely, and those who are different. Fear of unpleasant consequences paralyzes many, giving evil more strength to continue its destruction and pain.

What did God mean in the promise that all would acknowledge those who do justice as being blessed? History seems to contradict that. Maybe one needs to lay down one's life to suffer persecution as the seeds of justice are planted. The harvest may be long in coming, and so blessedness on earth may be delayed.

Prayer: **Jesus, you have said, "Blessed are those who are persecuted for righteousness' sake, for theirs is the kingdom of heaven."*** **Grant me the courage to act in the directions you call me. Amen.**

---

*Matthew 5:10

Wednesday, December 11   Read Psalm 126.

Those who risked giving up the comforts of Babylon returned home to Jerusalem to the task of rebuilding. Generations had passed and those returning had never seen the Holy City. Destruction lay all around them, yet they remembered the stories of Jerusalem's glory that their ancestors had told them. Their return was a dream, and the exiles wondered what the reality would be.

The psalmist's trust is implicit. The Lord has done great things for the people in bringing them back from captivity. And so the psalmist pleads for the restoration of their fortunes. He compares them to the living water found in the streams of the desert. He hopes they are now ready to forget their tears and to sing and dance with joy. The people understood well the process of planting and harvesting, and so the psalm expresses itself in these images.

With God, time is non-existent; everything is an everlasting now. The rhythm of sowing and reaping is parallel to the rhythm of sorrowing and rejoicing. The Exile was a sorrowing period, a period of death, both physical and spiritual. In that dying, however, there was the promise of new life. Returning to the Holy City was exultation for this new generation that would birth a new Jerusalem.

Our lives carry a similar rhythm. Disappointments, separations, and sometimes even spiritual exile are to be expected and encountered. If we allow a hibernation period at these times, then in *God's time* one's spirit will be rejuvenated and new birth will follow.

Prayer: **I need your wisdom, O God, to recognize these moments of death that bring sorrow and disillusionment. Let me rest in your time as I wait for new birth. Help me recognize the joy of resurrection and new life when it occurs. Amen.**

Thursday, December 12   Read Luke 1:46-55.

It is likely that Mary was confused, uncertain, questioning when the angel appeared with this heavenly message. Although every Jewish child-bearing woman yearned for the privilege of bearing the expected Messiah, it must have been overwhelming for this young teenager to realize that she was the one chosen.

If we put ourselves in her place and let our emotions and fears take over, we can begin to sense what Mary's consent must have meant. Living in a small, confined village, she knew the pregnancy would be visible and condemnation would follow. She needed to die to all these concerns, and so instead of focusing on them she focused on the God who chose her. She trusted that the Spirit would heal what was broken.

Perhaps she found a caravan on its way to Jerusalem, by which she could safely travel to see her kinswoman Elizabeth, about whom the angel had spoken. That long journey would have given her time to assimilate the wonder of what was happening to her. I can imagine that she struggled with the wilderness in which she found her spirit.

Yet her meeting with Elizabeth was one of exultation. By the very fact that Elizabeth acknowledged the child in her womb, Mary was affirmed in the mystery within her. She could not contain her joy.

She burst forth in that song of praise which is so familiar to us. Her song did not focus on herself but on the God who had done great things for her. Accusations and isolation might rend her heart in the months ahead, but now it was enough to savor God's love. She acknowledged the power God had to bless the poor and the lowly.

Prayer: **God, help me to confirm the great things you have done for me in a spirit of praise and humility as Mary did. Amen.**

Friday, December 13   Read 1 Thessalonians 5:16-24.

Paul makes clear his firm belief that regardless of what happens in life, whether it is painful or joyful, disappointing or elating, Christians need to rejoice. He also insists that Christians are called to pray and give thanks to God at all times.

Such a stance is possible because the Lord Jesus calls us to this lifestyle. We respond because the Lord is trustworthy and will be with us always.

Paul also cautions Christians to discern the character and behavior of contemporary prophets by weighing the values of the gospel against contemporary social values.

Paul's admonitions are as meaningful today as they were almost 2,000 years ago. How joyful and trusting are we in times of distress? When and how do we pray? Do we listen to the prophets of our day as they call us to examine our societal values? How much do we trust that the Lord Jesus will guide us both in the valley and on the mountaintop, in darkness and in light? How do we keep our body, soul, and spirit irreproachable by avoiding evil? What evil persists in our lives? How aware are we of the impact that television, magazines, and the electronic highway can have in negating the call to live out our lives as followers of Jesus Christ?

Prayer: **Lord Jesus Christ, your demands are frequently greater than those made by the secular culture in which I live. They require courage, stamina, and trust to withstand selfish desires and satisfactions that draw us away from you. Empower me to be true to you. Amen.**

Saturday, December 14   Read John 1:6-8.

The focus on this section of the Prologue in John's Gospel is on John the Baptizer. He was a man sent by God as a witness to testify about the Light that was to come.

We met John earlier as we read of his miraculous conception and birth. Now, when he appears on the scene as an adult, he makes clear that he is simply preparing a way for the person who is to come. He is testifying to a Light that would dispel the darkness.

The Hebrews had waited for centuries for such a Light, and after hearing John their hopes were high that, finally, this long waiting period would be over.

Most likely, John, who had come from the desert and spoken so vehemently and chastisingly, repelled some of his listeners. His forceful voice burst forth as he encouraged them to acknowledge their sins publicly and wash themselves so as to be ready for the Light (the Messiah).

The Jews were familiar with ritual bathing, so John's requirement of cleansing carried weight. As they listened to the accusations about their lives, they were moved to purify themselves. And John's repetitive caution kept reminding them that all this was in preparation for the Light that was to come.

Suggestion for meditation: **When have you been like John the Baptizer, setting your own preferences aside so that the Spirit could shine through you? In addition, how have you prepared yourself to dispel the darkness within your heart to make room for the Light? What courage is required of you to allow that Light to shine through?**

Sunday, December 15   Read John 1:19-28.

It is important to recognize that the particular Jews who are mentioned in this reading were hostile. They awaited a political Messiah. When they sent the priests and Levites from Jerusalem, they were trying to trap John by the questioning.

They were not only curious but also anxious to find out who this man was, who on his own initiative began to preach and baptize. There had always been an expectation that Elijah, taken up to heaven in a flaming chariot, would return just prior to the Messiah's coming. It was important for them to know the identity of this man. Was he Elijah?

When John was asked, "Are you the Messiah?" he recognized their hostility. However, this did not keep him from being truthful. "No, I am not the Messiah; or Elijah, the Prophet," he answered. But the emissaries needed a response. His reply was familiar to them, for he quoted Isaiah. "I am the voice of one crying out in the wilderness, 'Make straight the way of the Lord.'"

As they pressed him to identify himself, John emphasized that someone was coming whom they did not know but who would baptize with the Spirit and not simply with water. Again he let them know the greatness of this man as he told them that he was not worthy to unfasten the strap of his sandal.

Suggestion for meditation: **How do I respond when someone is hostile to me? How would I identify myself if I were asked, "Who are you?" How do I point the way to Jesus? What can I do in the ten days before the Nativity to make straight the ways in my life for the coming of the Lord?**

FROM DAVID TO JESUS—A GOD OF GRACE

December 16–22, 1996   **Ira Gallaway✤**
Monday, December 16   Read 2 Samuel 7:1-11, 16.

We are in the season of Advent, moving toward Christmas. As I think about Advent as a time of penitence, as a time of darkness before the coming of light, I am deeply aware again of our total dependence upon God for all that is good in our lives.

In the Wesleyan tradition, there is a strong emphasis upon the grace of God. Grace is the unmerited love of God, given freely and generously to all who will turn to God, seek forgiveness, and accept God's love. John Wesley* made much of prevenient grace, the "grace that goes before," before anything that we can think or do. You see, God is always working to establish the Kingdom in our lives. The initiative is with God.

As we look at the promise of God to establish the Davidic kingdom (v. 16), we see a God who wills his love and salvation upon David and his descendants. This was the fruition of God's plan even though David later committed a grievous sin with Bathsheba.

I am grateful that we worship and serve a God who loves us and wills the Kingdom of heaven into our lives, even though we fall, even though we fail at times to be true to God's love. God's grace, the grace that goes before, is working and is freely available to us now as we turn to receive the love and forgiveness offered through Jesus Christ.

Prayer: **Dear Lord, whatever unlit and needy places there are in my life, let your light shine brightly into all the corners and bring hope and joy. Amen.**

✤United Methodist clergy; author; currently ministering to the Navajos through the Four Corners Native American Ministry; resides in Pagosa Springs, Colorado.
*John Wesley (1703-91), founder of the Methodist tradition.

Tuesday, December 17   Read Psalm 89:1-4.

As we read yesterday in 2 Samuel 7:16, God promised to establish the kingdom of God in and through David. This would be a kingdom that would last forever. In Psalm 89, the psalmist gives praise and testimony to the faithfulness of God in keeping the promise made to David.

The Hebrew word for God's loving-kindness is *hesed*. The English language does not have a word or words to adequately express what *hesed* means. Our word *love* has been so diluted in its meaning that it can refer to love of apple pie, the erotic love of sex, or, in its highest human expression, a mother's or father's love for their child. Our use of the word *love* has been so colloquialized and trivialized that to speak of love, even the love of God, has ceased to speak to our hearts and souls.

God's *hesed* is a kind of love that transcends any expression of love that we can imagine. The psalmist here sings a song to that kind of love. During Advent as we look toward Christmas, the song to sing is about a God who loves us. No matter what we may have done or have not done or will do, God loves us and wills for us salvation. The poet George Matheson says it best:

> O Love that wilt not let me go,
> I rest my weary soul in thee;
> I give thee back the life I owe,
> That in thine ocean depths its flow
> May richer, fuller be.

That is God's plan and will for us, to rest in the divine love and to have life that is rich and full.

Prayer: **God, touch us with your everlasting love and make us aware that you are with us no matter what our circumstances. Amen.**

Wednesday, December 18   Read Psalm 89:26.

Most of us, as modern day Christians, have at best a limited knowledge of the writings of the Hebrew scriptures (the Old Testament) and the theology of the story unfolded therein. Because of this we can read passages as rich as a mother lode of gold and fail to get the true meaning or to be moved at the center of our lives.

As David writes about his God and Father, who is the "rock of my salvation," he is talking about a foundation for living which is unmovable and everlasting. The Hebrew word for rock here is *sûr*, which has as its basic meaning the massive stone foundations which are the building blocks of mountains. As I write these words here in the San Juan Valley on the western slope of the majestic Rockies, I look out toward Pagosa Peak and Eagle Mountain. The word *rock* (or *sûr*) has a rich and gratifying meaning for me. The mountains I look at and the "rock" that is their foundation are solid and truly majestic. I cannot imagine the power it would take to move them.

God's love, shown through God's salvation, is so much greater and unshakeable that it is beyond my imagination. To try to build our lives on success or fame or fortune instead of on God's *hesed* is surely to build on sand and to live always in uncertainty. As Christians we need not live in uncertainty but in the sure knowledge and experience of God's love in Jesus Christ.

It is truly wonderful that with David, we can cry out to our God, "My Father and my God, and the Rock of my salvation!"

Prayer: **Lord, in this time of complexity and uncertainty in things spiritual and temporal, plant our feet upon the rock of faith in Jesus Christ. Amen.**

Thursday, December 19   Read Romans 16:25-27.

As Paul writes to the Christians in Rome, he speaks of the God "who is able to establish you according to my gospel and the preaching of Jesus Christ" (NASV; NKJV). One of the meanings of *establish* is "to set on a firm basis, to make permanent."

David had spoken of a God who had promised a kingdom to God's people. This kingdom was to be founded upon God's unending love. Certainly, Israel had not fully understood the nature and extent of that love on many occasions. Of course, this is true of us today as well; our understanding is limited and not always clear.

In some real sense the essence of God's love has always been a mystery. Paul says that the mystery has now been revealed in Jesus Christ. The real and wonderful nature of God's unmerited grace, *hesed* love, can *now* be known and expressed in Jesus Christ. When we come to know and experience God's love in Christ, we find our lives established on a firm basis. We can live without fear as we face the future with our faith upon the "rock of our salvation," which is Jesus Christ.

In First John 4:18, we read, "There is no fear in love, but perfect love casts out fear." For the longest time that verse was troublesome and perplexing to me. If I could live out perfect love, surely I could live without fear, but somehow, perfect love seemed beyond my grasp. Then one day as I was meditating on this verse, the insight came to me that perfect love has a name, and that name is Jesus Christ. Jesus Christ *can* cast out all fear. To live in Christ is to live in hope, not in fear.

Prayer: **Lord, help me depend not upon myself, but upon Jesus, the "rock of my salvation." Amen.**

Friday, December 20   Read Luke 1:26-29.

As I read the Nativity stories this Advent, I am deeply aware that we live in a skeptical age. This is a time in which truth is looked upon as relative rather than objective, especially in spiritual or moral matters. Some would even say that there is no such thing as objective truth or absolutes—that all truth is relative. Such a statement is false on the face of it, for if there is no such thing as an absolute or objective truth, then that statement itself becomes an absolute and therefore is an illogical statement.

When someone asks me if I believe in the Virgin Birth, my reply is, "That's the wrong question." The key that unlocks the mystery of Jesus Christ is the Cross and the Resurrection. I believe that Jesus Christ was crucified and raised from the dead. You see, I read the Nativity story as a believer in the crucified and resurrected Lord. And if God raised Jesus from the dead, then the mystery of the Angel Gabriel and a baby born to a virgin named Mary poses no problem for me at all.

The Angel Gabriel addressed Mary and said, "Hail, favored one! The Lord is with you" (NASV). When she heard this, Mary was troubled and did not fully understand what this meant. *Favored one*—filled with grace! This is God's promise for you and me. I do not pretend to understand this fully, but I am grateful that the promise given to David has been fulfilled in Jesus Christ. I am grateful that as I approach the throne of grace in the name of Jesus, this grace is available to me. Yes, even to me. The darkness of Advent is pierced and lighted by God's love and grace.

Prayer: **Lord, in an age of skepticism, let us still be open to the word that you want to share with us in the scriptures and in the presence of your Spirit. Amen.**

Saturday, December 21   Read Luke 1:30-33.

We began this week talking about the Davidic kingdom promised by God. We have seen where the promise of this kingdom has been fulfilled in Jesus Christ. The "rock of salvation" for David has been made personal to us and for us by the Incarnation, in the birth, life, death, and resurrection of Jesus Christ.

The Angel Gabriel spoke to Mary and said, "Do not be afraid, Mary, for you have found favor with God." Perhaps the angel went even further, as recorded in the Gospel of Matthew in a conversation with Joseph, and said to Mary as well that the name of this baby would be Jesus, ". . . for it is He who will save His people from their sins" (NASV). The message of the angel to both Mary and Joseph was that this baby would be the Savior of the world. Although both Mary and Joseph had questions about this extraordinary event in their lives, their response was one of faith and obedience.

The heritage of Mary and Joseph included the promise:

For a child will be born to us, a son will be given to us;
And the government will rest on His shoulders;
and His name will be called Wonderful Counselor,
    Mighty God,
Eternal Father, Prince of Peace.   —Isaiah 9:6, NASV

In Luke 1:32-33, the angel is really saying to Mary, "Israel has waited a long time, Mary, for the fulfillment of the promise to David and the word of the prophets. The time has now come. 'Immanuel, God is to be with us.'"

Isn't this what God is saying to each of us now? "In Jesus Christ, I am with each of you." We, too, can believe in the promise of God. Let all the world know!

Prayer: **O Jesus, who saves us from our sins, it is less than a week until we celebrate your birth on Christmas Day. Please, dear Jesus, may we be aware of the reality of your presence each day. Amen.**

Sunday, December 22   Read Luke 1:34-38.

Today is Christmas Sunday. I began this week of devotions by noting John Wesley's strong emphasis upon the grace of God, especially the prevenient grace of God—the grace that goes before.

That is what Christmas means to me. We worship and love and serve a God who promises always to come and bless us with forgiveness and unmerited love. The prevenient grace of God that always goes before was made present to the world and to each of us in Jesus Christ. Yes, God has come in Jesus Christ, and God will come to us again and again as we open our hearts to him. I believe in Christmas! I believe in a God who has come as Immanuel—God is with us—and who will always come.

You may ask, "How can I know this reality for myself?" In Mary's response to the angel we can find a clue—no, a model. As the angel explains to Mary that this Jesus will be born of the Holy Spirit and that "nothing will be impossible with God," Mary responds, "Behold, the bondslave of the Lord; be it done to me according to your word" (NASV). Or as another translation reports it, "I belong to the Lord, body and soul. . . . let it happen as you say" (J. B. PHILLIPS).

That is the most difficult affirmation of faith for each of us to make. To release control of our lives and to give that control to the Holy Spirit is the foundation act of faith for the Christian. But Oh! If we can honestly and hopefully make the same responses Mary did, then Christmas *will* come; God will enter anew into our lives!

Prayer: **Dear God, enter my life anew this day. Amen.**

PROCLAIMING THE PROMISE

December 23–29, 1996   **Elizabeth Canham**✤
Monday, December 23   Read Galatians 4:4-7.

Advent invites us to wait, recalling God's coming to us in the past, looking for God's daily visitation, and anticipating God's future coming in glory. We live these weeks like children longing for the moment when the gifts are unwrapped, and cries of joyful surprise escape us as we receive what we have longed for. Sometimes, though, we have waited impatiently, wondering if our desires will be met and not even sure we have been heard. Like the psalmist we sometimes ask agonizingly, "How long, O LORD?" (Psalm 13:1); and our hope grows dim.

A startlingly different waiting is explored in the Epistle to the Galatians, and it offers a clue to our puzzled wondering why God does not act. Here it is God who waits—for the *kairos*, the time of fullness—then participates in that moment of history that will change the world. God becomes flesh in order to set us free and make us members of the family—children and heirs. It was for this right time that God waited.

Aware now of our adoption, we cry from a place of loved intimacy, *"Abba!"* As we experience the promise's fulfillment, we are compelled to proclaim it. By so doing we express our joy in God.

God continues to wait for *kairos*. In our personal and corporate life there are many moments yet to come when we will reach a point of readiness and, like Mary, say yes to the divine word (see Luke 1:39).

Suggestion for meditation: **Who will we become if we dare to believe that *Abba* delights in us and waits to transform our experience?**

✤Episcopal priest; author; Director of Stillpoint Ministries and Assistant to the Bishop, the Episcopal Diocese of Western North Carolina, Black Mountain, North Carolina.

Christmas Eve

Tuesday, December 24   Read Luke 2:1-20.

Luke is the proclaimer of good news to those who are poor, despised, powerless, and disenfranchised. Included in Luke's Gospel are many stories about women, children, Samaritans, and lepers, all of whom were marginalized by the purity laws of Judaism. It is to God's *anwim*, those who need protection, that Jesus comes with words of welcome and hospitality. Luke names the shepherds as the first recipients of the message of Christ's birth, for they, too, were ostracized by the orthodox hierarchy. While they went about their ordinary work in the long, watchful night hours, God's messenger announced that the Savior had come.

Once their fear had been dispelled, these simple peasant folk made their way to Bethlehem where they found the Christ sheltered in circumstances of poverty and need. Matthew makes no mention of the stable or of the cattle feeding trough which provided a cradle for Jesus. Luke seems to be telling us that God's presence is revealed where few would expect such encounter and to those overlooked by the elite and culturally respectable.

Soon the shepherds began telling their story, and people were amazed by the message and the messengers. They passed on what was told them, "good news of great joy for all the people" in the coming of the Messiah. Thus, they became the heralds of the gospel.

Today we share the shepherds' joy in God. We know that we, too, are invited to participate in the proclamation that is communicated most powerfully by those in whom Christ is born and given shelter.

Prayer: **Gracious God, give us open hearts to perceive your presence within us. Give us joyful words to proclaim good news to all those you send to us in the spirit of your Son, who shared our humanity. Amen.**

Christmas Day

Wednesday, December 25　　　　　　　　　　Read John 1:1-14.

> In the beginning when God created the heavens and
> the earth, the earth was a formless void and darkness
> covered the face of the deep. . . . God said, "Let there
> be light"; and there was light.　　　—Genesis 1:1-3

> In the beginning was the Word, and the Word was with
> God, and the Word was God. . . . All things came into
> being through him, . . . in him was life, and the life
> was the light of all people.　　　—John 1:1, 3*a*, 4

Before time began, God spoke into the darkness of chaos
bringing light and order. Throughout history the divine word continued, often through reluctant messengers, frequently in times of
dreary waiting and chaotic loss. Then God came as the Word made
flesh—the ultimate proclamation of the Creator's love—dwelling
among us. God consented to share our humanity and so to sanctify
our struggle to live faithfully in a fearful world.

A compelling picture emerges in this passage. Christ comes
into the world bringing light, offering new life to all who are ready
to receive the gift. The Word is rejected by some but welcomed by
those ready to receive the invitation and become children of God.

Today grace upon grace is poured out for us as we celebrate the
gift of Godself. The Word is again given that we, too, might receive,
embody, and speak, into the struggling confusion of our day, the
life-giving word of hope. God is with us and for us. How can we
be afraid?

Prayer: **O God the Creator, fill our lives with wonder as we
witness new things coming to be. Grant that Christ the Word
may be heard above the cacophony of the world's fears and that
the Holy Spirit energize us to proclaim hope in a darkened
world. Amen.**

Thursday, December 26   Read Isaiah 61:10–62:3.

The rich images offered in these verses have the impact of a collection of rare and beautiful paintings gathered together for a special exhibit. The pictures are full, breathtaking, and leave the viewers in wonder that such creative genius has been set like a feast before them. The author of this section of Isaiah gives voice to the joy of God's blessing as the covenant people celebrate deliverance. They are covered with garments of salvation and robes of righteousness; shimmering wedding clothes and jewels sparkle as they move; like a lush garden bursting into spring life, they bloom in fruitfulness; and, finally, they are compared to a crown of beauty in God's hand, a royal diadem.

As the author contemplates what God has done, he rejoices. With his whole being he exults in God. This miracle of newness must be proclaimed aloud so that others can enter into the blessedness of being chosen and see themselves with fresh eyes. We catch the vision today as the spirit of this season enables us to know once again that we are loved and beautiful in God's sight.

To these transformed people of the old covenant of promise, God gave a new name to mark the movement from loss to life. We who participate in the new covenant inaugurated by the coming of Christ are also invited to live into newness. What "new name" best announces who we are today? As you listen to God's gracious word in the scriptures, be ready to hear your new name spoken with endearment and to find yourself living fully into its meaning.

Suggestion for prayer: **As you pray today, listen to hear God speak your new name. Consciously enter into a dialogue with God and make a response. You may wish to write down your conversation with God so you can reread it later.**

Friday, December 27   Read Psalm 148.

The natural world celebrates God's goodness by being fully what it was made to be. Angels, sun, moon, stars, water, sea monsters, hail, snow, frost, stormy wind, mountains, trees, and creatures—all participate in praise to the Creator. People whether of high or low status, young or old, are also called upon to praise the Maker of all. Saint Irenaeus once wrote that the glory of God is the human person "fully alive," and today's psalm awakens us to the potential of that aliveness. We learn our capacity for living and growing fully into the persons God created us to be by joining our proclamation of praise with the rest of the created universe.

Taking time to be in creation, to see and listen to the voiceless ones, enables us to find our own songs of praise. Out in the ocean the whales play, and awe fills us by the thought of them. Watching the sun rise behind mountain peaks we see God's grandeur; the first blooming crocus invites our wonder as the long winter months end. These are "big" moments, but every day there are small miracles of life to be celebrated by those with eyes to see. The city pigeons perched on a lamppost above early morning gridlocked traffic cause us to smile, give thanks, and slow down a little. The housefly that has somehow survived the cold weather and bug spray reminds us of the tenaciousness of God's creatures. The weed that thrusts its way through concrete causes us to remember those hard times through which we have grown in our faith, and a "Praise the Lord" escapes our lips. We are coming to life, coming to fullness as we give voice to all creatures in our daily prayer of praise and gratitude.

Suggestion for meditation: **Take a short walk outside with the intention of noticing the natural world, allowing it to "speak" God's promise.**

Saturday, December 28   Read Luke 2:22-35.

Epiphanies are always happening to surprise us with God's presence in ordinary life. They are moments when we move beyond the obvious, the surface meaning of things, and see the holy clothed in everyday events. For Simeon, waiting prayerfully for many years to see God's promise of a Savior come to pass, such an epiphany occurred when Mary and Joseph entered the Temple with the infant Jesus. Ordinary peasant people bringing a newborn child to present to the Lord, offering the sacrifice deemed acceptable for the poor, was not an unusual event. However, Simeon had learned to listen to God's spirit. Sensing that this was a pivotal moment, he entered the Temple where he found the Holy Family and knew his waiting was over.

Luke offers three hymns (canticles) in celebration of the events surrounding the coming of Christ. At the time of her visitation with Elizabeth, Mary burst into the song of thanksgiving we call the *Magnificat* (Luke 1:46-55); when John is born, his father, finally able to speak again, praises God in the word of the *Benedictus* (Luke 1:67-79); and here the old man Simeon recognizes in this "ordinary" child the presence of the long-awaited Savior and utters the *Nunc Dimittis* (Luke 2:29-32). There is nothing more that requires his waiting, for he senses life's completion in the revelation of Christ.

Simeon, like Mary and Zechariah, tells his joy in God. The three invite us to be open to those surprising and long-awaited moments when Christ is made known. They also encourage us, by their example, to speak the good news of God's promise fulfilled in human experience.

Prayer: **Open our eyes to see you, living Christ, in the ordinariness of life. Continue to surprise us with your daily visitation. Amen.**

Sunday, December 29   Read Luke 2:36-40.

In a culture that venerates the opportunities of youth and rewards persons for youthful appearance and staying active, there is a tendency to neglect the beauty and wisdom of age. The story of Anna is a timely reminder of the grace of aging when faith is the guiding principle and love for God the primary focus. The eighty-four-year-old prophet-widow was constantly in the Temple worshiping and fasting as she delighted in her lifelong journey with God. For her, there was immediate recognition when she saw Jesus and a pressing need to "praise God and to speak about the child to all who were looking for the redemption of Jerusalem."

In many traditions the grandmothers are the bearers of wisdom, greatly honored for their life experience and looked up to by the young. Many Christians can identify profound moments of faith shared with a grandmother or grandfather whose love for scripture, whose ready embrace, have enabled them to experience their own preciousness. The Annas of our own past history remind us that a lifetime of prayer and expectation is a rare gift that enriches us beyond measure. It is only natural for such a wise one to talk readily and with delight about the child who transforms the world.

A new year brings new opportunities to give thanks for those wise women and men who have shaped our lives and enabled us to see the Christ. They will bless us for our gratitude, and will delight in our willingness to proclaim the promise fulfilled among us.

Suggestion for meditation: **Consider some of the Anna figures (both women and men) whose lives have touched and guided you in the faith.**

December 30–31, 1996
Monday, December 30

Justo L. González✤
Read Jeremiah 31:7-9.

One of Israel's most traumatic experiences was the exile to Babylon. God had brought the people out of Egypt and into a rich land "flowing with milk and honey" (Exod. 3:8). There they had built a kingdom that had reached the zenith of its power under David and Solomon. Their future seemed assured. Then something went wrong. The people and their rulers went astray. The kingdom was divided, and decline set in. Eventually, Israel was conquered, and many were carried away into captivity.

As we come to the end of 1996, perhaps we can understand something of the deep disappointment faced by Israel. Most of us began this year with great expectations. We made resolutions. We established goals. We promised ourselves and others that this year we would do certain things, that our lives would be more faithful.

Now the year comes to an end. As we look back at those resolutions and promises, we realize how far we have strayed. We did not do all the good we had intended. We did some evil we had not intended. We have allowed ourselves to stray, and now we find ourselves exiled from our hopes, distanced from our lofty goals.

But there is the possibility of a return. God said, "With weeping they shall come, and with consolations I will lead them back." Through the same prophet, God calls us today to newness of life, to a new beginning, to a return to God.

Prayer: **Thank you, God, that even when we look back at our lives in despair, you are always there for us, that we may look to you for hope. Lead us into a newness of life and new beginnings. Through Jesus, your Son, our life. Amen.**

✤Retired clergy, Río Grande Annual Conference of The United Methodist Church; resides in Decatur, Georgia.

Tuesday, December 31   Read Jeremiah 31:10-14.

The period of exile in Babylon is also called the Babylonian captivity. The people of Israel were captives of the most powerful empire of their time. To them the situation must have seemed hopeless. Yet, the prophet proclaims the power of God that will free Israel even from such a mighty master: "The LORD has ransomed Jacob, and has redeemed him from hands too strong for him."

There are many powers that can enslave us. But none of them is mightier than the past. Against any other master, we can rebel. But the past we cannot change. That is what makes our feelings of failure at the end of the year so overwhelming. A year has gone by, and we are powerless to undo what we did, or even to recover the time we lost, when we failed to do what we ought to have done. We may try to undo the consequences of our past—and in most cases we should. But the past itself, these last twelve months, we cannot undo. It is there, apparently forever, with a givenness we cannot challenge. No matter how hard we try, we cannot undo it. It is a far mightier master than the Babylonians were to Israel. Just as Jacob (Israel) was bound by "hands too strong for him," so are we burdened by the weight of a past we cannot change.

But the God who ransomed Jacob from "hands too strong for him" can also ransom us from whatever binds us no matter how strong—even from the weight of the past.

That is the meaning of forgiveness. God ransoms us from the power of our sin, from the shame of our failures, from the weight of the past. Thus, as we approach a new year, we can do so with joy similar to that of the prophet Jeremiah's words. Read them again, and rejoice with him!

Prayer: **Cast away from us, O God, all our failures and sin of the year past, as you cast away the yoke of Babylon. Grant us the joy of those who return to you from the exile of sin and guilt. Amen.**

The Revised Common Lectionary* for 1996
Year A – Advent/Christmas Year B
(*Disciplines* Edition)

January 1–7
BAPTISM OF THE LORD
Isaiah 42:1-9
Psalm 29
Acts 10:34-43
Matthew 3:13-17

EPIPHANY, January 6
Isaiah 60:1-6
Psalm 72:1-7, 10-14
Ephesians 3:1-12
Matthew 2:1-12

January 8–14
Isaiah 49:1-7
Psalm 40:1-11
1 Corinthians 1:1-9
John 1:29-42

January 15–21
Isaiah 9:1-4
Psalm 27:1, 4-9
1 Corinthians 1:10-18
Matthew 4:12-23

January 22–28
Micah 6:1-8
Psalm 15
1 Corinthians 1:18-31
Matthew 5:1-12

January 29—February 4
Isaiah 58:1-12
Psalm 112:1-10
1 Corinthians 2:1-12, (13-16)
Matthew 5:13-20

February 5–11
Deuteronomy 30:15-20
Psalm 119:1-8
1 Corinthians 3:1-9
Matthew 5:21-37

February 12–18
THE TRANSFIGURATION
Exodus 24:12-18
Psalm 2 (*or* Psalm 99)
2 Peter 1:16-21
Matthew 17:1-9

February 19–25
First Sunday in Lent
Genesis 2:15-17; 3:1-7
Psalm 32
Romans 5:12-19
Matthew 4:1-11

ASH WEDNESDAY
Joel 2:1-2, 12-17
(*or* Isaiah 58:1-12)
Psalm 51:1-17
2 Corinthians 5:20*b*–6:10
Matthew 6:1-6, 16-21

February 26—March 3
Second Sunday in Lent
Genesis 12:1-4*a*
Psalm 121
Romans 4:1-5, 13-17
John 3:1-17

March 4–10
Third Sunday in Lent
Exodus 17:1-7
Psalm 95
Romans 5:1-11
John 4:5-42

March 11–17
Fourth Sunday in Lent
1 Samuel 16:1-13
Psalm 23
Ephesians 5:8-14
John 9:1-41

March 18–24
Fifth Sunday in Lent
Ezekiel 37:1-14
Psalm 130
Romans 8:6-11
John 11:1-45

March 25–31
PASSION/PALM SUNDAY

Liturgy of the Palms
Matthew 21:1-11
Psalm 118:1-2, 19-29

Liturgy of the Passion
Isaiah 50:4-9*a*
Psalm 31:9-16
Philippians 2:5-11
Matthew 26:14–27:66
(*or* Matthew 27:11-54)

Week of April 1–7
HOLY WEEK
(selected lections)

Monday, April 1
Psalm 36:5-11
John 12:1-11

Tuesday, April 2
Psalm 71:1-14
John 12:20-36

Wednesday, April 3
Psalm 70
Hebrews 12:1-3
John 13:21-32

Maundy Thursday
Exodus 12:1-14
Psalm 116:1-2, 12-19
1 Corinthians 11:23-26
John 13:1-17, 31*b*-35

Good Friday
Isaiah 52:13–53:12
Psalm 22
Hebrews 10:16-25
John 18:1–19:42

Holy Saturday
Lamentations 3:1-9, 19-24
1 Peter 4:1-8
Matthew 27:57-61

April 7
EASTER SUNDAY
Acts 10:34-43
Psalm 118:1-2, 14-24
Colossians 3:1-4
John 20:1-18

April 8–14
Acts 2:14*a*, 22-32
Psalm 16
1 Peter 1:3-9
John 20:19-31

April 15–21
Acts 2:14*a*, 36-41
Psalm 116:1-4, 12-19
1 Peter 1:17-23
Luke 24:13-35

April 22–28
Acts 2:42-47
Psalm 23
1 Peter 2:19-25
John 10:1-10

April 29—May 5
Acts 7:55-60
Psalm 31:1-5, 15-16
1 Peter 2:2-10
John 14:1-14

May 6–12
Acts 17:22-31
Psalm 66:8-10
1 Peter 3:13-22
John 14:15-21

May 13–19
Acts 1:6-14
Psalm 68:1-10, 32-35
1 Peter 4:12-13; 5:6-11
John 17:1-11

> **ASCENSION DAY, May 16**
> *(These readings may be used
> for Sunday, May 19.)*
> Acts 1:1-11
> Psalm 47 (*or* Psalm 93)
> Ephesians 1:15-23
> Luke 24:44-53

May 20–26
PENTECOST
Numbers 11:24-30
Psalm 104:24-34, 35*b*
Acts 2:1-21
John 20:19-23 (*or* 7:37-39)

May 27—June 2
TRINITY SUNDAY
Genesis 1:1–2:4*a*
Psalm 8
2 Corinthians 13:11-13
Matthew 28:16-20

June 3–9
Genesis 12:1-9
Psalm 33:11-12
Romans 4:13-25
Matthew 9:9-13, 18-26

June 10–16
Genesis 18:1-15
Psalm 116:1-2, 12-19
Romans 5:1-8
Matthew 9:35–10:8, (9-23)

June 17–23
Genesis 21:8-21
Psalm 69:7-18
Romans 6:1*b*-11
Matthew 10:24-39

June 24–30
Genesis 22:1-14
Psalm 13
Romans 6:12-23
Matthew 10:40-42

July 1–7
Genesis 24:34-38, 42-49,
   and 58-67
Psalm 45:10-17
Romans 7:15-25*a*
Matthew 11:16-19, 25-30

July 8–14
Genesis 25:19-34
Psalm 119:105-112
Romans 8:1-11
Matthew 13:1-9, 18-23

July 15–21
Genesis 28:10-19*a*
Psalm 139:1-12, 23-24
Romans 8:12-25
Matthew 13:24-30, 36-43

July 22–28
Genesis 29:15-28
Psalm 105:1-11, 45*b*
Romans 8:26-39
Matthew 13:31-33, 44-52

July 29—August 4
Genesis 32:22-31
Psalm 17:1-7, 15
Romans 9:1-5
Matthew 14:13-21

August 5–11
Genesis 37:1-4, 12-28
Psalm 105:1-6, 16-22, 45*b*
Romans 10:5-15
Matthew 14:22-33

August 12–18
Genesis 45:1-15
Psalm 133
Romans 11:1-2*a*, 29-32
Matthew 15:(10-20), 21-28

August 19–25
Exodus 1:8–2:10
Psalm 124
Romans 12:1-8
Matthew 16:13-20

August 26—September 1
Exodus 3:1-15
Psalm 105:1-6, 23-26, 45*c*
Romans 12:9-21
Matthew 16:21-28

September 2–8
Exodus 12:1-14
Psalm 149
Romans 13:8-14
Matthew 18:15-20

September 9–15
Exodus 14:19-31
Psalm 114 (*or* Exodus
    15:1*b*-11, 20-21)
Romans 14:1-12
Matthew 18:21-35

September 16–22
Exodus 16:2-15
Psalm 105:1-6, 37-45
Philippians 1:21-30
Matthew 20:1-16

September 23–29
Exodus 17:1-7
Psalm 78:1-4, 12-16
Philippians 2:1-13
Matthew 21:23-32

September 30—October 6
Exodus 20:1-4, 7-9, 12-20
Psalm 19
Philippians 3:4*b*-14
Matthew 21:33-46

October 7–13
Exodus 32:1-14
Psalm 106:1-6, 19-23
Philippians 4:1-9
Matthew 22:1-14

October 14–20
Exodus 33:12-23
Psalm 99
1 Thessalonians 1:1-10
Matthew 22:15-22

 **THANKSGIVING DAY,
  CANADA, October 14**
 Deuteronomy 8:7-18
 Psalm 65
 2 Corinthians 9:6-15
 Luke 17:11-19

October 21–27
Deuteronomy 34:1-12
Psalm 90:1-6, 13-17
1 Thessalonians 2:1-8
Matthew 22:34-46

October 28—November 3
Joshua 3:7-17
Psalm 107:1-7, 33-37
1 Thessalonians 2:9-13
Matthew 23:1-12

ALL SAINTS DAY,
November 1
Revelation 7:9-17
Psalm 34:1-10, 22
1 John 3:1-3
Matthew 5:1-12

November 4–10
Joshua 24:1-3a, 14-25
Psalm 78:1-7
1 Thessalonians 4:13-18
Matthew 25:1-13

November 11–17
Judges 4:1-7
Psalm 123
1 Thessalonians 5:1-11
Matthew 25:14-30

November 18–24
Ezekiel 34:11-16, 20-24
Psalm 100
Ephesians 1:15-23
Matthew 25:31-46

> *Year B lections begin the*
> *First Sunday in Advent, 1996.*

November 25—December 1
First Sunday of Advent
Isaiah 64:1-9
Psalm 80:1-7, 17-19
1 Corinthians 1:3-9
Mark 13:24-37

THANKSGIVING DAY, USA,
November 28
Deuteronomy 8:7-18
Psalm 65
2 Corinthians 9:6-15
Luke 17:11-19

December 2–8
Second Sunday of Advent
Isaiah 40:1-11
Psalm 85:1-2, 8-13
2 Peter 3:8-15a
Mark 1:1-8

December 9–15
Third Sunday of Advent
Isaiah 61:1-4, 8-11
Psalm 126
   (*or* Luke 1:47-55)
1 Thessalonians 5:16-24
John 1:6-8, 19-28

December 16–22
Fourth Sunday of Advent
2 Samuel 7:1-11, 16
Psalm 89:1-4, 19-26
Romans 16:25-27
Luke 1:26-38

December 23–29
First Sunday after
Christmas Day
Isaiah 61:10–62:3
Psalm 148
Galatians 4:4-7
Luke 2:22-40

   CHRISTMAS EVE
Isaiah 9:2-7
Psalm 96
Titus 2:11-14
Luke 2:1-20

CHRISTMAS DAY
Isaiah 52:7-10
Psalm 98
Hebrews 1:1-4, (5-12)
John 1:1-14

December 30—
  January 5, 1997
Jeremiah 31:7-14
Psalm 147:12-20
Ephesians 1:3-14
John 1:10-18

   NEW YEAR'S DAY
Eccesiastes 3:1-13
Psalm 8
Revelation 21:1-6a
Matthew 25:31-46